W9-CRA-021

TAXATION
ONLY WITH
REPRESENTATION

TAXATION
ONLY WITH
REPRESENTATION

Richard W. Painter

Foreword by John Pudner

Taxation Only with Representation:
The Conservative Conscience and Campaign Finance Reform

Copyright © 2016 by Richard W. Painter
All rights reserved
Published by Take Back Our Republic
Produced by Keen Custom Media (**keencommunication.com/keen-custom-media**)
Printed in the United States of America
First edition, first printing

Published by: Take Back Our Republic
                  246 E. Glenn Ave., Ste. B
                  Auburn, AL 36830
                  www.takeback.org

Cover design by Scott McGrew
Text design by Annie Long and Steve Jones
Charts by Steve Jones
Cover image: Bronze Franklin Mint Boston Tea Party Bicentennial 1973 by Kevin
Dooley (Chandler, AZ)/Flickr, made available under an Attribution 2.0 Generic license
(creativecommons.org/licenses/by/2.0)

ISBN: 978-1-939324-12-2

TABLE OF CONTENTS

FOREWORD

BY JOHN PUDNER

I HIT SEND shortly after 7 p.m. on June 10, 2014, and 93,000 people received the e-mail "Dave Brat Surging Ahead of Eric Cantor." Sitting in Brat headquarters, we had received only three precinct reports, but with 1% of the precincts in, I knew Dave had won based on my matrix.

My cell phone exploded as the nation learned from my e-mail that the Majority Leader had lost. "Are you sure?" "Is this serious?" A little later in the evening, I was with Dave Brat, his family, and three others behind a locked door as I called the county police department for an escort to get his children home through the enthusiastic crowd. Meanwhile, Dave was on the phone with Sean Hannity, who was flying a plane to Richmond, Virginia, to cover the hottest story of the day.

Two days later, Gretchen Carlson concluded her Fox News interview with me by saying, "You believe that the 21st-century tools even out money in races . . . and you think that this race would not have happened 30 years ago. And I think it is fascinating for politics moving forward, because everyone thinks unless you have a ton of dough you can't do it. And this is proof that you can."

Soon after the Fox News interview, I was talking with Richard Painter, the author of this book, and telling him how the Brat race actually almost made me give up. There were three key points that needed to be addressed:

1. TAX CREDITS. In January *National Review* announced that I was running Brat's effort, but almost two months later, only $16,000 had been raised. I begged a room of 200 people to put checks in a basket that I was holding at the exit. We more than doubled our money at that time, but some chose not to give once they learned that political contributions were not tax deductible. I asked Painter, "Why can't we give a tax credit to small donors to give them a chance to offset the mega-donors?" Painter gave me details on how this could be done. He supported these details by sharing the history of such tax credits and their use. He also explained how Ronald Reagan was elected president

viii

through the use of the Federal Small Donor Matching Fund System we used to have.

2. TRANSACTIONAL GIVING. I asked Painter if I was the only conservative who was worried about Big Money interests [unions, the entertainment industry, the gambling industry, special interest groups] swelling the deficit and pushing to enact their special interest agendas. I feared that the faith-based voters in the 16 battleground states that I helped recruit for the Bush/Cheney 2000 election were becoming irrelevant due to the current campaign finance rules and accepted practices. Painter gave me quotes going back more than 50 years from Barry Goldwater, who foresaw these perils many decades ago.

3. DARK MONEY AND SUPER PACS. I almost gave up on the fight to reform the influence of Big Money in campaigns. This occurred at the low point of the campaign, when I e-mailed Dave to let him know I wanted to save him from having to pay me for the last two months of consulting retainers and to break off strategy communications. I could not tell Dave that the reason for this went beyond saving him money. In talking to my associate, Cole Muzio, we decided that the only way we could produce the digital TV and Get Out the Vote phone calls that we thought necessary in the campaign was by going "outside" and forming a super PAC.

    This decision came with personal sacrifice. The terrible downside was that I could not do any of the things I truly enjoyed and had done for decades—talking to the candidate at midnight every night, knocking on doors, and making phone calls in headquarters with volunteers. Instead, I would spend all my time talking to a lawyer to make sure we did not trip on any coordination laws while producing a TV commercial praised by the likes of Laura Ingraham, Mark Levin, and Breitbart in the closing days of the campaign as Cantor's 32-point lead disappeared. Leaving the campaign also allowed me to spend what I wanted to ensure the correct production of the commercial and its digital targeting.

My having to leave a campaign to make a commercial seemed ludicrous. I asked Painter if there was some way to change this ridiculous process. The process also suppressed voter participation by making the system seem too complex. I wanted to stop incentivizing donors to give to dark sources and/or super PACs by toughening up disclosure laws, thus freeing up a little more money to go directly to candidates to make them part of the campaigns. I'm not for unlimited giving by billionaires to candidates, as some on the right advocate, because I think our elections should belong to everyone, especially average Americans. But it would have been great to be able to spend a little bit of my company and personal money to produce our commercials and still be able to continue talking to the candidates. Painter walked me through case law on this particular issue. He also pointed out that *Citizens United v. FEC* specifically praised full disclosure as being important to our democracy and consistent with the reading of the First Amendment argument that prohibited the government from restricting independent political expenditures.

When Painter started reviewing main points from the chapters for what would become this book, I was ecstatic.

Having been in the political field for 20 years, I was thrilled to find the intellectual backing for many of the rough ideas I had for reforming a system that was making grassroots activists irrelevant. I thought it was just me and my tea party and social conservative friends who felt they were being overwhelmed by Big Money billionaires and corporations in primaries and Big Money unions and environmental groups in general elections.

Learning that there are many who share these concerns gave me hope that this was a fight worth fighting. Top leaders from the political field, including Painter, Mark McKinnon (creator of the Bush/Cheney TV commercials that ran while I was going state to state on the ground and drafting Catholic and social conservative phone scripts), and Juleanna Glover (who had worked for George W. Bush, Phyllis Schlafly, Jesse Helms, and John Ashcroft) were at the forefront of this issue.

I finished running some campaigns, including a great upset of a union-backed, Big Money candidate first elected in 1982, and then announced I was opening Take Back Our Republic. To our surprise, many conservative leaders are interested in our message, including Republican Congressional offices.

The one piece that was missing was a guidebook to provide the intellectual foundation for this movement—for that, I turned to Painter to ask if he would consider allowing Take Back Our Republic to publish this book.

Certainly, Painter could have gone with a prestigious academic press, but the hunger for a book such as this from conservatives across the country was astounding. They wanted to see this book, which gives hope to conservatives and like-minded voters everywhere. Fortunately, Painter agreed. I am thrilled that you are preparing to turn the pages.

PREFACE

ON A BRIGHT Sunday morning the USS *Republic*—the multibillion-dollar pride of the U.S. Navy—is anchored in a harbor. The ship lists sharply to port, visibly taking in water and slowly sinking. The starboard side tilts high in the air at a 60-degree angle.

Thousands of crates of money—all heavy coins—are stored aboard the ship, mostly on the port side. The captain protests that the ship will sink, but the government ignores his warning and continues to bring more and more crates of coins aboard, almost all of them immediately placed on the port side and only a scattered few on the starboard side, if only to maintain the illusion of balance for external observers.

The coins are brought aboard because America's powerful politicians and their supporters use the *Republic* to exchange money for political favors. If such an exchange took place anywhere else the parties involved could go to jail for bribery, but the law allows this exchange aboard the *Republic, provided the money is kept on board.* The stored money legally belongs to the ship, even though a particular politician has a claim to individual crates of money and has exclusive control over where it is stored (politicians can also transfer money aboard the ship to each other and use it to trade favors). For whatever reason, the politicians and their supporters prefer to keep the money mostly on the port side of the ship. Money stays on board because those who are caught taking it off the ship risk going to jail.

A decade ago, Congress, worried that the *Republic* would sink, passed a law restricting the amount of money that could be brought aboard. The Supreme Court, however, found the law unconstitutional, ruling that politicians and their supporters had a right to bring as much money as they want on board the *Republic*.

Local citizens and taxpayers, having watched this strange sight for years, become furious that this ship—one far more valuable than its heavy cargo—is sinking. A crowd begins to form, and demonstrators begin to chant, "Save the *Republic*! We paid for it!" They rush aboard and divide into two groups. One group quickly throws overboard as many crates of coins as they can. Another group moves some of the remaining crates from port to starboard in an attempt to right the ship. The inspiration for the frustrated taxpayers' actions is remarkably similar to that of the Boston Tea Party in 1773. This time, however, the problem is not a British tax on tea, but American money sinking the ship of state.

THIS BOOK DISCUSSES how the fundamental principles and values of American citizens, particularly those who identify themselves as conservatives, are threatened by our current system of campaign finance. This book is also about solutions to the problem that conservatives can support in order to restore to American citizens a meaningful say in who runs their government.

The Tea Party patriots of 1773 demanded such a say, and with their fellow patriots proved willing to put their lives on the line and shed blood to gain it. Now more than 200 years later, we have lost this ability to have our voices heard in choosing the composition of our own government—not to England or any other foreign power (although foreign powers can easily manipulate our current system of campaign finance) but to our own money-drenched system of funding elections to public office. We are throwing away our right to self-governance.

This book presents a clear and impassioned case for why conscientious Americans, and politically conservative Americans in particular, must respond to the campaign finance problem. This book is also about the specifics of a plan to take back our Republic and restore the right of the American people to govern themselves.

ACKNOWLEDGMENTS

THE AUTHOR IS grateful to Eric Yang of Harvard University and Michael Burke, Jonathan Thomas, and Lindsey Krause of the University of Minnesota for invaluable research for this book. Most of the work on writing the manuscript was funded by a one-year residential fellowship at the Edmond J. Safra Center for Ethics at Harvard University. The author also benefited greatly from comments on prior drafts from Safra Center faculty, staff, and fellows. The author thanks the officers and staff of Take Back Our Republic for commenting on prior drafts and for publishing this book.

INTRODUCTION

"The enemy of freedom is unrestrained power, and the champions of freedom will fight against the concentration of power wherever they find it."
—Barry Goldwater, *The Conscience of a Conservative* (1960)

ARIZONA SENATOR AND 1964 presidential candidate Barry Goldwater understood the importance of individual liberty in the face of the growing concentration of power in America—big government, big labor, and big corporations. And he understood the role of campaign finance, even if the role of money in politics then was only a shadow of what it is now. As Goldwater wrote in *The Conscience of a Conservative,* "In order to achieve the widest possible distribution of political power, financial contributions to political campaigns should be made by individuals and individuals alone. I see no reason for labor unions—or corporations— to participate in politics. Both were created for economic purposes, and their activities should be restricted accordingly."[1]

Goldwater spoke about this and many issues from the heart as well as the mind, emphasizing that one's political perspective was not just a matter of utilitarian preference or convenience, but a matter of conscience. At the height of America's struggle against global communism, Goldwater expressed a vision of moral truth to guide our politics. Even if modern conservatives do not embrace some of his positions, particularly his opposition to federal civil rights legislation, many other principles Goldwater articulated still have enormous appeal for conservative voters and some other voters as well. Goldwater was also able to identify problems that, if left unaddressed, would become progressively worse and threaten the vitality and perhaps even the existence of our country. Campaign finance was one of those problems.

Ironically, Goldwater's loss of the 1964 presidential race was an early demonstration of the power of money in politics. Democrats paid for the infamous "Daisy Girl" commercial that ran on television nationwide in 1964. More than 50 million Americans watched a little girl picking daisies in a field and then being blown up by a nuclear bomb because Goldwater

---

1 Barry Goldwater, *The Conscience of a Conservative* (1960. Princeton, NJ: Princeton University Press, 2007), 49.

had been elected president.[2] President Lyndon Johnson, hardly a pacifist, was instead reelected in what would be the largest landslide in American history. Political advertising would never be the same after that commercial; neither would the campaign fundraising needed to pay for commercials. The landscape of American politics had been irrevocably altered.

Goldwater reiterated his concerns about campaign finance in a March 22, 1983, statement on the Senate floor:

> Instead of achieving an intimate relationship between the public and their government, this distorted election process leads to a system in which the force of government will be imposed on the people in the course of their daily lives for the advantage of selfish interests who are removed from the general public. It is important to notice that the Framers wanted elections to be free of the corruption that was then so widespread in England. The Founders of our Constitutional Government were disgusted at the deluge of corruption that overwhelmed British Parliamentary elections.[3]

Goldwater expressly advocated for reversal of the Supreme Court's decision in *Buckley v. Valeo* (1976)[4] declaring limits on campaign spending unconstitutional. Goldwater observed:

> Candidates must be more than caricatures who front for donors with the most money. Candidates should reach the public on the human level. They should communicate honest principles and values of interest to the entire public and demonstrate their personal qualities of leadership. They should not be the paid hands of any vested interest group nor appear to be so.[5]

For many who lived through both the international struggle against communism and the domestic turmoil of the 1960s, Goldwater personified what it meant to be a conservative. The noun *conservative* has the same root as the verb *conserve*. There are many things that a conservative should want to conserve—including the essential character of the American political system. Goldwater was committed to that cause, whether

---

2 Steven Seidman, "The 'Daisy Spot'—The Most Famous Political TV Ad," *Posters and Election Propaganda,* Ithaca College, ithaca.edu/rhp/programs/cmd/blogs/posters_and_election_propaganda /the_daisy_spotthe_most_famous_political_tv_ad (accessed 15 September 2015).
3 John W. Dean and Barry M. Goldwater Jr., *Pure Goldwater* (New York: Palgrave MacMillan, 2008), 353.
4 Buckley v. Valeo, 424 U.S. 1 (1976).
5 Dean and Goldwater, *Pure Goldwater,* 359.

the enemy be communism, moral decay, big government, or big money in government.

In the four decades since Goldwater's impassioned statements, the campaign finance system has only gotten worse. Public servants, voters, journalists, and scholars have all repeatedly observed that, because of the role of money in elections, our political system is not what it used to be.[6] There has been a radical change away from representative democracy, a radical change that conservatives should strongly oppose. Voters no longer have the choices they once had, and elected officials do not respond to voters' concerns the way they once did. Admittedly, the past was not perfect; women and minorities were denied the right to vote, while rampant direct bribery and other forms of corruption did even more to undermine the system. Yet our current system of campaign finance has transformed our "republican" form of government into a peculiar barter system that departs dramatically from the ideals of the founders of the United States.

After Goldwater, the campaign finance problem was taken up by another Republican senator from Arizona and eventual presidential nominee, John McCain. McCain had endured years of torture and imprisonment in Vietnam because of his participation in a war that our government believed was a necessary part of America's fight against communism. In the 1990s McCain confronted a different enemy that he believed had the potential to destroy our country from within—big money in politics.

Like Goldwater, McCain sought to reduce the impact of big money on politics by restricting the activities of corporations, unions, and other principally economic organizations. The new prohibitions, however, would go beyond limiting contributions to campaigns. By the 1990s unofficial, or "shadow," campaigns to support or oppose candidates had become so pervasive that reformers believed they had to focus on the organizations that funded such electioneering communications.[7] This approach imposed restrictions on political speech about candidates and clashed with principles of individual liberty. As a result, many conservatives object to such reform initiatives, while other critics believe such

---

6 Michael J. Malbin and John Fortier, "An Agenda for Future Research on Money in Politics in the United States" (Washington, D.C.: Campaign Finance Institute and Bipartisan Policy Center, 2013), cfinst.org/pdf/books-reports/scholarworkinggroup/CFI-BPC_Research-Agenda_Report_Webversion.pdf (accessed 15 September 2015).

7 Section 203 of the McCain–Feingold Act prohibited corporations and unions from using funds from their general treasury to pay for electioneering communications mentioning a candidate within 30 days before a primary or 60 days before a general election.

restrictions will be ineffectual anyway.[8] But, believing that some reform was better than no reform, a bipartisan coalition in Congress passed the Bipartisan Campaign Reform Act of 2002, better known as McCain–Feingold in recognition of its chief sponsors, and President George W. Bush signed it into law.[9]

Despite initially upholding the constitutionality of McCain–Feingold in *McConnell v. FEC* (2003), the Supreme Court, under the leadership of newly appointed Chief Justice John Roberts, shifted positions in *Randall v. Sorrell* (2006),[10] *FEC v. Wisconsin Right to Life* (2007),[11] and, most explosively of all, *Citizens United v. FEC* (2010),[12] which struck down important provisions of McCain–Feingold that had restricted corporate funding of electioneering communications. The court gave corporations and unions the same First Amendment rights as individuals, including the constitutional right to spend unlimited amounts of money to influence political campaigns. The court's decision may have vindicated certain principles of individual liberty espoused by some conservatives, but it greatly expanded the reach of case law to which Goldwater had strongly objected when he criticized the court's holding in *Buckley v. Valeo*. And the court's *Citizens United* decision opened the floodgates of campaign money even further because it was now possible for a corporation or union to spend as much money as it wanted to elect or defeat a candidate.

In the six years following *Citizens United*, Congress declined to respond to the court's decision with new campaign finance reform legislation. Instead, in the past six years, members of Congress have intensified their efforts to raise campaign money. Even proposals to require more disclosure of expenditures on electioneering communications have foundered in Congress, with efforts such as the Real Time Transparency Act and Senate Campaign Disclosure Parity Act failing to even move out of committee.[13]

Time and time again, Congress has failed to heed the warnings of Goldwater, McCain, and other conservative leaders about the corrupting influence of money in politics. Even if conservatives today ultimately do

---

8 James Campbell, "The Stagnation of Congressional Elections," in *Life After Reform*, ed. Michael J. Malbin (New York: Rowman & Littlefield Publishers, 2003), 141.

9 George W. Bush, "President Signs Campaign Finance Reform Act," press release, 27 March 2002, georgewbush-whitehouse.archives.gov/news/releases/2002/03/20020327.html (accessed 15 September 2015).

10 Randall v. Sorrell, 548 U.S. 230 (2006).

11 FEC v. Wisconsin Right to Life, 551 U.S. 449 (2007).

12 Citizens United v. FEC, 558 U.S. 310 (2010).

13 Introduced by Beto O'Rourke (D-TX) in the House and Angus King (I-ME) in the Senate; introduced by Jon Tester (D-MT) in the Senate.

not embrace the solutions that Goldwater and McCain supported, they cannot continue to deny or ignore that the current role of money in politics is a serious problem. And this, too, is not enough; conservatives also need to support a solution to that problem.

Voters across the political spectrum are demanding a solution.

A CBS News/*New York Times* nationwide telephone poll, conducted May 28–31, 2015, of 1,022 adults, with a margin of sampling error of plus or minus three percentage points, showed overwhelming support for campaign finance reform from Democrats, Republicans, and Independents. Respondents in the poll were asked the following question and gave the responses indicated below:

> Which of the following three statements comes closest to expressing your overall view of the way political campaigns are funded in the United States:

1) On the whole, the system for funding political campaigns works pretty well and only minor changes are necessary to make it work better.

   Democrat: 14%

   Republican: 16%

   Independent: 10%

   All adults: 13%

2) There are some good things in the system for funding political campaigns but fundamental changes are needed.

   Democrat: 38%

   Republican: 45%

   Independent: 37%

   All adults: 39%

3) The system for funding political campaigns has so much wrong with it that we need to completely rebuild it.

   Democrat: 46%

   Republican: 36%

   Independent: 53%

   All adults: 46%

Three quarters of self-identified Republicans also supported requiring more disclosure by outside spending organizations. Republicans in the poll were almost as likely as Democrats to favor additional restrictions on campaign donations.[14]

Political operatives inside the Beltway may see campaign finance reform as an issue for liberals that conservatives can safely ignore, but conservative voters clearly don't see it that way.

THIS BOOK USES a broad definition of a political "conservative" that includes at least four categories of Americans: first, those concerned about excessive government regulation, taxation, and spending (small-government or free-market conservatives often associated with the modern-day tea party); second, those concerned that our government is not doing enough to preserve traditional moral values in a range of areas, including protection of human life (social conservatives); third, those concerned that our government is not doing enough to protect the United States against threats to our national security and to our national interests (so-called neoconservatives, among others, fit into this category, which favors a robust military and foreign policy); and fourth, those philosophically committed to having a republican form of government as close as possible to that envisioned by our country's founders (this perspective emphasizes, among other things, a strict interpretation of the actual language of the Constitution with an emphasis on the intent of the founders—an approach known as originalism—and all three branches of government being faithful to the founders' vision as they act within their Constitutional powers). Many conservatives do not fit within all four of these categories, although many fit into more than one.

First, there are the contemporary tea party activists, who, like their 1773 predecessors, complain of increasing taxation and diminishing representation. They have become increasingly frustrated by the growth of Washington's "insider culture," dominated by earmarks and entrenched incumbents that steadily expand the size of government. Unilateral government actions, from executive orders used to implement President Barack Obama's health-care law to the growing national debt, strip

---

14 Nicholas Confessore and Megan Thee-Brennan, "Poll Shows Americans Favor an Overhaul of Campaign Financing," *The New York Times,* 3 June 2015, A1; "A New York Times/CBS News Poll on Money and Politics," *The New York Times,* 2 June 2015, nytimes.com/interactive/2015/06/01/us/politics /document-poll-may-28-31.html (accessed 15 September 2015).

political power from citizens.[15] A fundamental problem for these voters is that government is increasingly remote from the governed. Many decisions are made not at the state and local levels but by a national government hundreds or thousands of miles away. This government in turn is chosen through a process from which many Americans—conservative, liberal, and moderate—feel increasingly alienated. At the same time, the federal government continues to grow relentlessly in size.

Big campaign finance and big government reinforce each other. Politicians need a lot of money to get elected, particularly in federal elections. They attract contributions to their campaigns and to the shadow organizations that support them, in part by spending taxpayers' money in ways that benefit special interests, from pork barrel construction projects to allowing health-care providers to overbill Medicare. It matters little whether the government is led by Republicans or Democrats; from 2002 to 2006 the federal government grew significantly in size and cost in years when Republicans controlled both the White House and Congress.[16] When politicians spend taxpayer money on defense contracts, public works projects, and speculative investments such as renewable energy ventures, they first look to who supports the spending and whether these people and organizations also support their political campaigns. The merits of an expenditure, and its costs, may be secondary. When federal contractors overcharge the government, their friends in Congress hinder rather than help efforts to investigate. Big campaign finance and big government depend on each other to grow as ordinary voters—and taxpayers—are pushed into the background.

Big campaign finance also encourages excessive regulation of business. Regulated businesses are much more worried than unregulated businesses about what government does, and regulated businesses will likely make more generous campaign contributions to get the access they feel they need.[17] Businesses that support political campaigns also have another advantage in the regulatory state: They can lobby for regulation

---

15 "Tea Party Youth Blast Debt, 'Taxation Without Representation,' " *The New American,* 24 January 2014, thenewamerican.com/usnews/politics/item/17479-tea-party-youth-blast-debt-taxation-without-representation (accessed 15 September 2015).

16 See "Federal Debt: Total Public Debt as Percent of Gross Domestic Product," Federal Reserve Bank of St. Louis Economic Research, 25 September 2015, research.stlouisfed.org/fred2/series/GFDEGDQ188S (accessed 15 September 2015); "Historical Source of Revenue as Share of GDP," Tax Policy Center, 4 February 2015, taxpolicycenter.org/taxfacts/displayafact.cfm?Docid=205 (accessed 15 September 2015).

17 See Andrea Dua et al., "How Business Interacts with Government: McKinsey Global Survey Results" (2010), mckinsey.com/insights/public_sector/how_business_interacts_with_government_mckinsey_global_survey_results (accessed 15 September 2015); Edward T. Walker and Christopher M. Rea, "The Political Mobilization of Firms and Industries," *Annual Review of Sociology* 40 (2014), 281–304.

that benefits themselves and disadvantages competitors. Businesses that don't contribute may find the burden of regulations to be even more onerous. Politicians know that this dynamic grinds to a halt, and campaign contributions from business are likely to dry up, if Congress decides that regulation of an industry is unnecessary or is best left to individual states. Broad repeal of regulations is promised, but in most instances the best that regulated industry can hope for is to fall under the exception and not the rule. These exceptions are most likely delivered against a background of constant reminders that Congress and executive agencies have the power to increase regulation. And fear of that is what keeps the campaign contributions coming.

The past decades have seen an enormous increase in regulation in two areas in particular: financial services and health care. And it is no coincidence that these two industries are very generous contributors to the campaigns of both political parties.[18]

Because the campaign finance system gives politicians no incentive to decrease the power and cost of government, excessive government spending and regulating won't stop until political fundraising is brought under control. A better campaign finance system could at least restore integrity to the political party that—without the perverse incentives created by campaign fundraising—would be disposed to regulate less and spend less. Conservative voters who want to be represented by real conservatives who act upon rather than just talk about their preference for smaller government should want to do something to fix the system of campaign finance.

These and other concerns about our system of campaign finance that should trouble conscientious limited-government conservatives are addressed in Chapter 3.

Campaign finance also presents obstacles for socially conservative voters who fear that our country has turned away from its Judeo-Christian heritage as well as voters whose traditional views of public morals are grounded in the Islamic, Hindu, Buddhist, and a diverse range of other faiths. A system in which money buys power and defines laws is antithetical to any natural law theory of government in which temporal laws ought to be rooted in eternal truths, not fleeting and fallible human thinking.

---

18 "Finance/Insurance/Real Estate Interest Groups Summary," Center for Responsive Politics, opensecrets.org/industries/indus.php?Ind=F (accessed 15 November 2015); "Health Interest Groups Summary," Center for Responsive Politics, opensecrets.org/industries/indus.php?Ind=H (accessed 15 November 2015).

Faith-based voters seek to accomplish much of their agenda through churches and other nonprofits. A government controlled by money will instead reflect the social values of the country's dominant centers of profit. In an economy increasingly dominated by services, these profit centers include the entertainment sector, the media and gambling industries, drug companies (soon to include sellers of legal recreational drugs), and the health-care establishment. Under the current system, ordinary people are disempowered, no longer able to convey their values because their voices are drowned out by financial backers who preselect the major party candidates. Some of society's most vexing questions, including questions central to the existence of human life itself, will be measured in nothing more than dollars and cents.[19]

As the role of money in elections increases, for-profit enterprises find their hands strengthened, whereas those of churches and other tax-exempt nonprofits, even the largest ones, grow weaker. For faith-based voters the problem should be clear. Our Pledge of Allegiance invokes "One Nation under God," but the genuineness behind those words has been lost to the ravages of our campaign finance system. These words, a shell of their former selves, exist only as lip service to the faithful, while people in power worship money as a false god they believe will shape our nation's destiny.

These and other concerns about our system of campaign finance that should trouble conscientious social conservatives are addressed in Chapter 4.

Then there are the national security concerns that come to mind when one realizes that corporate wealth—and thus corporate political speech in American elections—is not all American. With growing concentrations of wealth in the Middle East, China and the Far East, and Latin America, more corporations in the United States will be owned and/or controlled from overseas. If corporate money dominates elections, American citizens will have a limited role in choosing their own government. Our independence as a country could even be at stake, particularly if it is easier for foreign businesses to influence our government than it is for Americans to influence foreign governments.

These and other concerns about our system of campaign finance that should trouble conscientious national security–oriented conservatives are addressed in Chapter 5.

---

19 This author has personally disagreed with parts of the agenda of some "religious conservatives" in areas such as equal rights for gays and lesbians yet agreed with religious conservatives in many other areas. The important point is that faith-based voters of all types are very poorly represented in a political system dominated by big campaign contributors.

Finally, there is the participation problem, which should trouble all Americans but particularly conservatives who want our government to adhere as closely as possible to its founders' vision of a participatory democracy.

Political philosophers from John Locke to George Will have long embraced a vision of a government that embodies the core values of all citizens, independent from the distribution of economic power, a government in which the rich, the middle class, and the poor all have the opportunity to participate in the process of representative democracy. The campaign finance system by contrast fits well within the economic determinism of Marxists, who believe that distribution of political power is commensurate with distribution of material wealth, and who argue that political equality can only come when material wealth is distributed equally.[20]

Very few grassroots conservatives—who are overwhelmingly middle class—participate in the campaign finance system as major donors. Some participate as smaller donors, but face enormous collective action problems vis-à-vis the larger donors who know what they want and know how to use their donations to get it. The electoral map has undergone tremendous change since Goldwater ran for president more than 50 years ago, and increasingly conservative voters live in so-called red states that on the whole have lower per capita income than their wealthier blue state counterparts. (See pages 55–56 of this book for a list of red and blue states ranked by per capita income.) This phenomenon can give liberal candidates an advantage in raising the hard-dollar donations that go directly to fund ground operations critical to electoral success (fundraising tours in New York, Boston, San Francisco, and Los Angeles alone can go a long way toward reaching fundraising goals). The problem is that middle-class and low-income voters, conservative and liberal alike, are shut out of the political process. Regardless of which side has an advantage in the money race, this money-saturated electoral system has drifted far from the founding fathers' vision of participatory democracy, and on that basis alone many political conservatives should strenuously object.

Even financially successful Americans on the whole opt out of the campaign finance system, putting them in a position not much better than people who have far less money to spend. These wealthier donors often face collective action problems, particularly if they try to get politicians to focus on a broader vision of effective government rather than on narrowly tailored special interests. An astonishingly small percentage of millionaires give large donations, and only a fraction of the billionaires

---

20 See Allen Wood, *Karl Marx* (London: Routledge and Kegan Paul, 1981), chapters 9 and 10.

in the Forbes 400 make political contributions close to the maximum amount allowed by law. This lack of participation even by those who can afford to participate belies the notion that campaign finance is an issue of class dominance, as some observers on the left would have us believe. It could be said that what unites 21st-century Americans of all socioeconomic classes is our inability to actively participate in and meaningfully finance political campaigns. Though many of our nation's founders were men of wealth, and part of their influence in society surely came from that wealth, it is hard to imagine them wanting to create a government in which that very influence could be bought and sold. They, like the many financially successful Americans today who opt out of campaign finance, would probably say "thanks, but no thanks."

These and other concerns about our system of campaign finance that should trouble conscientious conservatives who seek to model our government after the ideals of its founders are addressed in Chapters 2 and 6.

What brings together these seemingly disparate groups of conservatives is that they cannot logically or in good conscience claim to hold onto their core beliefs, values, and chosen policy positions yet still defend or remain indifferent to the status quo on campaign finance. That status quo is fundamentally opposed to what each of these groups of conservatives purports to want for our country. Different types of conservatives will find the arguments presented in different chapters of this book more or less appealing, but they all face the same question of conscience if they ignore a system of campaign finance that undermines what they themselves say is good for our country.

WHEN IT COMES to resolving the campaign finance problem, this book seeks a practical and feasible solution that will prove acceptable to many if not most people who identify with one or more of these four groups of conservatives, as well as to other people who do not identify themselves as conservative at all. This book seeks a solution that will unite, not divide, our country, that will allow us to once again become a republic of which we can all be proud.

There are several ways to reduce the inordinate influence of money on American politics.

One alternative is regulation of political campaigns and their financial backers, the approach taken by the 1971 Federal Election Campaign Act and the 2002 Bipartisan Campaign Reform Act. Regulation aimed at reducing corruption in the electoral process is arguably justified when t itself has such enormous power to regulate and tax. Allowing control over the reins of government to be sold to the highest bidder is absurd from the vantage point of voters who believe government power is too often abused.

Still, conservatives are skeptical of regulation as a solution to any problem. Most conservatives do not oppose all regulation, but they ask hard questions about whether regulation really works and whether it unduly interferes with individual liberty. Efforts to regulate political contributions and political campaigns arguably fall short by both measures. Efforts to regulate political speech, including methods of paying for political speech, are even less likely to be effectual and constitutional. Many conservatives will look for alternative solutions besides regulation to address the campaign finance problem. A few will deny there is a problem, an approach that has some short-term political advantages and may please some campaign contributors, but that in the long run undermines the credibility of the conservative movement with voters.

This book focuses on one solution in particular. This solution is premised on the observation that the problem is not too much money in politics, but not enough money in politics and, in particular, not enough money from the citizenry as a whole (as opposed to a very small percentage of the citizenry). This solution also assumes that the government should not provide the money, but the citizens themselves should. The principal role of the government should be to empower citizens to overcome their collective action problems and enact a system in which citizens can support candidates of their choice out of their own money.

The core premise of this solution is that the United States would have a better democracy if citizens could support political campaigns of their choice with a modest portion of their money that goes to pay taxes.

The most frequent launching point for public financing of political campaigns, proposed by President Theodore Roosevelt and more recently by professor Lawrence Lessig in his book *Republic, Lost,* is that public financing will need to be substantial to make a real difference in reducing the impact other campaign expenditures have on who wins elections and on decisions people make in public office. The public financing we have today is nowhere near enough, and indeed it is so little that many campaigns don't even want public money when it comes with strings attached.

The cost of financing political campaigns with taxpayer money would be substantial, but it pales compared to the economic loss caused by ineffective regulation and wasteful government spending that often occurs when campaign contributors get the quid pro quos they seek. On balance, taxpayer financing of political campaigns would probably save mc the long run, reducing the size of the federal government. That alone reason why many conservatives should support it.

The problem with many public financing proposals is political. Most of these proposals involve government subsidies of political campaigns and/ or vouchers distributed by government to citizens who would use them for political campaigns. Advocates of small government will pounce at any mention of government "handouts" to political campaigns in an era of trillion-dollar deficits. A voucher will be likened to food stamps or some other coupon program. Controversy over any of these ideas will be stirred up by beneficiaries of the present system of campaign finance who don't want to see their expenditures diluted by an influx of public money.

Yet the public debate does not need to be this way if we stop to think about whose money it is to begin with. The distinction between public money and private money is artificial—it was all private money before government took some of it. And perhaps citizens should get a meaningful say in who runs their government before the government has the opportunity to take their money.

To change the tone of the conversation, public campaign expenditures should be discussed in terms of a tax cut or tax rebate instead of a subsidy or a voucher. This is about returning to taxpayers a portion of their own money so they can have a real voice in what is done with the rest of their money. The idea would be to return to American taxpayers a flat sum taken out of taxes paid (perhaps $200 per taxpayer) for use by them in political contributions of their choice. The tax rebate program would be an acknowledgment of the fact that the right to vote is not enough in a world where money determines electoral success. Each taxpayer also needs some money with which to "vote," and government can make this possible by sending some of the money back to be used for that purpose.

The government could send a tax rebate check of $200 to every citizen over the age of 18, with one condition: The rebate check can only be endorsed over—in hard copy or electronically—to a bona fide political campaign or political party organization for expenditures in connection with an election. The check could not be used for any other purpose. Every citizen over age 18 should get a $200 check because every citizen pays some type of taxes (income tax, sales tax, gas tax, etc.; the federal government could subtract amounts sent to persons who don't pay federal income taxes from federal revenue sharing with states in which those persons live and pay taxes). The point would be that every citizen is entitled to use some of his or her tax money ($200) to help choose the people who decide how the rest of the tax money is spent, and it would be up to the individual citizen to decide whether and how to "vote" with his or her $200 in federal, state, or local elections. People could of course increase the size of their monetary vote by also using after-tax money on political expenditures (corporations already use some pretax money for this purpose after *Citizens United*). But *everybody* would get to spend $200 to help choose their government before paying *any* taxes to support that government.

This tax rebate concept is similar in function to the many voucher ideas being proposed by advocates for government-funded political campaigns. But there is a critical difference. This is not about the government paying for anything with "its" money. This is about the government allowing us to use a portion of *our money* that would otherwise go to taxes for the purpose of choosing the public officials who spend the rest.

Taxation should be conditioned upon this fundamental right to meaningful representation. State constitutions and the federal constitution thus should include an amendment providing for taxation only with representation, stating that:

> No person eligible to vote in the United States shall be required to pay any federal, state, or local income tax or any other tax, and no sales tax shall be levied with respect to transactions entered into by such person, unless such person has an opportunity to designate once each year out of federal, state, or local tax receipts an amount of not less than $200 for expenditure in support of a candidate or candidates of the person's choice for elected office in the federal, state, or local governments.

This provision could also be enacted by Congress or state legislatures as a statute because, unlike restrictions on campaign contributions and spending, there are no constitutional issues with the government simply allowing taxpayers to make a decision about how to spend their own money.

The objective of this book is to convince conservatives to support such an amendment or a federal or state statute that accomplishes the same thing. Taxation is only justified when the taxpayer has a meaningful opportunity to choose who taxes him and spends his money. Politicians will be more accountable to people who vote for them and who help pay for their political campaigns, and the people in this country should be given a chance to do both.

Chapter 1

From Magna Carta to *McCutcheon*:
The Controversy over Taxation Without Representation

TAXATION WITHOUT REPRESENTATION has been the norm for most of human history. And it has been bitterly resented, generating social upheaval and revolution time and time again. The decree of Caesar Augustus ordering a census of the entire Roman Empire for purposes of taxation is a familiar part of the Christmas story ("And it came to pass in those days, that there went out a decree from Caesar Augustus, that all the world should be taxed." Luke 2:1, King James Version). A few decades later Roman taxation of the Jews would be a major factor in the disastrous Great Revolt of 66–73 AD.[21]

The revolt against taxation without representation in English-speaking countries goes back at least 800 years.

1215: The 1% Rebel Against Taxation Without Representation

KING JOHN, THE youngest of Henry II's five sons, ascended to the throne in 1199 upon the death of all of his brothers. In a war with Philip II of France, his difficult financial situation contributed to the collapse of his entire empire in northern France (England had controlled this territory since the Norman conquest of 1066). John would spend the next decade raising money to recapture his land in Normandy, and he

---

21 Flavius Josephus (ancient), *The Jewish War: Revised Edition,* trans. G. A. Williamson (New York: Penguin Classics, 1984).

imposed on his noblemen highly unpopular scutage, taxes on inheritances and town charters. The magnitude of the tax hikes he imposed was simply staggering, as shown by the following chart, prepared by professor Deborah Boucoyannis:

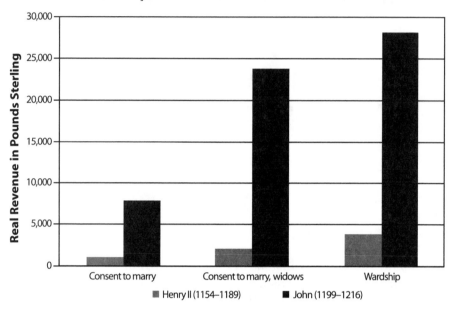

Feudal crown exactions from English nobles, 1154–1216, in pounds, adjusted for inflation. (Data: Waugh 1998; Barratt 1999. Figure: Deborah Boucoyannis)[22]

By 1215 noblemen in the north and east of England organized an armed revolt, leading their self-proclaimed Army of God to capture Lincoln, Exeter, and London. King John, on the verge of losing his throne, negotiated a meeting with the rebel leaders at Runnymede, where he agreed to the Magna Carta, or Great Charter. One of the most famous sections

---

22 Deborah Boucoyannis, "Taxing the rich leads to representative government. Happy 800th birthday, Magna Carta!," *The Washington Post,* 15 June 2015, washingtonpost.com/blogs/monkey-cage /wp/2015/06/15/taxing-the-rich-leads-to-representative-government-happy-800th-birthday-magna-carta (accessed 4 December 2015). See also Deborah Boucoyannis, "Strong Rulers, Land, and Courts: The Origins of Representative Institutions" (Cambridge, England: Cambridge University Press, forthcoming). Boucoyannis demonstrates that growth in the capacity to tax historically precedes demands for government accountability through representation.
Scott L. Waugh, *The Lordship of England: Royal Wardships and Marriages in English Society and Politics, 1217–1327* (Princeton, NJ: Princeton University Press, 1998); Nick Barratt, "English Royal Revenue in the Early Thirteenth Century and Its Wider Context, 1130–1330," in *Crises, Revolutions and Self-Sustained Growth: Essays in European Fiscal History, 1130–1830,* ed. W. M. Ormrod, M. Bonney, and R. Bonney (Stamford, CT: Shaun Tyas, 1999).

of this document designated a committee of noblemen from whom the king was required to obtain consent before imposing any new taxes. In the 16th year of his reign, on the south bank of the Thames River, King John promised:

> To obtain the general consent of the realm for the assessment of an 'aid'—except in the three cases specified above—or a 'scutage', we [the King] will cause the archbishops, bishops, abbots, earls, and greater barons to be summoned individually by letter. To those who hold lands directly of us we will cause a general summons to be issued, through the sheriffs and other officials, to come together on a fixed day (of which at least forty days notice shall be given) and at a fixed place. In all letters of summons, the cause of the summons will be stated. When a summons has been issued, the business appointed for the day shall go forward in accordance with the resolution of those present, even if not all those who were summoned have appeared.[23]

Not only did the Magna Carta seek to restrain the prevailing principle of *vis et voluntas* (force and will), but it also sought to enforce the agreed-upon terms through representative government by majority rule (albeit for men at the top of the social order), laying the groundwork for what would later become Parliament:

> The barons shall elect twenty-five of their number to keep, and cause to be observed with all their might, the peace and liberties granted and confirmed to them by this charter. . . .
>
> If one of the twenty-five barons dies or leaves the country, or is prevented in any other way from discharging his duties, the rest of them shall choose another baron in his place, at their discretion, who shall be duly sworn in as they were. In the event of disagreement among the twenty-five barons on any matter referred to them for decision, the verdict of the majority present shall have the same validity as a unanimous verdict of the whole twenty-five, whether these were all present or some of those summoned were unwilling or unable to appear. The twenty-five barons shall swear to obey all the above articles faithfully, and shall cause them to be obeyed by others to the best of their power.[24]

---

23 "English translation of Magna Carta," British Library, bl.uk/magna-carta/articles/magna-carta-english-translation (accessed 9 November 2015).
24 *Ibid.*

Most of England's citizens did not even know the Magna Carta existed,[25] much less had their lives affected by its statutes, but the political rights enshrined in the now-iconic parchment was the first glimmer of representative democracy in England. The momentous events of 1215 demonstrated to future rulers and governments the dangerous instability of a society in which those who paid for government had little or no power over it.

For the 99% of English society, the fight for taxation only with representation dragged on for another six centuries. The upward march of taxation that began under King John also did not come to an end with Magna Carta—indeed, it only accelerated.

By the 18th century, the burden of taxation fell not only upon the landed aristocracy but upon England's rising commercial classes as well. In addition to more common taxes on land and various commodities, Parliament resorted to stranger measures such as the infamous Window Tax, first levied during the height of the British currency crisis of 1696 to finance recoinage.[26] In addition, Britain's expensive wars waged first in the Western Hemisphere and India and then on the Continent required continuous military investment and generated massive budget deficits, forcing William Pitt the Younger to levy the first British income tax in 1798 to compensate for a decline in government revenues from import duties.

Yet until the Reform Act of 1832, representative democracy in England was limited, even in the so-called House of Commons. Most of the nation's population growth, which exploded with the advent of the Industrial Revolution, was concentrated in the urbanized middle and working classes. And these disenfranchised groups, who paid heavy taxes to finance Continental wars and the interests of British grain farmers without any voice in Parliament, began to work together to demand change.

Despite domestic unrest in the two decades following the Napoleonic wars, including the 1819 Peterloo Massacre that killed 15 and injured hundreds more protesters demanding reforms to representation, Parliament successfully avoided the type of violent revolution that had separated Great Britain from its American colonies in the 1770s and that had engulfed France in 1789 and then much of Europe again in the 1830s and 1840s. Buoyed by immense political pressure and public anger that the House of Lords had defeated the first two editions of the

---

25 Edward I issued the *Confirmatio Cartarum* (Confirmation of Charters, 3) in 1297, which required that the Magna Carta be "read before the people two times by the year" in cathedrals throughout England.
26 Andrew E. Glantz, "A Tax on Light and Air: Impact of the Window Duty on Tax Administration and Architecture, 1696–1851," *Penn History Review* 15 (2008), repository.upenn.edu/phr/vol15/iss2/3 (accessed 15 September 2015).

Reform Bill, its members recognized that a legislative fix to taxation without representation was possible and Parliament had the foresight to enact it.

The Reform Act of 1832 for the most part only extended the franchise to the commercial upper classes and a portion of the middle class (from approximately 500,000 to 813,000 out of a total population of 14 million); it was not until the Reform Act of 1867 (which doubled the British electorate) that the urban working class would begin to gain the right to vote. These acts launched a century-long process of expanding the franchise in Great Britain's electoral system, which was still dominated by the property-owning upper classes through the early 20th century. The House of Lords continued to possess (and frequently exercised) the power to reject legislation until the power was sharply curbed by the Parliament Acts of 1911 and 1949.

And throughout this period the franchise, for Englishmen who had it, was threatened by another phenomenon: corruption. The political commentator Edmund Burke, a founder of modern conservative political thought, spent much of his career in Parliament and in his publications combating corruption. He saw the cost of political campaigns as a significant part of the problem:

> Theory, I know, would suppose that every general election is to the representative a day of judgment, in which he appears before his constituents to account for the use of the talent with which they intrusted him, and for the improvement he has made of it for the public advantage. It would be so, if every corruptible representative were to find an enlightened and incorruptible constituent. But the practice and knowledge of the world will not suffer us to be ignorant that the Constitution on paper is one thing, and in fact and experience is another. We must know that the candidate, instead of trusting at his election to the testimony of his behavior in Parliament, must bring the testimony of a large sum of money, the capacity of liberal expense in entertainments, the power of serving and obliging the rulers of corporations, of winning over the popular leaders of political clubs, associations, and neighborhoods. It is ten thousand times more necessary to show himself a man of power than a man of integrity, in almost all the elections with which I have been acquainted. Elections, therefore, become a matter of heavy expense; and if contests are frequent, to many they will become a matter of an expense totally ruinous, which no fortunes can

bear, but least of all the landed fortunes, incumbered as they often, indeed as they mostly are, with debts, with portions, with jointures, and tied up in the hands of the possessor by the limitations of settlement. It is a material, it is in my opinion a lasting consideration, in all the questions concerning election. Let no one think the charges of elections a trivial matter.[27]

This was an old problem with representative government. Burke pointed out in the same speech that frequent elections and "the monstrous expense of an unremitted courtship to the people" had also destroyed republican government in ancient Rome:

So was Rome destroyed by the disorders of continual elections, though those of Rome were sober disorders. They had nothing but faction, bribery, bread, and stage-plays, to debauch them: we have the inflammation of liquor superadded, a fury hotter than any of them. There the contest was only between citizen and citizen: here you have the contests of ambitious citizens of one side supported by the crown to oppose to the efforts (let it be so) of private and unsupported ambition on the other. Yet Rome was destroyed by the frequency and charge of elections, and the monstrous expense of an unremitted courtship to the people. I think, therefore, the independent candidate and elector may each be destroyed by it, the whole body of the community be an infinite sufferer, and a vicious ministry the only gainer.[28]

The cost of becoming and staying a member of Parliament contributed to specific corruption problems that Burke also worried about. These included the influence of offices and pensions bestowed by the Crown on members of Parliament as well as the corrupt influence of one of the earliest and most infamous government-sponsored enterprises: the East India Company. These instances of corruption—and their modern counterparts[29]—are discussed further when Chapter 3 turns to the relationship between big government and the cost of political campaigns.

---

27 Edmund Burke, "Speech on a Bill for Shortening the Duration of Parliaments" (1780), gutenberg.org/files/16292/16292-h/16292-h.htm (accessed 15 September 2015).
28 *Ibid.*
29 Modern variations on the government-sponsored enterprise (GSE) concept include the mortgage giants—and campaign contributors—Fannie Mae and Freddie Mac that contributed to the financial crisis of 2008; see Chapter 3.

1770s: Americans Rebel Against Taxation Without Representation

IN THE 1760S England's Parliament had a hereditary upper house, the House of Lords, and an elected lower house, the House of Commons. Any new taxes levied on Englishmen required the consent of both. Yet as mentioned earlier, with representative democracy in Britain still in its early stages, the House of "Commons" represented little more than the interests of landed aristocracy, including some lesser landowners. Electoral participation for the 99% of British society, despite prominent reform advocates such as the Whig prime minister William Pitt the Younger, would have to wait until the 19th century. The situation in the American colonies was even worse, as Americans had no representation at all in Parliament, no matter how rich they were and no matter how much they paid in taxes.

By the 1750s England was—again—at war with France. Unlike earlier conflicts, this time the dispute revolved not around European territorial issues, but around disputed territorial boundaries in North America. Americans had little say in the decision to go to war, but many Americans supported England (George Washington, among others, fought in the war). Despite the territory they had acquired from the French as a result of the 1763 Treaty of Paris, the French and Indian War proved immensely costly to the British, whose national debt had doubled to nearly £130,000,000, the equivalent of £16 *billion* in today's values.[30] Caving to additional political pressure to keep a large standing army in the colonies, Prime Minister George Grenville shifted this financial burden to the colonies through unprecedented direct internal taxation.[31]

The English government fired its opening salvos with the Sugar Act of 1764 (which halved the existing sixpence-per-gallon import duty on molasses, in an attempt to incentivize compliance) immediately followed by the Stamp Act of 1765 (which required printed materials such as newspapers, legal documents, and even playing cards be printed on paper that bore a tax stamp). Facing fierce colonial opposition, street protests, and merchant boycotts, the latter was repealed in March 1766.

However, the English government, despite a leadership change (King George III's frustration with Grenville led to his replacement by Lord Rockingham in 1765), remained recalcitrant, simultaneously passing the

---

30 Edmund S. Morgan and Helen M. Morgan, *The Stamp Act Crisis* (Chapel Hill, NC: University of North Carolina Press, 1995), 21.
31 Peter David Garner Thomas, *British Politics and the Stamp Act Crisis: The First Phase of the American Revolution 1763–1767* (Oxford, England: Clarendon Press, 1975), 37.

Declaratory Act, which reinforced parliamentary sovereignty "in all cases whatsoever," alongside the repeal of the Stamp Act.[32] Next came the Townshend Acts, which, beginning in 1767, imposed taxes on a wide range of imported consumer goods such as glass, lead, paint, paper, and tea. British Chancellor of the Exchequer Charles Townshend proposed these acts because he believed Americans would be more willing to accept a tax on imported goods.

He was wrong. The Americans again rebelled. Leaders of the revolt predominantly hailed from the upper echelons of American society (including John Dickinson, who penned the highly influential and widely published "Letters from a Farmer in Pennsylvania"), but they recognized the need to include "the whole of political society, involving all of its social and economic subdivisions"[33] to ensure the protest's eventual success. Indeed, some of the strongest supporters of rebellion, those who took to the streets to demonstrate and burn effigies, were tradespeople and professionals in Boston and other urban areas, understandable as the most hated English taxes were not directed at landed estates of the aristocracy as much as consumer products such as newspapers, books, and tea. "Taxation without representation" was a popular phrase for describing the British tyranny, and to this day has been a phrase associated with the American Revolution.

As John Hancock wrote in 1768 on behalf of Boston selectmen[34] protesting the Townshend Acts:

> *You are already too well acquainted with the melancholy and very alarming Circumstances to which this Province, as well as America in general, is now reduced. Taxes equally detrimental to the commercial interests of the Parent country and the colonies are imposed upon the People, without their consent; Taxes designed for the Support of the Civil Government in the Colonies, in a Manner clearly unconstitutional, and contrary to that, in which 'till of late, Government has been supported, by the free Gift of the People in the American Assemblies or Parliaments; as also for the Maintenance of a large Standing Army; not for the*

---

32 *Declaratory Act 1766.* Available at ushistory.org/declaration/related/declaratory.htm (accessed 15 September 2015).

33 Pauline Maier, *From Resistance to Revolution* (New York: Knopf, 1972), 87.

34 Selectmen were citizens chosen to oversee the day-to-day running of New England towns (essentially serving as the executive branch of local government).

Defence of the newly acquired Territories, but for the old Colonies, and in a Time of Peace.[35]

Furthermore, in that same year the Massachusetts House of Representatives ratified a circular letter drafted by Samuel Adams stating in part:

The House have humbly represented to the ministry, their own sentiments, that . . . his Majesty's American subjects, who acknowledge themselves bound by the ties of allegiance, have an equitable claim to the full enjoyment of the fundamental rules of the British constitution; that it is an essential, unalterable right, in nature, engrafted into the British constitution, as a fundamental law, and ever held sacred and irrevocable by the subjects within the realm, that what a man has honestly acquired is absolutely his own, which he may freely give, but cannot be taken from him without his consent; that the American subjects may, therefore, exclusive of any consideration of charter rights, with a decent firmness, adapted to the character of free men and subjects, assert this natural and constitutional right.

It is, moreover, their humble opinion, which they express with the greatest deference to the wisdom of the Parliament, that the acts made there, imposing duties on the people of this province, with the sole and express purpose of raising a revenue, are infringements of their natural and constitutional rights; because, as they are not represented in the British Parliament, his Majesty's Commons in Britain, by those acts, grant their property without their consent.[36]

The Massachusetts House circular went on to elaborate on an important theme—that the constitutional problem could not be solved by giving the colonists a voice in Parliament because their representation in a distant capital would be far too difficult and too expensive to match the level of representation they had in colonial legislatures:

This House further are of opinion, that their constituents, considering their local circumstances, cannot, by any possibility, be

35 John Hancock, *Letter of Boston Selectmen Protesting the Townshend Acts (1768),* historywiz.com /primarysources/hancockletter.html; digitalhistory.uh.edu/disp_textbook.cfm?smtID=3&psid=137 (accessed 15 September 2015).
36 Massachusetts Circular Letter, Province of Massachusetts Bay, 11 February 1768, in J. Jackson Owensby, *The United States Declaration of Independence (Revisited),* (Kernersville, NC: A-Argus Better Book Publishers, LLC, 2010), 252.

*represented in the Parliament; and that it will forever be imprac-
ticable, that they should be equally represented there, and consequently, not at all; being separated by an ocean of a thousand
leagues. That his Majesty's royal predecessors, for this reason,
were graciously pleased to form a subordinate legislature here,
that their subjects might enjoy the unalienable right of a representation: also, that considering the utter impracticability of their ever
being fully and equally represented in Parliament, and the great
expense that must unavoidably attend even a partial representation there, this House think that a taxation of their constituents,
even without their consent, grievous as it is, would be preferable to
any representation that could be admitted for them there.*

The message from the circular was clear: Even though taxation could
theoretically be predicated on full and equal representation of the colonists in Parliament, as a practical matter full and fair representation in a
distant central government was not possible. The Massachusetts legislature argued for local representation and decision-making because the
substantive quality of representation matters (voters too far away from
the government that taxes them are not really represented). Hence began
a debate in American politics about not only the extent of the formal franchise but the quality of representation itself. In the 250 years since their
dispute with Great Britain, Americans have frequently revisited this question: Is representation in a central government so expensive and imprac-
tical for ordinary citizens that important decisions, including imposition
of taxes, should be made as much as possible at the state and local levels?

Undaunted, Parliament passed the Tea Act in May 1773, allowing the
East India Company to directly ship tea to the colonies while validating
the tax on tea implemented under the earlier Townshend Acts (this was
one of the few taxes not repealed in 1770). (The corrupt influence on
Parliament of the East India Company, one of the earliest government-
sponsored enterprises, is discussed further in Chapter 3.) The British
prime minister, Lord North, fully expected that colonists would embrace
lower tea prices, upholding Parliament's ability to tax. But new protests
quickly followed with angry colonists vehemently rejecting British claims
over the power to tax. Cities such as New York and Philadelphia forced
East India Company ships to return to England, while Charleston and
Boston residents simply refused to unload the tea.

In Boston, faced with a rapidly approaching deadline to unload the
tea on December 16, a tense standoff between the Loyalist governor
Thomas Hutchinson and colonists culminated in the now-infamous
Boston Tea Party: A group of men associated with the Sons of Liberty

boarded the *Dartmouth, Eleanor,* and *Beaver* and dumped more than 300 boxes of tea worth around £1.2 million into Boston Harbor. British officials, even those considered sympathetic to the colonial cause, were shocked and outraged, inciting Parliament to pass the Intolerable Acts as punishment, but the daring act and the backlash it generated also rallied the colonists behind a shared belief in liberty, constitutional rights, and fair representation. Writing in his diary the following day, John Adams immediately recognized that "this Destruction of the Tea is so daring, so firm, intrepid and inflexible, and it must have so important Consequences, and so lasting, that I can't but consider it as an Epocha in History."[37] Even today, the Tea Party serves as an inspiration for Americans who continue to courageously resist taxation by a centralized government in which they have little voice in choosing.

Emerging triumphant from the Revolutionary War, American political leaders sought to form a new government markedly different from England's. The drafters of the Constitution were careful to avoid creating a powerful and potentially corrupt central government that could levy arbitrary taxes at will; consequently, they designed a federal government with limited powers to tax, primarily through excise taxes on specific goods as well as tariffs (an income tax would require a constitutional amendment over a hundred years later in 1914). Most of the people who paid taxes believed they had a meaningful say in their government, and they probably did.

As with any nation, there was corruption in the early days of the Republic. William Blount, a senator from Tennessee, was evicted from his seat in 1797 after going heavily into debt through land speculation and conspiring with the British to seize the Louisiana Territory from Spain. Another senator, William Maclay of Pennsylvania, complained of bribery, insider trading on government information, and more in his diary while serving from 1789 to 1791.[38] But the corruption was largely isolated instances rather than systemic (the federal government was relatively

---

37 John Adams, *Diary of John Adams, Vol. 2* (17 December 1773) in *Founding Families: Digital Editions of the Papers of the Winthrops and the Adamses,* ed. C. James Taylor (Boston: Massachusetts Historical Society, 2015), masshist.org/publications/apde2/view?id=DJA02d100 (accessed 10 November 2015).

38 *Journal of William Maclay: United States Senator from Pennsylvania 1789–1791,* ed. Edgar S. Maclay (New York: D. Appleton & Co., 1890), 174–175. See also Richard W. Painter, "Ethics and Corruption in Business and Government: Lessons from the South Sea Bubble and the Bank of the United States," lecture, University of Chicago Fulton Lecture, Chicago, 11 May 2006 (University of Minnesota Law School Legal Studies Research Paper, No. 06-32, papers.ssrn.com/sol3/papers.cfm?abstract_id=920912 [accessed 15 September 2015]).

"These crooked dealings in government bonds increased Jeffersonian Democrats' hostility to the rest of Hamilton's economic plan, hostility which culminated in Congress allowing the charter for the First Bank of the United States to lapse in 1808." *Ibid.*

small and most government continued to be at the local level), and there is little evidence that large portions of the voting population believed themselves to be excluded from a meaningful say over the composition of their government.

The Rise of Taxation in the United States

IN THE EARLY 1900s, populist Democrats and progressive Republicans appealed to the public to support an income tax to raise revenue and reduce the federal government's dependence on import duties. The public was told that only the richest Americans would be required to pay the tax. By February 13, 1913, Congress had enacted and three-fourths of the states had ratified the Sixteenth Amendment to the Constitution:

> The Congress shall have power to lay and collect taxes on incomes, from whatever source derived, without apportionment among the several States, and without regard to any census or enumeration.

For a few years politicians lived up to their word and the new federal income tax was only imposed on the very highest incomes. In 1914 the tax was 1% on income over $3,000 for individuals or $4,000 for married couples. There was a surtax between 1% and 6% on some higher incomes. Most people, however, could ignore the tax, as a mere 2% of Americans earned over the minimum.[39] The average annual income for most Americans at the time was about $600.

It did not take long, however, for politicians to change the rules. To finance American involvement in World War I, President Woodrow Wilson raised the tax rate to 2% for income over $1,000 for individuals and $2,000 for couples. By then the average American income was about $1,000, so many more Americans were subject to the tax. The federal government did not lower tax rates once an armistice ending the war was signed in 1918, resulting in corporate and individual income taxes making up more than half of government revenue by the 1920s, while tariffs, which previously occupied a significant portion of government receipts, fell to less than 15%.[40]

The Great Depression gave politicians yet another opportunity to raise taxes, as the country rallied behind old-age social insurance and other spending programs in President Franklin Roosevelt's New Deal. During

---

39 Brian Roach, "Taxes in the United States: History, Fairness, and Current Political Issues," (Global Development and Environment Institute, Tufts University, 2010), ase.tufts.edu/gdae/education_materials/modules/Taxes_in_the_United_States.pdf (accessed 15 September 2015).
40 *Ibid.*

World War II, Roosevelt argued that paying taxes became a matter of patriotism and national duty, claiming "in this time of grave national danger, when all excess income should go to win the war, no American citizen ought to have a net income, after he has paid his taxes, of more than $25,000."[41] By the late 1940s the top tax rate was over 90%.

Tax rates are down somewhat from their peak, but the government is enormous. The federal government alone spent 20% of the United States Gross Domestic Product in 2014, down from 24% in 2011.[42] Much of this money comes from taxes; the rest is borrowed, meaning that future generations of taxpayers will have to pay it back (the total national debt is now about $18 trillion).[43] State and local governments tax, spend, and borrow yet more money, putting many Americans in combined tax brackets of around 50% on earned income. Despite all this taxing, some state and local governments spend so much they are still on the brink of insolvency.

Do ordinary Americans at least have a say in choosing the government that taxes them and spends so much of their money?

The Rise and Decline of Representation in the United States

IN 1913 THE YEAR the income tax began, many American citizens did not have the right to vote. Women, like men, were subject to the income tax but were denied a voice in choosing the government. In much of the country, African Americans were de facto denied the right to vote through poll taxes, literacy tests, and other mechanisms of discrimination.

From the end of the 1910s through the 1960s, however, the franchise expanded.

Some states, including much of the West and Midwest, gave women the right to vote prior to 1917. The American entry into World War I and the corresponding surge in women working on the domestic front was another impetus. New York, then the most populous state, overwhelmingly voted to implement full suffrage in December 1917, convincing

---

41 W. Elliot Brownlee, *Federal Taxation in America: A Short History* (New York: Cambridge University Press, 2004), 109.

42 Sean Higgins, "Federal Spending Drops to 20 Percent of GDP," *Washington Examiner*, 29 December 2014, washingtonexaminer.com/federal-spending-drops-to-20-percent-of-gdp/article/2557957 (accessed 15 September 2015).

43 Josh Zumbrun and Nick Timiraos, "Q&A: What the $18 Trillion National Debt Means for the US Economy," *The Wall Street Journal*, 2 February 2015, blogs.wsj.com/economics/2015/02/01/qa-what-the-18-trillion-national-debt-means-for-the-u-s-economy (accessed 15 September 2015).

increasing numbers of politicians, even President Wilson himself, that suffrage could no longer be denied to women.[44] In 1920—seven years after the Sixteenth Amendment allowed Congress to impose a direct tax on personal income—the Nineteenth Amendment gave women the right to vote in every state.

Another suffrage movement gained steam in the aftermath of a global military struggle—this time the civil rights movement in the years following World War II. Hard-fought federal and state legislation, including the Voting Rights Act of 1965, ensured a larger percentage of the African American population a meaningful right to vote. Two centuries after the delegates at the Constitutional Convention enshrined their vision of a new nation whose government derived legitimacy "from the great body of the society, not from an inconsiderable proportion, or a favored class of it,"[45] the United States was finally moving closer to a model of representative democracy in which all citizens had a meaningful right to participate.

But there were also dark clouds on the horizon. Accompanying the dramatic expansion of suffrage in the 20th century was a stealthily growing threat to representation. This was a threat not to the right to vote in elections but to equal representation in the selection of candidates and the ultimate winners.

The way in which political campaigns were conducted increasingly made candidates and elected officials dependent upon the very small portion of the population that paid for their campaigns. This was not a new problem; recall that Edmund Burke had complained about the corrupting influence of the cost of Parliamentary elections in the 1770s. But it was a problem that was exacerbated by a large central government with power and influence concentrated in one place removed from much of the electorate, whether it be London in the 18th century or Washington, D.C., in the 20th and 21st centuries. As the United States grew bigger and elected officials represented more people (the House of Representatives is permanently fixed at 435 members, and each state has only two senators), personal contact with voters became more difficult and campaigns were forced to rely on expensive media outlets to reach voters.

---

44 In a September 1918 speech before the Senate, President Woodrow Wilson argued, "We have made partners of the women in this war; shall we admit them only to a partnership of suffering and sacrifice and toil and not to a partnership of privilege and right?"
Woodrow Wilson, "A Vote for Women," speech, US Capitol, Washington, D.C., 30 September 1918, senate.gov/artandhistory/history/minute/A_Vote_For_Women.htm (accessed 15 September 2015).
45 James Madison, "Federalist Paper No. 39," in *The Federalist Papers: Hamilton, Madison, Jay*, ed. Clinton Rossiter (New York: Mentor, 1961), 412.

As a result, it became more likely that those who bankrolled political campaigns, not ordinary Americans, would wield outsize influence over government, particularly at the national level where campaigns needed the most money. And the more power—including the power to tax and spend—the national government had compared with state and local government, the more drastic the impact this representation problem would have on people's lives.

The campaign finance problem confronting Americans was a modern variant of the "taxation without representation" problem that the Massachusetts House of Representatives confronted in 1768: Taxes were imposed without consent of the people being taxed, yet representation in the central government was not an acceptable solution if it would be too difficult and expensive to ensure it was full and equal. The United States once again faced the risk that the cost of political campaigns, particularly in federal elections, could make representation for ordinary Americans less than the full and equal representation envisioned by the country's founders.

First there were the newspaper barons. Up through the mid-20th century, newspapers' owners, who controlled the flow of information to the general public through content they chose to publish, wielded enormous weight with politicians. Some, such as William Randolph Hearst, had eccentric political views, but most backed either the Democratic or the Republican Party. Many, but by no means all, politicians depended on newspaper owners for support. Candidates paid for some political ads but for the most part also did whatever was necessary to stay on the good side of the newspaper owner, ensuring that the editorials, and often much of the news, would support the candidate's case for election. Controlling a newspaper was a highly effective way to get politicians to do what one wanted them to do.

And that aspect of the problem remains to this day. Though media has expanded to include radio, television, and in recent years the Internet and social media, many major supporters of political campaigns, including Rupert Murdoch and the late Richard Mellon Scaife, make control over media outlets an important part of their strategy for supporting candidates. This is an important point to remember because ownership and subsidization of media outlets that support or oppose candidates for practical purposes falls under the definition of a campaign "contribution" (which includes anything that significantly helps a campaign), but this type of contribution is almost impossible—as well as undesirable—for government to regulate. These media outlets are bought and sold in private markets and their communications are unquestionably protected by the First Amendment guarantee of freedom of speech and of the press, making this type of campaign contribution very difficult to control.

On the other hand, despite the influence of powerful newspaper barons, ordinary voters still had an important role in elections because political campaigns required people as much as money. Footwork on the ground—getting voters to the polls and persuading them to vote for a candidate—was probably the most important part of campaigning. The powerful Ohio political machines that sent William Howard Taft to the White House in 1908 had strong backing in the business community. Democrats relied heavily on labor unions. Both parties used religious organizations, including Catholic and evangelical Protestant churches. Money kept these machines running, but people—individual volunteers, clergy, labor leaders, and employers, among others—were important too.

The 1950s, however, saw the advent of paid political advertising on television, which increased the cost of campaigns significantly. In 1952 General Dwight D. Eisenhower's campaign filmed 40 20-second television spot commercials titled "Eisenhower Answers America." Twelve years later, President Lyndon Johnson plunged into negative advertising with the highly controversial Daisy Girl ad that featured a nuclear weapon exploding over a child picking daisies in a field—an ominous suggestion of what could happen if the Republican nominee, Barry Goldwater, were elected. All of this advertising was expensive and would continue to grow, and campaigns needed to raise cash to pay for it.

Congress and the Supreme Court Enter the Fray

RICHARD NIXON'S CAMPAIGNS, like many others, emphasized political fundraising when he ran for president in 1968 and 1972. The illegal activities his campaign and others conducted, including the 1972 burglary of the Watergate complex, scandalized the nation and pressured Congress to enact some measures of campaign finance reform, most notably the Federal Election Campaign Act of 1971 (amended in 1974), which imposed both reporting requirements and limits on campaign contributions and expenditures.

Political strategists and their lawyers soon figured out ways to bypass these measures, however, while also challenging them in the courts. The Supreme Court would thus assume a commanding role in the field of campaign finance, determining what Congress and state legislatures could and could not do to address a problem that the public was increasingly frustrated about.

The first major constitutional challenge to the Federal Election Campaign Act of 1971 was *Buckley v. Valeo*,[46] in which the Supreme Court struck down limits on campaign expenditures as unconstitutional but allowed caps on individual donations to particular campaigns to stand. Further opinions, including *Colorado Republican Federal Campaign Committee v. FEC* (1996),[47] upheld political parties' right to fund both mixed-purpose and candidate-directed activities with soft money, money that was donated to political parties and not specific candidates.

In response to the increasing influence of unregulated political donations, Congress enacted the Bipartisan Campaign Reform Act of 2002, which is better known as the McCain–Feingold Act.[48] Not only did McCain–Feingold ban political parties from soliciting or spending soft money, but it also sought to curb the use of issue advertisements by noncandidate individuals and organizations. This act, cosponsored by Senator and later GOP presidential candidate John McCain (R-AZ), regulated soft-money contributions to political parties and imposed additional requirements for campaign communications, including the requirement of a disclaimer on political committee communications and candidate-authorized media. In addition, for those advertisements not authorized by a candidate, the name and contact information for the responsible organization must be clearly provided. Most important, the act included restrictions on electioneering communications (advertisements) that are publicly distributed for a fee and that refer to a clearly identified federal candidate but do so with regard to a particular issue rather than specifically advocating for the candidate's victory or defeat. Under the act, these types of communications must be disclosed if the direct costs of producing and airing the advertisement total $10,000 or more. Finally, the act contained the restriction on use of corporate treasury funds to pay for electioneering communications, a restriction that was struck down by the Supreme Court in the now famous *Citizens United* case[49] in 2010.

In that case, a conservative political research and advocacy organization sought an injunction against the Federal Election Commission to prevent it from applying the McCain–Feingold Act regulations to a film the organization created critiquing Hillary Clinton shortly before the 2008

46 Buckley v. Valeo, 424 U.S. 1 (1976).
47 Colorado Republican Federal Campaign Committee v. FEC, 518 U.S. 604 (1996).
48 Bipartisan Campaign Reform Act of 2002, PL 107–155 (2002), 116 Stat. 81.
49 Citizens United v. FEC, 130 S.Ct. 876 (2010).

campaign in which she ran in the Democratic primary.[50] The Supreme Court held by a 5-4 vote that, under the First Amendment, corporate funding of independent political broadcasts in elections cannot be limited.[51] The opinion held that political speech may not be suppressed based on the speaker's corporate identity, and that the federal ban on independent corporate expenditures for electioneering communications violated the First Amendment.[52]

Then came *McCutcheon v. FEC*.[53] During the 2011–2012 election cycle, Shaun McCutcheon donated funds to several candidates and nonpolitical committees, all in compliance with the aggregate donation limits in place at the time. Wishing to donate more, McCutcheon partnered with the Republican National Committee to file a lawsuit, alleging that the limits are unconstitutional under the First Amendment.[54] They sought an injunction to prevent the FEC from enforcing the limits. In *McCutcheon* the Supreme Court struck down the aggregate limits on the amount a particular individual may contribute to all federal candidates, parties, and PACs combined in a two-year period.[55] The court reasoned that the aggregate limits "intrude[d] without justification on a citizen's ability to exercise 'the most fundamental First Amendment activities.' "[56]

The Supreme Court has not yet overturned individual donor caps on contributions to particular campaigns, but the court has struck down a provision that would adjust such caps based on how much money an opponent spends. In *Davis v. FEC*[57] it ruled that political speech was substantially burdened by the McCain–Feingold Act's "Millionaires Amendment," which tripled contribution caps for the opponent of a candidate who spent over $350,000 of his personal funds on his campaign. The court held that this provision unconstitutionally forced a candidate "to choose between the First Amendment right to engage in unfettered political speech and subjection to discriminatory fundraising limitations." This "unprecedented penalty" "impose[d] a substantial burden on the exercise of the First Amendment right to use personal funds for campaign speech" that was not justified by a compelling government interest.[58]

---

50 *Id.*, at 888.
51 *Id.* at 906.
52 *Id.* at 912–913.
53 McCutcheon v. FEC, 134 S.Ct. 1434 (2014).
54 *Id.* at 1443.
55 *Id.* at 1462.
56 *Ibid.* (citing Buckley v. Valeo, 424 U.S. 1, 96 S.Ct. 612, 643–644, 652).
57 Davis v. FEC, 554 U.S. 724, 128 S.Ct. 2759.
58 *Id.* at 739–740.

The Supreme Court has also rejected public financing schemes that tied one candidate's public funding to how much money is spent by or on behalf of another candidate (the taxpayer rebate plan described in Chapter 8 avoids this problem by allowing taxpayers to allocate $200 of their tax receipts to any candidate they choose, regardless of how much other money is spent by or on behalf of that candidate). Despite legislative initiatives in 11 states and four municipalities that incorporated public financing in state law, these provisions have been repeatedly struck down as violations of the First Amendment (freedom of speech), first in Vermont's *Randall v. Sorrell* (2008), then in Arizona's *Arizona Free Enterprise Club's Freedom Club PAC v. Bennett* and *McComish v. Bennett* (2010).[59] The Arizona case was notable in that the relevant law, the 1998 Arizona Citizens Clean Elections Act, enabled matching funds for publicly financed candidates if an opposing privately financed candidate's expenditures, combined with the expenditures of independent groups supporting the latter candidate, exceeded the publicly financed candidate's initial allotment. The publicly financed candidate was to receive roughly $1 for every dollar spent by or on behalf of the privately financed candidate. Citing the *Davis* decision as precedent, the Supreme Court struck down this provision of the Arizona law, ruling that Arizona was in effect penalizing political speech by and on behalf of the privately financed candidate by providing the publicly financed opponent with a dollar-for-dollar match. "Arizona's matching funds scheme substantially burdens political speech and is not sufficiently justified by a compelling interest to survive First Amendment scrutiny," wrote Chief Justice John Roberts for the majority, although the opinion also points out that public financing is acceptable provided it is "pursued in a manner consistent with the First Amendment."

In these cases, the Supreme Court has for the most part proven hostile to campaign finance reform, often in 5-4 decisions split along the party lines of the president who appointed each justice. This situation inspires reformers who claim that, with the change of one vote on the Supreme Court (replacing one conservative justice with a liberal one) the campaign finance problem can be solved.

As explained in Chapter 7, it is unlikely that federal limits on both independent and campaign contributions, even if held constitutional, could make a considerable dent in the problem of money in politics. The influence that money wields over the political system incentivizes people to continually find new avenues to exert this influence, and many of these avenues are nearly impossible to regulate without infringements on

59 Arizona Free Enterprise Club's Freedom Club PAC v. Bennett, 564 U.S. (2011).

the First Amendment that no justice on the court would accept (such as restrictions on owning a politically biased newspaper, hosting an Internet site that provides free content in exchange for watching political messages, or making a movie or publishing a book about a candidate). Even constitutionally accepted regulations will be extremely difficult to enforce if violations cannot be detected.

But reformers who advocate changing the composition of the Supreme Court are at least recognizing that there is a problem with our current system of campaign finance and that the court has blocked repeated attempts by elected legislatures to address the problem. These reformers correctly point out that the court would probably have ruled 5-4 in favor of existing regulations had one more liberal justice been appointed in place of a conservative justice. They incorrectly believe that these regulations, if upheld by the court, would have come close to solving the problem.

And these reformers *also* know that accomplishing their objective through change in the composition of the Supreme Court requires election of a liberal president and a sympathetic Senate, which means that liberals would be able to make headway on progressive solutions to a wide range of unrelated issues. For some reformers, these agendas may be more important than curbing the influence of money in the electoral process.

Conservatives clearly do not want liberals to implement their "solution" to the campaign finance problem by gaining the upper hand in all three branches of government. But it remains to be seen whether conservatives will first recognize that there is a problem and then offer a solution of their own.

Elections as a Billion-Dollar Business

ELECTION CAMPAIGNING IS now a billion-dollar business, with spending on opposition research, staff and consultants, publicity and outreach events, and especially television and radio ads growing more and more expensive. To pay for these expenditures, candidates for public office rely almost exclusively on contributions.

In this environment, elected officials constantly have to focus on raising money. As Lawrence Lessig points out:

> When Ronald Reagan ran for reelection, he attended eight fundraisers. When Obama ran for reelection, he attended 228 fundraisers. You just get a clear sense from that statistic alone of the radical

change in priorities of the president—but I can tell you
dynamic in Congress.[60]

This not only diverts attention from the business of governing but also provides preferential access to elected officials for the people who provide the money they need to stay in office. The interests and voices of the 99% or more of Americans who cannot make substantial campaign contributions, along with the substantial percentage of the richest Americans who choose not to make substantial campaign contributions (lack of participation even by the rich is further discussed in Chapter 6) take a backseat because the officeholder does not depend on their money for reelection.

Our current system of campaign finance also dramatically reduces ordinary voters' meaningful ability to choose candidates. Though everyone might be able to vote in a general election, they can only choose from candidates who have already been preselected by both major parties' "green" primary, where money determines who continues to campaign and who is forced to drop out.[61] A select few of the wealthiest and most powerful people in the United States wield direct influence over who can stand as a candidate for election to political office. These people either have tremendous amounts of personal wealth they are willing to spend on politics or, as leaders of corporations, trade associations, or unions, are in a position to control and spend other people's money.

Political Action Committees (PACs), along with so-called super PACs (independent expenditure–only committees), are at the heart of this problem. PACs are set up by corporations, organizations, or occasionally individuals to fund political candidates. Corporations that sponsor PACs cannot contribute to them out of their own treasuries but can cover administrative costs and then solicit employees, shareholders, and others to contribute to their PACs. Super PACs can make unlimited expenditures on electioneering communications but cannot contribute directly to or coordinate with candidates or parties.

According to the Center for Responsive Politics:

> *Technically known as independent expenditure–only committees,*
> *Super PACs may raise unlimited sums of money from corporations,*
> *unions, associations and individuals, then spend unlimited sums*

---

60 Elias Isquith, "It Shocks People, but It's Important: Lawrence Lessig on the 'Radical' Shift in American Politics," *Salon*, 30 August 2014, salon.com/2014/08/30/it_shocks_people_but_its_important_lawrence_lessig_on_the_radical_shift_in_american_politics (accessed 15 September 2015).
61 Lawrence Lessig, "Corrupt and Unequal, Both," *Fordham Law Review* 84, no. 2 (2015): 249–50 (discussing the Green Primary, citing Jamin Raskin and John Bonifaz, "Equal Protection and the Wealth Primary," *Yale Law & Policy Review* 11, no. 2 [1993]: 273–74.)

to overtly advocate for or against political candidates. Super PACs must, however, report their donors to the Federal Election Commission on a monthly or quarterly basis—the Super PAC's choice—as a traditional PAC would. Unlike traditional PACs, Super PACs are prohibited from donating money directly to political candidates.

As of October 20, 2014, 1,220 groups organized as Super PACs have reported total receipts of $462,494,032 and total independent expenditures of $246,648,184 in the 2014 cycle.[62]

Super PACs have been around since 2010 but are quickly growing in number and are very easy to set up. Political consultants who set up super PACs make money by selling them their services. "It has an incredibly simple one-page form you file with the FEC," according to Trevor Potter, former chairman of the FEC. "You need a treasurer and a bank account, and that's it. You're off and running."[63] In the 2012 election cycle, super PACs spent approximately $1 billion, 73% of that money coming from 100 people.[64]

Another quickly growing source of funds is the 501(c)(4) and other nonprofit organizations that are allowed to keep their donors secret. These organizations serve as the dark pools of campaign finance, a term originally coined by the financial world to describe institutions, hedge funds, and sovereign wealth funds that trade in securities and derivatives markets off of organized exchanges. In October 2014 *The New York Times* reported that more than half of the general election advertising coming from outside groups in the 2014 cycle came from groups that disclose little or no information about their donors:

Fifty-five percent of broadcast advertising in the midterm elections has been paid for by groups that do not fully disclose their donors, according to an analysis by The New York Times *of advertising data from the Campaign Media Analysis Group, compared with 45 percent from super PACs, which are required to file regular financial disclosures with the Federal Election Commission. . . . secretly funded advertising is widely expected to surge in 2016, when there will be no incumbent running for the White House.[65]*

---

62 "Super PACs," Center for Responsive Politics, opensecrets.org/pacs/superpacs.php (accessed 15 November 2015).

63 David Gura, "Some Consultants See a Payday in Super PACs," Marketplace, 20 October 2014, marketplace.org/topics/elections/some-consultants-see-payday-super-pacs (accessed 15 November 2015).

64 Evan Osnos, "Embrace the Irony," *The New Yorker,* 13 October 2014, newyorker.com/magazine/2014/10/13/embrace-irony (accessed 15 November 2015).

65 Nicholas Confessore, "Secret Money Fueling a Flood of Political Ads," *The New York Times,* 11 October 2014, nytimes.com/2014/10/11/us/politics/ads-paid-for-by-secret-money-flood-the-midterm-elections.html?_r=0 (accessed 15 November 2015).

The New York Times also noted:

> *According to a new analysis by the Brennan Center for Justice, a*
> *New York–based think tank that supports tighter campaign rules,*
> *more than half of the reported outside spending in nine leading*
> *Senate races—in Alaska, Arkansas, Iowa, Colorado, Georgia, Ken-*
> *tucky, Louisiana, Michigan and North Carolina—has come from*
> *anonymous donors. Through Sept. 30, reported expenditures in*
> *those nine races by groups that shield their donors totaled $84*
> *million, well ahead of the pace in 2012.*[66]

Nobody knows who these donors are—and as discussed in Chapter 5, nobody even knows if the money paying for these ads is American or foreign. In the not-so-distant future, people in other countries could use the dark pools of our campaign finance system to decide who runs our government and how government wields its power, with potentially massive ramifications for our national security and independence.

Finally, the dependency relationship lasts even after a member leaves Congress because many members later become lobbyists. Their staff often do the same. These former members and staff who become lobbyists know the remaining members of Congress and ask them for favors, although since 2007 some such "representing back" contacts are prohibited for a one- to two-year period. These lobbyists also know the political donors because they raised money from many of these same people when they were in office. This means that former members and staff turned lobbyists can do an enormous amount to help their former colleagues stay in office by bundling campaign money and by arranging for spending via the dark pools of 501(c)(4) organization money—provided of course their former colleagues return the favors. And the returned favors invariably are accession to the requests of a lobbying client who has paid the lobbyist handsomely for the necessary arrangements and perhaps also thrown his contribution into the lobbyist's "bundle."

Big Labor—Big Money

THE BIGGEST BUNDLERS of campaign contributions, however, probably are not lobbyists but labor union leaders. They don't bundle by soliciting individual donors and sending in the donations together for maximum impact. Instead labor union leaders simply extract dues and

---

66 *Ibid.*

other contributions from members and then make political expenditures from this pool of money as they see fit.

Union leaders used to influence politics by getting their members to vote. Today, with fewer members, union leaders have shifted their focus to something that many politicians want more than union members' votes: their money.

According to the Center for Responsive Politics:

> *The past generation has been marked by a changing economy, a pattern of deregulation, and decreasing union membership. In 2012, only 11.3 percent of workers belonged to unions compared to 20.1 percent in 1983. Still, the past couple of election cycles have seen increased campaign contributions by the labor sector. In the 2012 election cycle, the industry contributed more than $141 million to campaigns and committees, nearly double the almost $76 million contributed in the 2008 election cycle.*[67]

Thus, unions represent only 11.3% of the workforce but by ramping up political contributions hope to have a disproportionate impact on national labor policy—and probably do have a disproportionate impact on labor policy when the politicians they support win. None of this changes the fact that for the vast majority of American workers, the labor union agenda is marginally relevant or irrelevant because they don't belong to a union. Furthermore, union members have only an indirect influence over how their money is spent in the political arena. Many complain that the process by which union leaders are elected is as corrupt if not more corrupt than the political process in government. Labor leaders benefit, but it is not at all clear that workers do.

A single union, the National Education Association (NEA), and its affiliates contributed an enormous amount, roughly $30 million in the 2014 election cycle.[68] As discussed in Chapter 4, the NEA contributions have undermined the education agenda of some parents, social conservatives, and school-choice proponents. These contributions also undermine the efforts of American business to improve the American primary and secondary education systems—unless one concludes that teachers' unions, rather than parents and employers, know best how to prepare young people for the modern workforce.

67 Monica Vendituoli, "Labor: Background," Center for Responsive Politics, opensecrets.org/industries/background.php?cycle=2014&ind=P (accessed 15 November 2015).

68 "National Education Association, Profile for the 2014 Election Cycle," Center for Responsive Politics, opensecrets.org/orgs/summary.php?id=d000000064 (accessed 17 November 2015).

Relatively few campaign expenditures are allocated for the purpose of opposing positions taken by the teachers' unions in federal elections or statewide elections. What corporation has so much vested in the future workforce years from now that it would want to spend millions of dollars to oppose the NEA agenda? Collective action problems for parents and other education reformers are probably even worse. The cost of moving to a location with quality public schools despite teacher union influence, or of paying for private school, is far less than what it would cost to counterbalance the unions in federal or statewide elections. Individuals who choose to confront teachers' unions usually focus their efforts locally, often on local school board elections. With a few notable exceptions, such as the recent statewide effort in California to revise teacher tenure, activists in the education arena have ceded the national and statewide political playing field to the teachers' unions that can pay to play.

Another big contributor—at $11.3 million in the 2014 election cycle—was the American Federation of State, County and Municipal Employees and its affiliates.[69] Chapter 3 explains how the enormous size and cost of government, including state and local government, results from our system of campaign finance. These public employee union campaign contributions are part, although by no means all, of the explanation for developments that alarm many fiscal conservatives and taxpayers.

Public sector unions also are among the few unions that are adding members. When they jump into campaign finance as well, they usually get what they want. Collective action problems make it very difficult for the broad segments of the population opposing the public sector unions to respond (the recent election and retention of Governor Scott Walker in Wisconsin was a notable exception). This is true even in states in dire financial condition such as Illinois, where public sector pension funds and benefits threaten the state government with insolvency.

Unlike the private sector unions, public sector unions have few if any corporate interests directly opposing them on particular issues—their negotiation counterpart and political adversary is the city, state, or federal government itself. This means that the taxpayer stands on the opposite side of them on most issues. Except in the very few states that have a rebate program similar to the "Taxation Only with Representation" provision discussed in Chapter 8, taxpayers have no right to make political contributions from their taxes.

---

69 "American Federation of State, County and Municipal Employees, Profile for the 2014 Election Cycle," Center for Responsive Politics, opensecrets.org/orgs/summary.php?id=D000000061 (accessed 17 November 2015).

Yet public sector and private sector union leaders will both claim that "what is good for the goose is good for the gander." If corporations can make political expenditures, unions can too. They raise money for traditional PACs but also for 501(c)(4) electioneering expenditures to which the Supreme Court has given First Amendment protection no matter who pays for them. And labor leaders, whose personal political power comes with the power to allocate members' money to support or oppose candidates, make a seemingly compelling case to their members that these expenditures are necessary because corporations spend so much. They will also argue that labor unions are entitled to the same First Amendment rights as corporations (they are probably right on this point). And they will argue that if corporations can spend money on politics without the consent of their shareholders, labor unions should be able to do so without the consent of their members.

Distortion of the Electoral Process

THE 2014 RACE in New York's Third Congressional District, on the North Shore of Long Island, presents a graphic illustration of how campaign finance affects the electoral process. Incumbent Congressman Steve Israel (D-NY) got only 2% of his money from small donors; the rest came from PACs and big donors.[70] These big donors include $39,150 from employees of Rubie's Costumes; $35,400 from employees of Amneal Pharmaceuticals; $25,600 from employees of Deloitte; and $23,800 from employees of the John P. Picone Company, a construction firm.[71]

Congressman Israel's Republican opponent for the Third District seat, Grant Lally, raised almost all of his money from individual donors and needless to say had a lot less money than Israel—one-twentieth as much.[72]

Going through this data, and looking at the one, two, or even three extra digits in Israel's totals, one wonders what is going on in a relatively wealthy district that has sent many Republicans as well as Democrats to Congress. What we do know is that Israel won the election in 2014 by getting 52.6% of the votes to Lally's 43.4%, a respectable margin for a losing candidate who had almost no money.

---

70 "Rep. Steve Israel: Summary Data," Center for Responsive Politics, opensecrets.org/politicians/summary.php?cid=N00013345 (accessed 15 November 2015).

71 "New York District 03 Race, Top Contributors in 2014," Center for Responsive Politics, opensecrets.org/races/contrib.php?id=NY03&cycle=2014 (accessed 15 November 2015).

72 "Geography Data, 2014 Race: New York District 03," Center for Responsive Politics, opensecrets.org/races/geog.php?id=NY03&cycle=2014 (accessed 15 November 2015).

The role of big money in elections does not favor one party over the other, but it does favor incumbents such as Steve Israel time and time again. According to the Center for Responsive Politics, in 1974 the average spending in competitive races by challengers was $100,435 versus $101,102 for incumbents, less than a 1% difference. In 2012 challengers spent $2,456,903 versus $3,108,968 for incumbents, which is about 26% more. And this difference applies to total expenditures more than 20 times those in 1972, not including the 501(c)(4) and other shadow spending, which does not count toward campaign spending by either candidate but is common now and was virtually unheard of in 1972.[73]

Yet another problem is that the biggest donors have now asserted a claim to a substantial voice, and perhaps a controlling voice, over who the political parties' nominees will be. At a January 2015 annual winter donor retreat near Palm Springs, California, the billionaire brothers Charles G. and David H. Koch unveiled plans to spend and raise from approximately 300 coordinating donors close to $900 million for the 2016 campaign, which will probably be more than the amount spent by either the Republican Party or the Democratic Party.[74] Much of this money presumably was to be raised before the primaries even began, very likely giving the Kochs and their coordinated group of donors a lot of influence over who the Republican nominee will be. According to *The New York Times,* at least five potential presidential candidates were invited to the Koch event this year, "and four attended, including Governor Scott Walker of Wisconsin. On Sunday evening, three of them—Senators Marco Rubio of Florida, Rand Paul of Kentucky, and Ted Cruz of Texas—took part in a candidate forum on economic issues."

For Republican voters other than those invited to attend this gathering, the question is whether a "Koch Caucus" such as this one will effectively replace traditional caucuses and primaries in the 50 states. By the time candidate selection is formally made, will the outcome be a done deal? And how credible will the winner of the Koch Caucus be as a candidate with voters in a general election?

Republicans, however, can take heart in the damage that campaign finance is also doing to the Democrats. The "Soros Caucus," the "Steyer Caucus," or some other group of donors will likely organize similar events vetting Democratic candidates, so the Democratic nominee

---

73 "The Dollars and Cents of Incumbency," Center for Responsive Politics, opensecrets.org/bigpicture/cost.php?cycle=2012 (accessed 15 November 2015).
74 Nicholas Confessore, "Koch Brothers' Budget of $889 Million for 2016 Is On Par with Both Parties' Spending," *The New York Times,* 26 January 2015, nytimes.com/2015/01/27/us/politics/kochs-plan-to-spend-900-million-on-2016-campaign.html?_r=0 (accessed 15 September 2015).

will also appear to be out of touch with the concerns of ordinary voters. Another risk the Democrats face in the 2016 presidential race is that one candidate—former First Lady, Senator, and Secretary of State Hillary Clinton—has loomed large for so long that the big donors could have rushed to choose and finance her before fully vetting her record. This rush by big money to anoint a nominee in the Democrats' "green" primary— as campaign finance reformer and 2016 presidential candidate Lawrence Lessig calls it[75]—discourages other qualified candidates from entering the primary and risks alienating ordinary voters. When other candidates do enter the primary, without sophisticated fundraising organizations and the campaign infrastructure big donors pay for, it may be too late.

Distortion of the Legislative Process When Bribery Is Almost Always Impossible to Prove

THEN THERE IS the impact of campaign money not only on elections, but on the legislative process itself. Do campaign contributors get concrete results in return for their contributions? Is campaign money a form of legalized bribery?

Supporters of the current system argue that campaign contributions do not buy influence because there is no evidence of a quid pro quo in which elected officials exchange favors for contributions. The Supreme Court pointed this out as a justification for its holding in the *Citizens United* case.[76] Chief Justice Roberts, writing for the majority in *McCutcheon* observed that regulation of campaign contributions must "target what we have called 'quid pro quo' corruption or its appearance. That Latin phrase captures the notion of a direct exchange of an official act for money."[77] Once again, in that case also, the court found such corruption to be lacking. The notion that officeholders do not adjust their official actions somewhat to accommodate campaign contributors—even in the absence of an express quid pro quo—is counterintuitive. It is also counterintuitive that contributors—particularly unions, corporations, and trade associations but also some individuals—would make very large contributions if they did not expect something in return. The problem is that a quid pro quo amounting to bribery is almost always impossible to prove (bribery is a criminal offense requiring proof beyond a reasonable doubt).

---

75 Lawrence Lessig, "Corrupt and Unequal, Both."
76 Citizens United, Section B2 of the opinion.
77 McCutcheon at 1441.

Almost always. In rare instances, a campaign contributor oversteps conventional boundaries in the number and types of favors requested (personal as well as business favors), in the magnitude of campaign contributions, and by combining those contributions with other more conventional gifts (or bribes) such as free travel for the officeholder. The right combination of facts can give prosecutors a chance to prove that not only are personal gifts an appropriate subject of bribery prosecutions, but also the much larger campaign contributions that come along with those gifts.

In 2015 the Justice Department announced a criminal indictment against Senator Robert Menendez (D-NJ) and Salomon Melgen, a West Palm Beach ophthalmologist who was paid $21 million by Medicare in 2012. That amount is apparently more than any other physician who billed Medicare that year.[78] Melgen and his family donated almost $50,000 to Senator Menendez's campaigns, and in 2012 Melgen's business contributed over $700,000 to Majority PAC, which in turn spent money on supporting Democratic Senatorial candidates, including Menendez.[79]

Menendez intervened on behalf of Melgen when Medicare officials accused his business of overbilling.[80] Menendez also backed a proposal by a Melgen business to get a port screening contract in the Dominican Republic. If these facts are true, there is some evidence that Menendez and perhaps other leading Democrats involved with Majority PAC helped Melgen overbill Medicare by millions of dollars and obtain other favors in exchange for campaign contributions. Such a quid pro quo, if proven, would be bribery but will be difficult to prove. The fact that Melgen also asked the senator and his staff for personal favors—such as facilitating visas for Melgen's girlfriends—may make it easier for prosecutors to prove their case.

The indictment alleges that the campaign contributions were given in exchange for official action by Senator Menendez. The indictment also focuses on private airplane trips that Menendez took in 2010 to the Dominican Republic as a guest of Melgen. In 2013, two years later, Menendez reimbursed Melgen $58,000 for the plane trips and said that "oversight" caused him to fail to disclose the flights on financial disclosure forms. If they can

78 Jay Weaver and Daniel Chang, "South Florida Ophthalmologist Emerges as Medicare's Top-Paid Physician," *Miami Herald,* 9 April 2014, miamiherald.com/news/local/community/miami-dade /article1962581.html (accessed 15 September 2015).

79 Indictment in *United States v. Robert Menendez and Salomon Melgen,* dated 1 April 2015, online.wsj .com/public/resources/documents/menendez04012015.pdf (accessed 15 September 2015). Indictment paragraph 16 alleges that Menendez solicited and accepted from Melgen thousands of dollars in contributions that benefited his 2012 Senate campaign in exchange for official action. Paragraphs 46–63 provide specifics on contributions to Menendez's campaign, to Majority PAC for the benefit of Menendez's campaign, and to another senator, not mentioned by name, to satisfy Menendez's commitment to raise money for that senator's campaign.

80 *Id.* at paragraph 23(d).

be linked with official action taken by Senator Menendez, these plane trips are not only chargeable as bribes or gratuities, but, as an evidentiary matter, may help prosecutors prove that the campaign contributions were also received in connection with official action. This is the first prosecution of a member of the United States Senate or House of Representatives alleging a connection between official action and campaign contributions in violation of bribery and gratuity laws, and it is unclear whether the Department of Justice would have pursued this case if Senator Menendez had not also accepted free travel on multiple occasions from the same person who also made the campaign contributions.

It is also unclear how many similar prosecutions the Department of Justice will pursue, even if it is successful in its case against Senator Menendez.

More generally, some academic studies have failed to uncover significant evidence of a quid pro quo connecting campaign contributions with official action. Recently an opponent of campaign finance reform quoted a single line from a 2014 Ohio State University study of the effect of campaign contributions on legislation, which stated, "If corruption is limited to the quid pro quo exchange of money for political favors . . . there is little threat of corruption from outside spending."[81]

Corruption, however, is not limited to the type of quid pro quo exchange of money for political favors that would expressly violate bribery statutes and put both contributors and officeholders in jail. Corruption is broader than that, including the fact that officeholders know that they are dependent upon the money to get elected and know where the money is coming from. This in itself creates a dependency relationship, making it very likely that the officeholder will do what campaign contributors want and will avoid doing things they don't want. The same Ohio State study concluded that there was evidence of "enhanced access and influence—particularly in the form of implied threats of spending if legislators do or don't act in accord with the wishes of outside groups."

Furthermore, both the appearance and the reality of campaign money influencing government reinforce public perceptions that government is corrupt, reducing public confidence in government and participation in the political process. On this point, the Ohio State study goes on to

---

81 Paul H. Jossey, "Beware 'Conservative' Political Reformers," *Daily Caller,* 22 January 2015, dailycaller.com/2015/01/22/beware-conservative-campaign-finance-reformers (accessed 15 September 2015), quoting Daniel P. Tokaji and Renata E. B. Strause, *The New Soft Money: Outside Spending in Congressional Elections,* 2014 (Project of Election Law at the Ohio State University Moritz College of Law), moritzlaw.osu.edu/thenewsoftmoney/wp-content/uploads/sites/57/2014/06/the-new-soft-money-WEB.pdf (this study was based largely on interviews of former government officials and others involved in campaigns).

observe, "There is also evidence that outside spending has an effect on the legislative agenda. In addition, we found some evidence of indirect effects on the legislative process, including increased time spent fundraising, deteriorating relationships among Members of Congress, party polarization, and a loss of public trust."[82]

Is It Oligarchy or Is It Even Worse?

IN SOME WAYS campaign finance is creating a situation in the United States that is similar to that in Great Britain before the Reform Act of 1832. There are two political parties that compete in elections, but a very small percentage of the people decides who runs for office in those two parties. And the politicians listen mostly to those people, not to the general public.

The situation in the United States today, however, is in some ways worse than that in Great Britain before the Reform Acts. First, the US government today is much bigger, more expensive, and more powerful than government was in any country in the 1800s; the government can do much more damage.

Second, as explained more fully in Chapter 6, it is not true that a coherent and organized "elite" controls the US government through campaign contributions. People with the means to make substantial campaign contributions can control discrete decisions of government, or block reforms or even emergency measures they don't like, and they can wreak havoc in doing so. But nobody can make our government conduct its affairs as a whole in a manner consistent overall with even the selfish interest of a coherent class of people, much less the common interest of all. The richest Americans, even if they tried to cooperate with each other in the current system of campaign finance (as pointed out above, the Koch brothers may be attempting to put together such a coalition), face enormous collective action problems. Even if such a coalition agrees upon what they want from government, they are unlikely to agree on what policy initiatives come first. And, as evidenced by coalition building among wealthy donors on the liberal side of the political spectrum led by people such as George Soros and Ted Steyer, while other donors support the conservative side, there are sharp divisions within the wealthiest donors as a group. And, as explained in Chapter 5, some of the people who use campaign finance to control our government may not even be Americans.

---

82 *Ibid.*

This situation is worse than oligarchy because it is more chaotic. No single group of people, whether small as in an oligarchy or large as in a well-functioning representative democracy, decides what is best for the country. Instead, with respect to each particular issue, a small but unique group (such as ideologically oriented individual donors, plaintiffs' lawyers, real estate developers, financial services firms, teachers' unions, military contractors, entertainment companies, supporters of foreign governments, or companies with links to foreign governments) uses campaign finance to get what they want. As political campaigns get more expensive and officeholders depend more on campaign funds, more money is needed to get representation in government, but different people's money determines what happens at a particular moment on a particular issue. This campaign finance system makes the United States government vulnerable to irrational and incoherent decision-making, in sharp contrast with the government of any other country—whether representative democracy or oligarchy—in which some group of people, large or small, consistently advances a vision of what is in the national interest.

In sum, our representative democracy is not gravitating toward oligarchy, but instead toward something even worse—corruption. Corruption is the deviation of an institution from its intended purpose, usually because decision-makers make decisions that they would not make absent the corrupting influence (Lawrence Lessig likens this influence to a compass pointing north that is diverted in a different direction by a magnet placed at its side).[83]

Oligarchies are also vulnerable to corruption, but that corruption is a very different phenomenon from the oligarchy itself. As Barry Goldwater pointed out in his 1983 speech on the Senate floor, quoted in the introduction to this book, Great Britain struggled with corruption in Parliament at the time of the American Revolution. In the 1770s and 1780s Edmund Burke constantly complained about corruption—and the cost of Parliamentary campaigns—but the English establishment did not listen to him. This corruption was one of the things that disgusted the American colonists; they saw Great Britain as not only an oligarchy but a corrupt oligarchy.

China today is an oligarchy similar in some respects to Great Britain at the height of the British Empire, particularly before the Reform Acts. The objective of such an oligarchy is for a small group of people to run a country as they see fit, which usually involves some combination of their collective self-interest and what they believe is good for the country. The system bestows enormous advantages upon a small class of people—in

---

83 Lessig, *Republic, Lost* (2011).

China it is people connected with powerful companies or the even more powerful Communist Party—but the ruling class usually exercises power by acting collectively. They have certain ideas about what is in the national interest and act together to pursue them.

Corruption, by contrast, involves individual actors using influence over officeholders to divert government from the objectives it would otherwise pursue (that is, the objectives of an elite in the case of an oligarchy and the objectives of the citizenry in the case of a representative democracy). China's ruling elite today are taking corruption of public officials very seriously because they know that it is a threat to their plans for China's prosperity and security. Ethics education of public officials is now undertaken in China on a massive scale, and enforcement is being made a priority, so much so that there have been many public corruption criminal trials.

What are we doing about the problem of corruption in the United States?

The Future of Representative Democracy

FOR MOST OF recorded history, people have been governed by a monarchy, with a single person in charge and hereditary succession; a dictatorship, with a single person and/or the military in charge; an oligarchy, with a small group of people in charge; or some combination of these forms of government (many kings and other monarchs were descended from military commanders). Ancient Athens had a direct democracy, and ancient Rome for part of its history had a representative democracy, albeit one that Edmund Burke correctly pointed out was corrupted by the cost of standing for election ("Yet Rome was destroyed by the frequency and charge of elections, and the monstrous expense of an unremitted courtship to the people").[84] Over thousands of years, however, direct democracy and representative democracy have been the exception—and a rare exception—rather than the rule.

The 18th century brought dramatic change when European and American political thinkers wrote about the value of representative democracy, and then in the 1780s a new country, the United States, had an opportunity to design a representative democracy after a successful rebellion against Great Britain. Representative democracy would prove a powerful competitor to monarchies, oligarchies, and dictatorships. And the United States was its champion. Today the majority of countries in the world

---

84 Burke, "Speech on a Bill for Shortening the Duration of Parliaments." See also page 20.

claim to have a representative democracy, although some of these work better than others.

Oligarchies, dictatorships, and other undemocratic systems, however, remain powerful competitors with representative democracy. Furthermore, many representative democracies have elements of oligarchy, with a few citizens having more political power than others. Great Britain overlaid oligarchy on representative democracy until well into the 20th century, a period when the British Empire reached the height of its power. As pointed out above, China today is also an oligarchy. Small groups of people—business leaders and Communist Party leaders—make decisions for the country and enjoy much of the nation's wealth.

Many Americans believe that our representative democracy is morally and practically superior to the British oligarchy that we rebelled against in the 1773 Tea Party as well as modern oligarchies in China, Russia, the Middle East, and elsewhere. That comparison is moot, however, if our system is corrupt. A government based on any type of system—representative democracy or oligarchy—that does a better job at fighting corruption will probably do better overall than a rival system that does a significantly worse job of fighting corruption. The less corrupt government will have the advantage of being able to implement a coherent plan for the country's future, whether that plan be the collective will of an elite or the collective will of the majority of its citizens. In the corrupt country, by contrast, the government will constantly be diverted and undermined by people who use government for their own personal advantage in discrete matters and who pay little attention to government's original objectives, the country's fiscal condition, its security, or anything else that affects the country as a whole. Government decisions will be wasteful, inconsistent, and at times chaotic.

Representative democracy has moral and practical advantages over other forms of government, but not so much that it can overcome the disadvantages of corruption. The American system of campaign finance is not only corrupt but a serious threat to the functioning and even the independence of our republic (as pointed out in Chapter 5, foreign powers can and probably do take advantage of our system of campaign finance to influence our government).

What is at stake is whether the United States will function well enough for us to remain competitive with other world powers in confronting the challenges of the 21st century: national security, cybersecurity, counterterrorism, controlling government spending and debt, economic stability, education, conserving the environment, and others. This book discusses the distorting impact of campaign finance on some of the specific issues that interest voters who support "conservative" candidates, for example, the business climate and the overall economy, social issues, foreign policy, military preparedness, and trade. The future competitiveness of the United States, the richest and most powerful representative democracy in the world, turns on whether we can disentangle our government from a domineering and dysfunctional system of campaign finance.

Complete or partial failure of the 200-plus-year-old representative democracy in the United States furthermore could reverse global progress toward representative democracy. Our failure could convince other nations that representative democracy cannot work, at least for a wealthy superpower. Some nations might choose instead—as did ancient Rome—to revert to oligarchy and other authoritarian forms of government that characterized human civilization for most of recorded history.

Taking Back Our Republic

AMERICANS ONCE AGAIN face taxation without representation, just as English nobles did in 1215 and as the Boston Tea Party demonstrators did in 1773. The government today taxes heavily and spends even more, running up massive deficits to be paid by future generations of taxpayers. How this money is spent is influenced by who funds the political campaigns of our elected officials. There is a dependency relationship between officeholders and donors in that officeholders who do what donors want get support; those who don't do what donors want get less support and risk losing their next election.

Most Americans have comparatively little say in who the candidates are or what elected officials do in office. As explained more fully in Chapter 6, many of the richest Americans also have little say because they choose not to play the campaign finance game. Up and down the income scale almost everybody pays taxes but almost everybody is shut out or opts out of significant participation in campaign finance and the influence that comes with it.

The United States Constitution established a representative democracy that would become a world power, and other nations eventually followed our example. Now, our system of campaign finance has presented a clear threat to our representative democracy.

Over the next few years Americans will have to decide whether to restore the republican form of government that our founders envisioned—a government in which every citizen has a meaningful voice. Powerful vested interests—lobbyists, campaign contributors, and politicians—have a stake in the current campaign finance system. Those vested interests will only become more powerful, and reform correspondingly more difficult, as time passes. We may only have a short window of time.

The next part of this book discusses ways in which the current campaign finance system undermines the civic republican ideal of our country's founders (Chapter 2). In particular, the current campaign finance system promotes big government (Chapter 3), undermines traditional moral values whenever they conflict with commercial interests (Chapter 4), undermines our national security by allowing foreign interests to infiltrate American politics (Chapter 5), and disadvantages most upper-income Americans just as it disadvantages the middle class and the poor (Chapter 6). This book then turns to solutions that conservatives can embrace (Chapters 7, 8, and 9). The centerpiece of this discussion is the "Taxation Only with Representation" constitutional amendment or statute that should be adopted nationwide but that can also be adopted at the state level (Appendix A).

It is time for another tea party—this time to throw overboard a system of campaign finance that is corrupting and slowly sinking our republic.

In January 2015 a group of conservatives, including this author, formed a group called Take Back Our Republic, dedicated to reforming our campaign finance system. We can no longer ignore this issue. We need to take back our republic from a campaign finance system that is out of control. And we need to identify and implement solutions that are consistent with the principles of individual liberty and minimal government to which we are committed.

Chapter 2

The Participation Problem:
The Founders' Vision Betrayed

MOST POLITICAL CONSERVATIVES in the United States want a government that conforms as closely as possible to the design of the men who founded our country and drafted the Constitution. As discussed further below, our present system of campaign finance is antithetical to the principles of participatory democracy upon which this country was founded.

The founders saw the need for public participation in government. James Madison wrote in *Federalist* No. 39:

> *If we resort for a criterion to the different principles on which different forms of government are established, we may define a republic to be, or at least may bestow that name on, a government which derives all its powers directly or indirectly from the great body of the people, and is administered by persons holding their offices during pleasure, for a limited period, or during good behavior. It is* essential *to such a government that it be derived from the great body of the society, not from an inconsiderable proportion, or a favored class of it; otherwise a handful of tyrannical nobles, exercising their oppressions by a delegation of their powers, might aspire to the rank of republicans, and claim for their government the honorable title of republic.* [85]

Some, such as Thomas Jefferson, went so far as to opine that genuine public participation in a centralized national government was close to impossible:

---

85 Madison, *Federalist* No. 39, 1788.

It must be acknowledged, that the term republic *is of very vague application in every language. . . . Were I to assign to this term a precise and definite idea, I would say purely and simply it means a government by its citizens in mass, acting directly and personally according to rules established by the majority; and that every other government is more or less republican in proportion as it has in its composition more or less of this ingredient of direct action of the citizens. Such a government is evidently restrained to very narrow limits of space and population. I doubt if it would be practicable beyond the extent of a New England township.*[86]

Others, particularly in the Federalist Party of George Washington and John Adams, disagreed with Jefferson and believed that a strong central government was essential and that adequate representation in that government could be achieved through a well-drafted constitution. But they also envisioned robust public participation in government. Few if any of the founders believed that public participation in government was not important.

The *Citizens United* court itself recognized this when emphasizing the value that the founders placed on free speech:

The great debates between the Federalists and the Anti-Federalists over our founding document were published and expressed in the most important means of mass communication of that era— newspapers owned by individuals. See McIntyre, 514 U.S., at 341–343; id., at 367 (Thomas, J., concurring in judgment). At the founding, speech was open, comprehensive, and vital to society's definition of itself; there were no limits on the sources of speech and knowledge. See B. Bailyn, Ideological Origins of the American Revolution, *p. 5 (1967) ("Any number of people could join in such proliferating polemics, and rebuttals could come from all sides"); G. Wood,* Creation of the American Republic 1776–1787, *p. 6 (1969) ("[I]t is not surprising that the intellectual sources of [the Americans'] Revolutionary thought were profuse and various").*[87]

Up through the 19th century, statesmen continued to emphasize the importance of the right, and obligation, of citizens to participate in government. For example, in 1840 Senator Daniel Webster urged Americans to:

---

86 Thomas Jefferson, "Letter to John Taylor," Monticello, 28 May 1816, let.rug.nl/usa/presidents
/thomas-jefferson/letters-of-thomas-jefferson/jefl245.php (accessed 15 September 2015).
87 Citizens United, 353.

Impress upon children the truth that the exercise of the elective franchise is a social duty of as solemn a nature as man can be called to perform; that a man may not innocently trifle with his vote; that every elector is a trustee as well for others as himself and that every measure he supports has an important bearing on the interests of others as well as on his own.[88]

The founders' vision of a participatory democracy and Webster's vision of a trusteeship between voters and the rest of society depend upon several factors. One is a government that is not so large and remote that most voters don't know the candidates they vote for and candidates don't know most of the voters. Another is a campaign and election process that does not make candidates more dependent upon political party bosses, large organizations, campaign contributors, or other sponsors than they are on the support of ordinary voters.

Dependency relationships between candidates and political party bosses, particularly in large urban areas, and dependency relationships between candidates and labor unions and other quasi-political organizations, have a long history going back at least to the 19th century (at times even organized crime has sponsored candidates for public office). In some instances, these dependency relationships are receding, although they are by no means absent from the contemporary political landscape. The urgent problem is that another type of dependency relationship has emerged that turns on the one thing candidates need most to run for office: money.

Today participation in our government at all levels, and particularly at the national level, is threatened by a campaign finance system that makes officeholders more and more remote from the voters they purport to represent. Our current campaign finance system excludes the vast majority of voters from participating in an important part of the political process: paying for increasingly expensive political campaigns and the influence over candidates and officeholders that comes with paying for campaigns. The people who pay for these campaigns—and on whom candidates depend—represent a small segment of our society. The political party bosses, labor unions, and corporations that seek to build dependency relationships with candidates know that in today's environment giving money or raising money for candidates is the best way to do it.

Dependency relationships thus solidify between candidates and the few individuals who give the money or raise the money that candidates

88 Daniel Webster, *The Works of Daniel Webster, Vol. 2* (Boston: Little, Brown and Company, 1853), 108, from remarks made at a public reception by the ladies of Richmond, Virginia, on 5 October 1840.

need to survive. Dependency relationships also solidify between can-didates and the labor union, corporate, and trade organization leaders who control organizations that give money or raise money for political campaigns. The vast majority of voters recede into the background, their "trusteeship" that Daniel Webster talks about being limited to the task of expressing their "preference" among the candidates that other more powerful people have already anointed.

Individual donors, particularly large donors, are an extremely small percentage of the electorate. According to the Sunlight Foundation, "In the 2012 election . . . [m]ore than a quarter of the nearly $6 billion in contributions from identifiable sources in the last campaign cycle came from just 31,385 individuals, a number equal to one ten-thousandth of the U.S. population"[89] According to Harvard Law professor Lawrence Lessig, who has studied the data on contributions to campaigns and to super PACs, "A tiny number of Americans—.26 percent—give more than $200 to a congressional campaign. .05 percent give the maximum amount to any congressional candidate. .01 percent give more than $10,000 in any election cycle. And .000063 percent—196 Americans—have given more than 80 percent of the individual super-PAC money spent in the presi-dential elections so far."[90] The title to the article in which Lessig reported these findings, "Big Campaign Spending: Government by the 1%," is mis-leading because the data clearly shows that large donations are coming from far fewer than 1% of the population, and that almost all Americans, including most Americans in the top 1% of income earners, don't make the large campaign contributions and super PAC contributions that get the attention of candidates and elected officials. As discussed in Chapter 6, this situation should alarm everyone, including the top 1% of income earners, who are often blamed for a system in which most of them, like other Americans, have no meaningful role. This is not government by the 1% but rather something even worse.

The participation problem has a geographic dimension as well. Wealth in the United States is concentrated in some states and not oth-ers, and within each state wealth is concentrated in some regions and not others. Big political donors are thus more likely to live in wealth-ier locations. Also, people who choose to participate in the campaign finance system by donating or raising money are more likely to have that

89 Lee Drutman, "The Political 1% of the 1% in 2012," Sunlight Foundation (blog), 24 June 2013, sunlightfoundation.com/blog/2013/06/24/1pct_of_the_1pct (accessed 15 September 2015).
90 Lawrence Lessig, "Big Campaign Spending: Government by the 1%," The Atlantic, 10 July 2012, theatlantic.com/politics/archive/2012/07/big-campaign-spending-government-by-the-1/259599 (accessed 15 September 2015).

opportunity in some locations than in others. Candidates, regardless of the people they "represent," go to these places where the money is because they depend on it to get elected.

The states are ranked below in per capita income (the color coding—gray for Republican and white for Democrat—shows which presidential candidate won that state in 2012):[91]

Rank	State	2014
1	Maryland	$70,004
2	Alaska	$69,825
3	New Jersey	$67,458
4	Connecticut	$65,753
	District of Columbia	$65,124
5	Massachusetts	$64,859
6	New Hampshire	$64,712
7	Virginia	$62,881
8	Hawaii	$62,814
9	Minnesota	$61,814
10	California	$60,287
11	Delaware	$57,954
12	Washington	$57,835
13	Wyoming	$56,322
14	Utah	$55,869
15	Colorado	$55,387
16	New York	$55,246
17	Rhode Island	$53,636
18	Illinois	$53,234
19	Vermont	$52,776
20	North Dakota	$51,704
	United States	$50,502
21	Wisconsin	$50,395

Continued on next page

91 "List of U.S. states by income," Wikipedia, 12 January 2015, en.wikipedia.org/wiki/List_of_U.S._states_by_income (accessed 12 November 2015).

Continued from previous page

Rank	State	2014
22	Nebraska	$50,296
23	Pennsylvania	$50,228
24	Iowa	$49,427
25	Texas	$49,392
26	Kansas	$48,964
27	Nevada	$48,927
28	South Dakota	$48,321
29	Oregon	$46,816
30	Arizona	$46,709
31	Indiana	$46,438
32	Maine	$46,033
33	Georgia	$46,007
34	Michigan	$45,981
35	Ohio	$45,749
36	Missouri	$45,247
37	Florida	$44,299
38	Montana	$44,222
39	North Carolina	$43,916
40	Idaho	$43,341
41	Oklahoma	$43,225
42	South Carolina	$42,367
43	New Mexico	$41,963
44	Louisiana	$41,734
45	Tennessee	$41,693
46	Alabama	$41,415
47	Kentucky	$41,141
48	Arkansas	$38,758
49	West Virginia	$38,482
50	Mississippi	$36,919

The wealthier states are heavily concentrated in the Northeast and the West Coast, with a few moderately wealthy states being in the Midwest. The South, with the exception of Texas, is almost entirely at the bottom of the income scale.

In each state per capita income is also heavily concentrated in a few regions, for example, New York City and surrounding suburbs have much higher per capita income than the northern and western parts of New York often referred to as upstate. The same is true of Chicago and its suburbs compared with downstate Illinois as well as the coastal regions of California compared with the eastern part of the state. Perhaps not surprisingly, these less prosperous regions tend to support a different political party (usually Republican) than the wealthier regions, but there is little that people in these regions can do to counter the influence of big campaign contributors on both political parties.

Per capita income data for geographic regions is important because it shows those regions where few people have the ability to make political contributions of more than perhaps $100 and probably less than that. These people are likely to be completely excluded from the campaign finance system because of enormous collective action problems; unless thousands and perhaps hundreds of thousands of them donate to the same candidate, they will have little if any impact. There are many similarly situated people in the wealthier states, but in the poorer states a larger percentage of the population is likely to fall into this category of complete exclusion because they cannot afford to make any significant political contributions at all.

These are also states and regions where candidates are most likely to have trouble raising money at home, leading them to aggressively search for funds elsewhere. Elections in these districts thus can be particularly vulnerable to influence by out-of-state money. And there is likely to be a lot more such out-of-state money because of the Supreme Court's *McCutcheon* decision striking down limits on aggregate campaign contributions by individuals.

Figuring out where campaign money is likely to come from requires a different calculation. While median income may be an indicator of the ability of a state's citizens to make small donations, only very high income earners can participate in the campaign finance system by making larger contributions. It is these donors who are most able to make substantial contributions not only to home state candidates but also to candidates in other states. According to IRS data, the top states for income tax filers earning more than $1 million are the following:[92]

State	Number of Returns with an Adjusted Gross Income of $1 Million–Plus
California	45,109
New York	38,240
Texas	27,347
Florida	20,921
Illinois	14,692
New Jersey	14,440
Massachusetts	11,395
Pennsylvania	10,180
Connecticut	9,493
Virginia	7,358

Only one notably conservative state—Texas—appears on the above list of highest income states. Two other states—Florida and Virginia—are swing states in presidential elections. The other seven states have consistently voted Democrat in the past several presidential elections (Pennsylvania is the only one of these states that Republicans seriously contest in presidential elections, and for over 20 years without success).

These states with high concentrations of millionaire earners are the states to which candidates from around the country will gravitate in their quest for hard-dollar donations. The Supreme Court's decision in *McCutcheon* to strike down limits on overall contributions by individual donors will accelerate this quest for money from out-of-state millionaire earners, who can now donate to as many candidates as they wish (for the moment, dollar limits on donations to individual campaigns remain intact, meaning donors who max out on home state candidates and still want to contribute to federal elections will likely direct their money out of state). Regardless of the political leanings of these donors, it should be clear to people not living in these states where hard-dollar funding for their local candidates will likely come from.

92 Ashlea Ebeling, "Where the 304,118 U.S. Millionaire Earners Live," *Forbes,* 14 February 2014, forbes.com/sites/ashleaebeling/2014/02/14/where-the-304118-u-s-millionaire-earners-live (accessed 15 September 2015).

If campaigns raised money only within the candidate's district, races in low-per-capita-income districts would probably be less expensive. But such is not the case; money in politics crosses state lines. Out-of-state money can thus have a stark impact on races, and on officeholders, in districts where less money can be raised at home. Candidates in wealthier districts also may use some out-of-state money but can turn to their own constituents (admittedly a very small percentage of their constituents) for much of the financial support they need to win.

People in lower-per-capita-income regions also have less impact on the presidential race. Even if early primaries are held in states without large cities and a high millionaire population, such as New Hampshire and Iowa, the "green" primary is held months earlier through multiple fundraisers in places such as New York, Los Angeles, Boston, Chicago, and the San Francisco Bay area. The likely nominee of both parties may already be determined in this green primary before New Hampshire and Iowa voters cast their first ballots.

This data illustrates two points. First, a campaign finance system that equates wealth with political influence will bestow disproportionate political influence on states and regions that have more wealth. That in itself should trouble anyone who believes in the founders' vision of participatory democracy. They did not want political influence to be skewed toward a certain geographic region at the expense of others. The founders studiously sought to avoid this problem when they drafted a constitution that achieved balanced representation of different geographic areas through proportionate representation in the House, equal representation of the states in the Senate, and a blended Electoral College. Such balance is destroyed when candidates for Congress or the presidency, regardless of whose votes they want on election day, spend much of their time appealing to the same groups of political donors in New York, Boston, Chicago, Palm Beach, San Francisco, and Los Angeles. Voters in geographic regions where those donors don't live are underrepresented in this system, regardless of the district where the candidate formally runs. As the East and West coasts and a few other places have a predominant influence on candidates who stand for election just about everywhere else, the constitutional design lies in shambles.

Second, this geographic concentration of political power is ideologically skewed as well. The states and regions where much of the wealth in this country resides—and with it disproportionate political influence under our system of campaign finance—are on the whole associated with the progressive end of the political spectrum. Donors are by no means all political progressives, but donors who live in these regions are more likely to be exposed in the neighboring population to political progressives than they are to political conservatives. For them, political conservatism may be a political philosophy, but they will have limited exposure to ordinary people who actually vote for conservatives and limited understanding of the reasons these ordinary people vote for conservatives. Some types of political conservatives—such as the social conservatives discussed in Chapter 4—may be almost entirely absent from the political landscape in these regions where most donors live. Even the most conservative donors, and the candidates who cater to those donors, may think that those types of conservatives can be ignored.

This is a situation that should deeply worry the conscientious conservative, and not just because high-level donors are likely to come from liberal states and regions (some of these donors are conservative regardless of where they live). The real problem is that in places where per capita income is below the national median, unless there is a tax rebate or voucher system similar to that described in Chapter 8, the exclusion effect is likely to be severe. Few citizens have any voice at all, even a small voice, in the campaign finance system. Furthermore candidates from both political parties are likely to develop dependency relationships with donors who live elsewhere. It is true that candidates running for office in solidly Republican or Democratic districts usually don't need out-of-state money to win, but in swing Congressional districts, and in close Senate races, out-of-state money can make a big difference. The combination of voter exclusion from the campaign finance system and out-of-state influence over elections and elected officials disillusions voters. Although voters around the United States are disillusioned by our campaign finance system, voters in low-per-capita-income states will likely sense the impact of big money on local elections more intensely. The result sooner or later will be voter disengagement from the political system entirely, occurring perhaps first in regions of the country that many political conservatives call home.

Disengagement of anyone—conservative or liberal—from the political system is not what the founders of our country envisioned. Both Republicans and Democrats, conservatives and liberals should worry about a system that purports to be a participatory form of government but that in fact excludes the vast majority of people from participation based on ability to pay.

Conservatives in particular should worry about their grassroots supporters who are not rich but overwhelmingly middle class. Grassroots conservatives care passionately about political principles such as individual liberty, free enterprise, and traditional values, but most cannot afford to make large contributions. In making smaller contributions they face collective action problems that are even worse than the collective action problems of larger donors that are described in Chapter 6. How much longer will these grassroots conservatives, as well as other Americans, continue to participate in the political process when candidates are chosen by, and depend on, somebody else?

Chapter 3

From New Deal to Bad Deal:
Big Government in the Era of Big Campaign Finance

As POINTED OUT in the previous chapter, the founders would have been shocked by the average citizen's lack of civic engagement with the political process in modern America. A campaign finance system that makes elected representatives beholden to vested interests, often geographically remote from their constituents, is a big cause of the problem. Another cause of the problem is the sheer size of government and its power to tax, spend, and regulate economic activity in all segments of society across a large geographic area, a phenomenon that, as discussed in Chapter 1, in Anglo-Saxon societies dates back at least to King John. Big government expanded with the British Empire and then yet more with the growth of the United States and its powerful federal government.

As discussed further in this chapter, there is ample historical evidence that when economic power and political influence are interdependent, it is likely that government will dominate a larger share of the economy and interfere more in whatever share remains. Individual free enterprise will be left with less.

Politicians' principal asset is their influence. Their personal capital is greater if government does more than if it does less (politicians who become lobbyists get to enjoy this personal capital even after they leave office). A government that takes people's money away and spends it, that tells people how they can and cannot make money, and that sponsors its own enterprises and gives them advantages over competitors in the private sector, brings power to the politicians who run the government.

Power brings in money, which wins elections and keeps politicians in office, which brings more power and more money. Big government and big money gravitate toward each other, and absent a popular rebellion—a Tea Party or some other focused movement that is determined to separate them—government and money will continue to converge.

People who don't like big government can try voting for politicians who promise to cut back on government. Will these promises, however, be kept? Our experience with many so-called small-government politicians is that once they are in office they do little to reduce the size of government. As discussed further in this chapter, the modern campaign finance system makes the problem of big government much worse.

The government-managed economy reached its modern rendition in the United States 80 years ago in the era of the New Deal and grew enormously in the decades that followed.

During the New Deal, Republicans, who had become the small-government party, knew that they could not stop the growth of government, but they did organize support in Congress for legislation that would limit politicization of government: the Hatch Act of 1939. The act recognized the dangerous link between government economic power and partisan politics, and expressly prohibited federal employees from, among other things, engaging in partisan political activity on the job or using their official titles. The act subjects state and local government employees who administer federal funds to similar restrictions. Keeping the greatly expanded business of government separate from the business of choosing government was vitally important to critics of the New Deal, and the Hatch Act was a valiant effort to limit convergence of the two.

Unfortunately, this legislation was only a partial solution to the problem because it did nothing about the growing influence of big government and the influence over government of campaign contributors and fundraisers. After the financial collapse of the early 1930s and the regulation of the securities industry that followed in 1933, for example, Wall Street knew that big business depended on the good graces of big government. Financiers got involved in raising money for politicians, including Democrats (one of President Franklin Roosevelt's most generous campaign contributors and fundraisers, financier Joseph P. Kennedy, was appointed as chairman of the Securities and Exchange Commission in 1934 and then in 1937 as United States ambassador to Great Britain—the latter appointment ended disastrously when Kennedy undermined Roosevelt's efforts in 1940 to help Great Britain in its war with Nazi Germany).

Today our government feeds on a combination of tax money and campaign money. Government management of the economy at times may help soften economic fluctuations (economic conditions probably would have been even worse without the 2008 bailouts of the financial sector, but that begs the question of how government-sponsored mortgage finance enterprises contributed to the crisis to begin with). Much of the United States still experiences the full impact of recessions big and small, but a rare exception is Washington, D.C., one of the richest metropolitan areas in the world where employment is steady in good times and in bad. Many Americans increasingly see the combination of government power over the economy and privileged access to government and inside influence fueled by campaign money as a Bad Deal.

The interaction of big money and big government has a long and unfortunate history, some of which is described below.

Government-Sponsored Enterprises

THE FOUNDERS OF the United States were well aware of the problem of big government. They saw it across the Atlantic—in all its glorious dysfunction. By the 1760s and 1770s they had had enough and they rebelled against it.

Big government in the British Empire in the 17th and 18th centuries was fueled in large part by Parliament bestowing monopoly powers on politically connected merchant companies. Two of the most infamous were the South Sea Company and the East India Company.

The South Sea Company was so badly handled by its promoters and their friends in Parliament that it precipitated one of the first financial crises in modern history, the South Sea Bubble of 1720. Members of Parliament bought South Sea Company stock for their own accounts while passing laws bestowing special privileges upon the company so it would appear to have a vibrant South Sea trade, which it did not. When the bubble in South Sea Company stock burst and the price collapsed, Parliament responded with an investigation and imposed more regulation of joint stock companies in the Bubble Act of 1720. The act bestowed more regulatory power on Parliament itself, the very entity that had precipitated the South Sea crisis to begin with. (The act prohibited limited liability companies from having publicly traded shares without prior consent of Parliament, something that the South Sea Company ironically had already had).⁹³ This pattern of politicians setting up government-sponsored enterprises (GSEs) that in turn do financial favors for politicians would repeat itself many times in both Great Britain and the United States. So would the pattern of politicians responding to mismanagement and financial crisis with regulation that purports to solve a problem that the politicians themselves created.

In *The Wealth of Nations*⁹⁴ Adam Smith in 1776 decried this mercantilist linkage of political power and commercial wealth and advocated instead a laissez-faire economy in which individual economic actors would decide their own destiny. Powerful politicians, however, saw no reason to restrain themselves, particularly when business promoters were willing to do financial favors for politicians in order to secure favors from government.

The East India Company had a crucial role in building the British Empire and, like the South Sea Company, was rife with mismanagement and corruption. As Judge John T. Noonan Jr. writes in his seminal book on the history of bribes, as early as 1695 the company was investigated for bribing government officials. Ninety thousand pounds was spent by Sir Thomas Cook, a governor of the company, "and accounted for vaguely in connection with the [Company's] charter. The inference was drawn that the money had been spent corruptly."⁹⁵ Some of the money was tracked to the Duke of Leeds, who was investigated by the Commons. Although the Lords failed to try him, the scandal helped end his political career.⁹⁶ One hundred years later in 1795, Warren Hastings, British governor of Bengal from 1772 to 1785 and an official of the East India Company, was tried before the House of Lords for receiving bribes from Indian princes and others. He was acquitted, although the evidence against him was overwhelming.⁹⁷ The East India Company—even though it was often in financial difficulty and depended on public funds—reimbursed Hastings's legal expenses of £71,000.⁹⁸

---

93 Richard W. Painter, *Ethics and Corruption in Business and Government: Lessons From the South Sea Bubble and the Bank of the United States* (2006 Maurice and Muriel Fulton Lecture in Legal History, published by the University of Chicago Law School), chicagounbound.uchicago.edu/cgi/viewcontent .cgi?article=1003&context=fulton_lectures (accessed 15 September 2015).
94 Adam Smith, *An Inquiry into the Nature and Causes of the Wealth of Nations* (London: W. Strahan and T. Caddell, 1776).
95 John T. Noonan Jr., *Bribes: The Intellectual History of a Moral Idea* (Oakland, CA: University of California Press, 1986), 760–761, n. 35.
96 *Ibid.*
97 John T. Noonan Jr., "The Bribery of Warren Hastings: The Setting of a Standard for Integrity in Administration," *Hofstra Law Review* 10, no. 4 (1982): 1073.
98 *Id.* at 1075.

The intellectual founder of modern conservatism, Edmund Burke (member of Parliament for Malton) was one of the most outspoken critics not only of the expense of Parliamentary elections and of government corruption in general (his views are discussed in Chapter 1) but of the East India Company in particular. Burke criticized the company's monopolization of trade and exclusion of free enterprise; its interference with private property rights; its connections with powerful politicians; and its corruption, cruelty, and misrule in India.[99] In a lengthy speech before Parliament in 1783, Burke denounced the charter the company had received from Parliament as being contrary to the rights of man recognized in the Magna Carta:

> *The charters, which we call by distinction* great, *are public instruments of this nature; I mean the charters of King John and King Henry the Third. The things secured by these instruments may, without any deceitful ambiguity, be very fitly called the* chartered rights of men.
>
> *These charters [such as Magna Carta] have made the very name of a charter dear to the heart of every Englishman—But, Sir, there may be, and there are charters, not only different in nature, but formed on principles the* very reverse *of those of the great charter. Of this kind is the charter of the East India Company.* Magna charta *is a charter to restrain power, and to destroy monopoly. The East India charter is a charter to establish monopoly, and to create power. Political power and commercial monopoly are* not *the rights of men; and the rights to them derived from charters, it is fallacious and sophistical to call "the chartered rights of men." These chartered rights, (to speak of such charters and of their effects in terms of the greatest possible moderation) do at least suspend the natural rights of mankind at large; and in their very frame and constitution are liable to fall into a direct violation of them.*[100]

The East India Company, however, was politically well connected and Parliament continued to support it. The company experienced financial difficulties, and in a series of East India Company Acts (1772, 1784, 1793, and 1813) Parliament extended government loans (bailouts) to the company in exchange for recognition of British authority over the Indian

---

99 Edmund Burke, "Mr. Burke's Speech, On the 1st December 1783 [Upon the Question for the Speaker's Leaving the Chair, in Order for the House to Resolve Itself into a Committee on Mr. Fox's *East India Bill*]", in *Miscellaneous Writings*, ed. E. J. Payne (Library of Economics and Liberty: 1990), econlib.org /library/LFBooks/Burke/brkSWv4c5.html (accessed 15 September 2015).
100 *Ibid.*

territories, while leaving the company in charge of managing (mismanaging) those territories. This policy required a military occupation in India that lasted until the late 1940s. The legacy of this GSE in India put a strain on relations between the two countries that lasts up to this day.

In the United States, the founders tried to set a different example, embracing a vision of limited government and an economy in private hands. However, economic necessity, or apparent necessity, quickly intervened. The political party favoring a powerful central government—first the Federalists and later the Whigs—promoted GSEs that solidified connections between money and political influence. The most prominent of these were the First Bank of the United States, founded by Alexander Hamilton in the late 1780s, and the Second Bank of the United States, headed by Nicholas Biddle in the 1830s. These banks embodied a vision of the GSE inherited from England (the Bank of England had been founded in 1696), and they brought with them similar risks. The experience of the United States with its first two national banks showed that a government that is bigger and does more in the economy is also at greater risk of corruption.

This is exactly what happened when Treasury Secretary Alexander Hamilton in 1789 used the First Bank of the United States to refinance, and ultimately pay at par (100%), the Revolutionary War debt of the United States and each of the individual states. This debt—much of it originally held by farmers and soldiers—was at the time trading at a fraction of par value because nobody believed it would be paid. Word of Hamilton's plan leaked to politically connected speculators who quickly began buying up the federal and state debt on the cheap. Members of Congress too joined the fray, leading one senator in the first Congress, William Maclay (D-PA) to complain at length in his diary about what was to be the first major insider trading scandal in United States history. This insider advantage bestowed on the New York–based speculators (the Capitol was in New York City at the time) infuriated Maclay's fellow Democrats, including Thomas Jefferson, and contributed to the bank's unpopularity with Congress, which eventually allowed the bank's charter to expire.[101]

The Second Bank of the United States also had a charter of limited duration from Congress. Nicholas Biddle, the bank's president, did what he could to keep powerful members of Congress committed to the bank. Dependency relationships in those days were created not as much by election campaigns as by the modest compensation of members of Congress, who usually worked second jobs to support themselves. The bank put some

101 Painter, *Ethics and Corruption in Business and Government supra,* quoting *Diary of William Maclay (1789–91).*

members of Congress on retainers and loaned money to others.[102] President Andrew Jackson's assault, however, continued and the bank eventually met its political demise in Congress. Biddle's influence peddling with Congress certainly did not help the bank's image in the eyes of the public.

Despite these setbacks, the growth of GSEs continued. The Federal Reserve itself was established in 1914, fortunately with more independence from Congress than its predecessors had and without the conflicting loyalties that inevitably arise when government is combined with for-profit enterprise (the Fed's purpose is not to make a profit for itself but to support the banking system). Although few people would support abolishing the Federal Reserve Board, its immense power to pick winners and losers in the economy has been salient in financial crises, most recently in 2008.

The New Deal of the 1930s brought about many more GSEs, mostly for massive public works projects such as the Tennessee Valley Authority for the generation of electricity.

Today two of the most powerful GSEs in the financial services sector are Fannie Mae and Freddie Mac, which securitize home mortgages, supposedly to increase access to affordable housing. Unlike the Federal Reserve Board and the GSEs of the Depression era, these two entities have shareholders and are intended to make a profit. They have executive officers who are chosen, and paid, in a manner similar to the executive officers of other companies. These officers are not employees of the government and are not subject to government conflicts of interest or ethics regulations.

Campaign contributions and lobbying are also an important part of their history. On July 16, 2008, on the eve of the financial crisis, the Center for Responsive Politics, in an article titled "Fannie Mae and Freddie Mac Invest in Democrats," reported that:

> The federal government recently announced that it will come to the rescue of Freddie Mac and Fannie Mae, two embattled mortgage buyers that for years have pursued a lobbying strategy to get lawmakers on their side. Both companies have poured money into lobbying and campaign contributions to federal candidates, parties and committees as a general tactic, but they've also directed those contributions strategically. In the 2006 election cycle, Fannie Mae was giving 53 percent of its total $1.3 million in contributions to Republicans, who controlled Congress at that time. This cycle, with Democrats in control, they've reversed course, giving

---

102 Painter, *Ethics and Corruption in Business and Government* supra.

the party 56 percent of their total $1.1 million in contributions. Similarly, Freddie Mac has given 53 percent of its $555,700 in contributions to Democrats this cycle, compared to the 44 percent it gave during 2006.

Fannie Mae and Freddie Mac have also strategically given more contributions to lawmakers currently sitting on committees that primarily regulate their industry. Fifteen of the 25 lawmakers who have received the most from the two companies combined since the 1990 election sit on either the House Financial Services Committee; the Senate Banking, Housing & Urban Affairs Committee; or the Senate Finance Committee. The others have seats on the powerful Appropriations or Ways & Means committees, are members of the congressional leadership or have run for president. Sen. Chris Dodd (D-Conn.), chairman of the Senate banking committee, has received the most from Fannie and Freddie's PACs and employees ($133,900 since 1989). Rep. Paul Kanjorski (D-Pa.) has received $65,500. Kanjorski chairs the House Financial Services Subcommittee on Capital Markets, Insurance and Government-Sponsored Enterprises, and Freddie Mac and Fannie Mae are government-sponsored enterprises, or GSEs.[103]

Fannie Mae and Freddie Mac, in the way they conducted business, were a significant factor in the 2008 collapse of the mortgage market, and with it the financial system. They were allowed to conduct business in this manner by a government that started them, paid for them, and bailed them out.

Peter Wallison wrote for *The American Spectator* in 2009:

Fannie and Freddie used their affordable housing mission to avoid additional regulation by Congress, especially restrictions on the accumulation of mortgage portfolios (today totaling approximately $1.6 trillion) that accounted for most of their profits. The GSEs argued that if Congress constrained the size of their mortgage portfolios, they could not afford to adequately subsidize affordable housing. By 1997, Fannie was offering a 97 percent loan-to-value mortgage. By 2001, it was offering mortgages with no down payment at all. . . .

The decline in underwriting standards is clear in the financial disclosures of Fannie and Freddie. From 2005 to 2007, Fannie

103 Lindsay Renik Mayer, "Fannie Mae and Freddie Mac Invest in Democrats," Center for Responsive Politics, 16 July 2008, opensecrets.org/news/2008/07/top-senate-recipients-of-fanni (accessed 15 September 2015).

and Freddie bought approximately $1 trillion in sub-prime and Alt-A loans. This amounted to about 40 percent of their mortgage purchases during that period. Moreover, Freddie purchased an ever-increasing percentage of Alt-A [loans made to speculative buyers or without the usual underwriting standards] and sub-prime loans for each year between 2004 and 2007. It is impossible to forecast the total losses the GSEs will realize from a $1.6 trillion portfolio of junk loans.[104]

By late 2008, virtually the entire financial sector became dependent upon government sponsorship, as the government propped up just about every financial institution, in many cases with direct loans or promises of credit or guarantees. For a few years many of the largest commercial banks, investment banks, money market funds, insurance companies, and other financial institutions were essentially GSEs in that their survival depended on credit from the American taxpayer.

And for years the recipients of this help had been keeping politicians well supplied with campaign contributions, enough so that arguably the politicians depended on the financial services industry for reelection as much as the industry depended on the government for bailouts.

On February 10, 2009, at the height of the bailouts, the Center for Responsive Politics reported that Congress would likely go easy on the banking executives:

The eight CEOs testifying Wednesday before the House Financial Services Committee about how their companies are using billions of dollars in bailout funds may find that the hot seat is merely lukewarm. Nearly every member of the committee received contributions associated with these financial institutions during the 2008 election cycle, for a total of $1.8 million. And 18 of the lawmakers have their own personal funds invested in the companies.

All of the companies represented at the hearing have received millions, even billions, from the government's Troubled Assets Relief Program (TARP), including Goldman Sachs, JPMorgan Chase, Bank of New York Mellon, Bank of America, State Street Corporation, Morgan Stanley, Citigroup and Wells Fargo. These companies' PACs and employees gave $10.6 million to all members of the 111th Congress in the 2008 election cycle, with 61 percent of that going to Democrats.

---

104 Peter J. Wallison, "The True Origins of This Financial Crisis," *The American Spectator,* February 2009, spectator.org/articles/42211/true-origins-financial-crisis (accessed 15 September 2015).

On the House Financial Services Committee, Rep. Jim Himes (D-Conn.), who is new to Congress this year and represents a state that is home to many hedge funds, insurers and other financial institutions, collected the most from these companies in the 2008 cycle at $195,350, followed by ranking member Rep. Spencer Bachus (R-Ala.), who collected $116,950. JPMorgan has been Bachus's second-largest donor over time, giving him at least $96,000 since 1989. The eight financial institutions at Wednesday's hearing have given $63,250 to the chairman of the committee, Rep. Barney Frank (D-Mass.), and JPMorgan has given him more money than any other company, union or organization since 1989. The House Financial Services Committee has jurisdiction over the housing and financial sectors.[105]

The national humiliation of massive mutual dependency in a supposedly free economy is a large part of what inspired the modern-day tea party movement. Ordinary citizens were disgusted at the financial services bailouts, not because the bailouts were bad economic policy (many of the bailouts were probably necessary to avoid a complete economic collapse) but because both government and the banking sector were so irresponsible to get into this situation to begin with and the individuals who caused the crisis were never held personally accountable. The financial industry's campaign contributions and the incessant revolving door between Wall Street and Washington—dubbed "Government Sachs" by the press—alienated ordinary Americans who paid their own debts and accepted the consequences of their financial decisions.

The founders did not intend it to be this way, and government's domination over the economy is nowhere enshrined in a constitution that envisioned a government of limited size and scope (as pointed out in Chapter 1, the income tax required a constitutional amendment that did not come until 1914). The relationship between government and money is one that the founders struggled with in their day, fully aware of the example that Great Britain was setting across the Atlantic and their desire not to follow that example if they could avoid it. This is an issue that modern-day Americans confront as well, only on a much bigger scale because our government is bigger and there is more money trying to influence it.

Taxing and Spending

THE CONNECTION BETWEEN taxing, spending, and political campaigns was summarized in a statement attributed to President Franklin Roosevelt's close advisor Harry Hopkins: "We will spend and spend, and tax and tax, and elect and elect." Taxing and spending is about winning political campaigns.

Campaign finance is also about winning political campaigns. And campaign finance affects taxing and spending. It should be clear that this influence is in one direction—toward more, not less. After all, how many campaign contributions are made with the explicit objective of convincing the government *not* to spend money on a particular thing?

Those campaign contributors who want something in return (some don't, but some do) weigh the anticipated return from political expenditures against alternative investments. They will allocate expenditures between politics and other investments depending upon where they are likely to get meaningful returns. As pointed out in Chapter 6, many businesses and financially successful individuals probably find campaign contributions to be a bad investment. Most don't contribute at all or make modest contributions compared to their financial wherewithal. Those who contribute—particularly businesses that contribute—are likely to expect some benefit, not necessarily an explicit quid pro quo, but sufficient influence on the legislative process to get what they want. For those businesses that are government contractors or that are downstream from government contractors or otherwise benefit from government contracts, it is usually quite clear what they want: the government's money, or rather taxpayers' money.

Government taxes away at least 30% of the gross national product, and then spends it. Much of this spending is discretionary.

A government that taxes and spends aggressively is a government worth paying to influence. A government that spends less is worth paying less to influence. Incumbent politicians know that bigger budgets—obtained through higher taxes—mean more campaign contributions. Smaller budgets and lower taxes mean smaller campaign contributions.

First, there is the enormous portion of the federal budget (over half) that goes to entitlement programs. Some of these programs, such as Social Security, may not be amenable to influence by campaign contributions, but Medicare and Medicaid expenditures are also enormous and are very much influenced by the amounts of money billed to the government by health-care providers. After a prescription drug entitlement was introduced in the Medicare Prescription Drug, Improvement, and Modernization Act of 2003 (this bill was passed by a Republican-controlled House of

Representatives and signed into law by President George W. Bush), drug companies had an even bigger interest in Medicare. These so-called entitlement programs benefit not just the ordinary Americans who use the health-care services and drugs, but also special interests that use political pressure to get what they want. In these entitlement programs, paid for by all taxpayers mostly through the Medicare payroll tax, some people are more "entitled" than others.

Health-care providers and drug companies are big contributors to political campaigns. The health-care industry as a whole contributed over a quarter of a billion dollars to campaigns in the 2012 election cycle. According to the Center for Responsive Politics, "Physicians and other health professionals are traditionally the largest source of federal campaign contributions in this sector, which contributed a record $260.4 million to federal candidates during the 2012 election cycle. Aside from doctors' associations, pharmaceutical companies and HMOs are consistently generous givers."[106]

Drug companies' campaign expenditures alone run well over $10 million per year, with three companies, Pfizer, Amgen, and Merck, each giving more than $1 million in the 2014 election cycle alone.[107]

Usually the relationship between campaign contributions by the health-care industry and specific political favors is not readily apparent. A quid pro quo that would amount to bribery is almost impossible to show, and a quid pro quo is not even necessary for contributors to have influence. As discussed in Chapter 1, campaign contributions create a dependency relationship whereby lawmakers depend on their contributors. Regulators of the health-care industry, including the Medicare and Medicaid programs, work under the watchful eye of lawmakers.

Once in a while, however, a health-care provider gives prosecutors an easy target by combining personal favors for politicians, such as free travel, with campaign contributions. This is what allegedly happened in the relationship between Senator Robert Menendez and Salomon Melgen, a West Palm Beach, Florida, ophthalmologist who was paid $21 million by Medicare in 2012. That amount is apparently more than any other physician who billed Medicare that year.[108] Melgen and his family donated more than $750,000 to support Senator Menendez's 2012 campaigns,

106 Monica Vendituoli, "Health: Background," Center for Responsive Politics, July 2014, opensecrets.org/industries/background.php?cycle=2016&ind=H (accessed 15 September 2015).
107 Alex Lazar, "Pharmaceutical Manufacturing: Background," Center for Responsive Politics, August 2015, opensecrets.org/industries/background.php?cycle=2016&ind=H4300 (accessed 15 September 2015).
108 Jay Weaver and Daniel Chang, "South Florida Ophthalmologist Emerges as Medicare's Top-Paid Physician," *Miami Herald,* 9 April 2014, miamiherald.com/news/local/community/miami-dade/article1962581.html (accessed 15 September 2015).

including $700,000 to the Democrats' Majority PAC, which in turn spent money on supporting Menendez.[109] Menendez intervened on behalf of Melgen when Medicare officials accused his business of overbilling.[110] The Department of Justice will seek to prove that this—and the other facts in the indictment—amount to bribery (this scandal was discussed in Chapter 1 as one of the rare instances in which it may be possible to prove that a campaign contribution is a bribe). Regardless of the outcome of that case, taxpayers are left with the regrettable fact that one of the defendants— someone who the government now alleges is a criminal—received $21 million from Medicare in 2012.

The story of Senator Menendez and Dr. Melgen is only the beginning. In 2014 *The Wall Street Journal* reported that Medicare investigations of hospitals and other health-care providers for overbilling frequently run into interference from members of Congress:[111] "Over the past five full years, medical providers and health-care interests spent $2.5 billion lobbying federal officials and lawmakers, according to the Center for Responsive Politics, fueled in part by a surge before passage of the 2010 health law. That constitutes 15% of all federal lobbying over that period."[112] These lobbying efforts are backed up by substantial campaign contributions. Contributions to the chairman of the House Ways and Means Committee, the budget watchdog, are apparently an important part of the strategy.[113]

In addition to entitlement programs such as Medicare and Medicaid, there is so-called discretionary government spending. Here also a lot of waste creeps into the federal budget. Nobel Prize–winning economist Joseph Stiglitz addressed this problem when he observed that rent-seeking wastes taxpayer money on unnecessary or inefficient government spending projects. He also observed that it crowds out other economic activity because "the rewards of rent seeking become so outsize that more and more energy is directed toward it, at the expense of everything else."[114]

109 Indictment in United States v. Robert Menendez and Salomon Melgen, 1 April 2015, discussed in Chapter 1, online.wsj.com/public/resources/documents/menendez04012015.pdf (accessed 15 September 2015).

110 Indictment paragraph 23(d).

111 Christopher S. Stewart and Christopher Weaver, "Medicare Overbilling Probes Run Into Political Pressure: Hospitals, Other Providers Seek Help from Elected Officials," *The Wall Street Journal*, 11 December 2014, wsj.com/articles/medicare-overbilling-probes-run-into-political-pressure-1418355002 (accessed 15 September 2015).

112 *Ibid.*

113 *Ibid.* (reporting substantial contributions from health-care providers to the chairman of the House Ways and Means Committee that he did not receive when he was not chairman).

114 Joseph E. Stiglitz and Linda J. Bilmes, "The 1 Percent's Problem," *Vanity Fair*, 31 May 2012, vanityfair.com/news/2012/05/joseph-stiglitz-the-price-on-inequality (accessed 15 September 2015).

Discretionary spending decisions are heavily influenced by individual senators and congressmen who can insert specific spending earmarks in legislation or persuade their colleagues and executive branch officials to support spending programs even if the formal earmarking process is not used. Executive branch officials also make spending decisions with respect to particular programs once their overall agency budgets are set by Congress. Executive branch agencies that want to spend more money than Congress has allocated to them will ask the president to seek a budget increase for the next year. The president then faces a choice between saying no to his cabinet officers and other agency heads, or submitting a larger budget to Congress. Saying no to agency heads who want spending increases may be the best thing for the budget but also may mean cutting politically popular programs. If these programs are supported by campaign contributors who help the president and members of Congress get reelected, the easier choice may be to increase spending.

And that appears to be the choice that is being made under both Republican and Democratic administrations, regardless of which party controls Congress.

A 2012 Heritage Foundation study looked at the 20-year period from 1992 to 2012, the presidencies of William Clinton, George W. Bush, and the first term of Barack Obama. Republicans controlled at least one house of Congress during most of this 20-year period. The Heritage study reports that:

- *Discretionary spending [as of 2012 was] about one-third of total federal spending.*

- *Since 2002, discretionary outlays surged 40 percent faster than inflation.*

- *In 2012, the federal government spent $1.289 trillion on discretionary programs. Of that amount, $669 billion went to national defense (including operations in Iraq and Afghanistan) and the remaining $620 billion funded nearly all other federal programs including education and transportation.*

- *Stimulus spending caused discretionary spending to peak in 2010. It is still 7 percent higher than its pre-stimulus level of $1,205 billion in 2008.*[115]

---

115 Alison Acosta Fraser, "Federal Spending by the Numbers - 2012," Heritage Foundation, 16 October 2012, heritage.org/research/reports/2012/10/federal-spending-by-the-numbers-2012 (accessed 15 September 2015).

Real Discretionary Outlays Have Grown 40% Since 2002 [116]

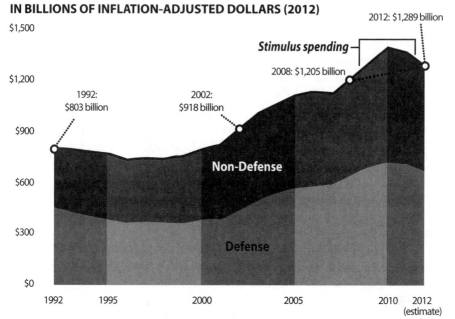

IN BILLIONS OF INFLATION-ADJUSTED DOLLARS (2012)

2012: $1,289 billion

$1,500

Stimulus spending

2008: $1,205 billion

$1,200

1992:
$803 billion

2002:
$918 billion

$900

Non-Defense

$600

$300

Defense

$0

1992   1995   2000   2005   2010   2012
(estimate)

Non-Defense Discretionary Spending Surged 78% [117]

PERCENT CHANGE SINCE 1992 IN INFLATION-ADJUSTED DOLLARS

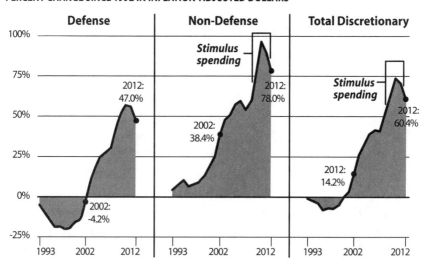

| Defense | Non-Defense | Total Discretionary |

100%

Stimulus
spending

75%

2012:
47.0%

Stimulus
spending

2012:
78.0%

2012:
60.4%

50%

2002:
38.4%

2012:
14.2%

25%

0%

2002:
-4.2%

-25%

1993   2002   2012   1993   2002   2012   1993   2002   2012

116 Office of Management and Budget, *Budget of the U.S. Government, FY 2013: Historical Tables, Table 8.7*, February 2012, whitehouse.gov/omb/budget/Historicals (accessed 15 September 2015). Congressional Budget Office, *An Update to the Budget and Economic Outlook: Fiscal Years 2012 to 2022, Table 1-1*, August 2012, cbo.gov/publication/43543 (accessed 15 September 2015).
117 *Ibid.*

The bottom line is that many politicians talk tough on spending, but the reality is that discretionary spending, and with it federal budgets, goes up and up.

In 2009 Taxpayers for Common Sense compiled data documenting more than 20,000 earmarks totaling over $35 billion. The Center for Responsive Politics, OpenSecrets.org, detailed $226.8 million in campaign contributions and lobbying expenditures. How members decide on earmarks is not very transparent, but occasionally media reports provide a glimpse of what is going on.[118]

For example, in 2007 *The New York Times* reported that Congressman Don Young (R-AK) sponsored an earmark in a 2006 transportation bill for a project costing $10 million in federal money, not in Alaska but at the proposed Coconut Road Interchange at Interstate 75 in Estero, Florida. Florida's elected officials were skeptical. Many favored widening the interstate to alleviate traffic jams, not an interchange. The site for the proposed interchange, however, was adjacent to land owned by a Michigan real estate developer who contributed and raised money for Young's reelection effort.[119] If the campaign finance system can cause a Republican congressman—who presumably tells his constituents that he favors lower taxes and lower spending—to behave this way, the impact on the overall federal budget, even if difficult to quantify, must be considerable. Those who favor a big federal government that taxes and spends may have no objections to the campaign finance system the way it is, but for those who want a smaller, less expensive government, the problem should be obvious.

Even fiscal conservatives such as former Senator Rick Santorum (R-PA)[120] and Senate Majority Leader Mitch McConnell (R-KY)[121] have played the earmarks game for campaign contributors, not because they like government spending but because it may be necessary for them to get reelected or elected to higher office.

---

118 Painter, *Getting the Government America Deserves* (Oxford, England: Oxford University Press, 2009), chapter 8 (discussion of earmarks).

119 David D. Kirkpatrick, "Campaign Funds for Alaskan; Road Aid to Florida," *The New York Times,* 7 June 2007, nytimes.com/2007/06/07/washington/07earmark.html?pagewanted=all (accessed 15 September 2015).

120 Michael Luo and Mike McIntire, "Donors Gave as Santorum Won Earmarks," *The New York Times,* 15 January 2012, nytimes.com/2012/01/16/us/politics/as-rick-santorum-secured-earmarks-2006-donations-flowed-in.html (accessed 15 September 2015); describes Rick Santorum's run for the presidency and provides examples of companies, such as JLG Industries, for which Santorum helped secure money in appropriations bills.

121 John Breshnahan, "Mitch McConnell Slammed for $110 Million in Earmarks," *Politico,* 10 March 2014, politico.com/story/2014/03/mitch-mcconnell-earmark-spending-104503.html (accessed 15 September 2015).

Occasionally the House Ethics Committee investigates links between campaign contributions and earmarks but, absent more than circumstantial evidence, formal allegations do not get very far. James P. Moran (D-VA) and Norm Dicks (D-WA) thus were both exonerated by the House ethics committee on February 26, 2010, after allegations that they had abused their offices by selling earmarks to donors. Both members claimed that they were unaware of who made donations to their campaigns or how much the donors gave. There was substantial overlap between defense industry contributions to their campaigns and earmarks,[122] but this was not sufficient to show the type of quid pro quo that would violate House ethics rules and antibribery laws.

And the earmarked projects that taxpayers pay for through this process range from wildlife preservation to defense and transportation. An aptly titled "pig book" report by Citizens Against Government Waste regularly identifies the most egregious examples.[123]

And then there is the defense budget. With recent cutbacks in the overall defense budget by the Obama administration, defense contractors have to fight for a share of a smaller pie. One approach would be to step up efforts to make higher-quality products and/or sell them to the government at a lower price. But there is another approach that is perhaps more expedient. By 2014, the top five federal contractors, all in the defense industry, had tripled their spending on political contributions within the past decade. Common Cause analyzed data from the Center for Responsive Politics and reported that PAC spending from the top five corporate recipients of federal contracts—Lockheed Martin, Boeing, Raytheon, General Dynamics, and Northrop Grumman—increased from $6.8 million in 2004 to $17.7 million in 2014. How much more these contractors gave to 501(c)(4)s and other dark money groups is not known.[124]

It is also not clear what these and other defense contractors get in return for their political expenditures. Presumably they get something or they wouldn't make these expenditures (after all, these and other businesses seek to make money, not promote political ideology for its own

122 R. Jeffery Smith, "Thin Wall Separates Lobbyist Contributions and Earmarks," *The Washington Post,* 7 March 2010, washingtonpost.com/wp-dyn/content/article/2010/03/06/AR2010030602374.html (accessed 15 September 2015).
123 See for example "Salmon Fund? 'Aquatic Plant' Control? Earmarks Soar Despite Supposed Ban, Report Finds," FoxNews.com, 13 May 2015, foxnews.com/politics/2015/05/13/salmon-fund-aquatic-plant-control-earmarks-soar-despite-supposed-ban-report (accessed 15 September 2015).
124 Jay Riestenberg, "Top Federal Contractors Disclosed Political Spending Tripled over the Last Decade. But What About Their Undisclosed Spending?" Posted on 11 March 2015, commoncause.org/democracy-wire/federal-contractors-disclosed.html (accessed 15 September 2015).

sake). It is also clear that members of Congress routinely inject themselves into debates about Department of Defense (DOD) contracts.[125]

Another area of increased federal spending is renewable energy. A particularly controversial expenditure was the Obama administration's approval of a $535 million loan guarantee to Solyndra, a solar energy company. A March 2009 Department of Energy press release announcing the $535 million loan guarantee for Solyndra said, "This loan guarantee will be supported through the President's American Recovery and Reinvestment Act, which provides tens of billions of dollars in loan guarantee authority to build a new green energy economy."

Solyndra, however, filed for bankruptcy about two and a half years after receiving the loan guarantee from the Department of Energy, leaving taxpayers holding the bag.[126]

As is almost always the case, the connection between fateful decisions such as this one and campaign contributions is opaque. George Kaiser, an Oklahoma billionaire, was very much interested in Solyndra. He was also a bundler who raised between $50,000 and $100,000 for Obama's 2008 campaign and later was a frequent visitor to the White House. In November 2011 the House Energy & Commerce Committee released several e-mails showing that Kaiser had discussed with his own business associates how to win White House and Department of Energy approval for the loan; some of these e-mails suggested that they may have discussed the project with the White House.[127]

Lobbyists are important players in the earmark game as well as in the campaign finance game that goes along with it. Many of these lobbyists

---

125 U.S. House of Representatives Office of Congressional Ethics, Report 14-1891, oce.house.gov
/disclosures/Review_No_14-1891_Referral.pdf (accessed 15 September 2015). See also Richard W.
Painter, "Yet Another Ethics Investigation That Misses the Point," *The Hill*, 10 October 2014, thehill.com
/blogs/congress-blog/politics/220170-yet-another-ethics-investigation-that-misses-the-point
(accessed 15 September 2015); discussing this report's failure to address the broader issues.

126 The guarantee program that Solyndra took advantage of was created under the massive economic
stimulus in the American Recovery and Reinvestment Act of 2009. This law amended the Energy Policy
Act of 2005 with a new Section 1705 allowing loans for "commercially available technologies."

127 Joe Stephens and Carol D. Leonnig, "Solyndra E-mails Show Obama Fundraiser Discussed Effort to
Win White House Help," *The Washington Post*, 9 November 2011, washingtonpost.com/politics/solyndra-
e-mails-show-obama-fundraiser-discussed-lobbying-white-house/2011/11/09/gIQAqPsq5M_story.html
(accessed 15 September 2015). In one e-mail, Kaiser said that when he and an official from his foundation visited the White House, staff members there showed "thorough knowledge of the Solyndra story,
suggesting it was one of their prime poster children" for renewable energy. Steve Mitchell, a managing
director of Kaiser's venture-capital firm, Argonaut Private Equity, who also served on Solyndra's board
of directors, wrote in a March 5, 2010, e-mail: "It appears things are headed in the right direction and
[Energy Secretary] Chu is apparently staying involved in Solyndra's application and continues to talk up
the company as a success story."

are former members of Congress or former Congressional staff members who push big spending projects for clients whose campaign contributions they bundle together for enhanced influence over their former colleagues in Congress.[128] They are not only lobbyists but bundlers—leading some commentators, including this author, to use the bagman image to describe what they are doing. Links between earmarks and lobbyist fundraising are abundant. For example, the Independent Center for Public Integrity did a computer analysis showing that John Murtha (D-PA), Peter Visclosky (D-IN), and Jim Moran (D-VA) steered a host of earmarks to PMA Group—a now defunct lobbying firm—and that PMA Group also raised campaign contributions for the lawmakers.[129]

Besides lobbying and campaign fundraising, government spending is the name of the game. Few if any of these lobbyists/bundlers are paid by clients to convince the government to spend *less* money on something; their job is to get the government to spend more. Taxpayers foot the bill and the size of government grows accordingly.

Regulating

REGULATED INDUSTRIES MAKE substantial political contributions. This may be because they want to, or because they have to.

In the past decade, two industries in particular have been subjected to increased regulation: financial services and health care. And these two industries are among the largest contributors to political campaigns. Commercial banks thus increased their contributions in the presidential races of 2008 and 2012.[130] The securities and investment industry, which had a key role in the financial collapse of 2008, was even more aggressive in increasing its political contributions beginning in 2008 when it became clear that increased regulation was inevitable.[131] And the healthcare industry substantially increased its contributions beginning in 2008

---

128 Richard W. Painter, "Lobbyists: Professional Intermediaries or Bagmen in Black Tie," in *Getting the Government America Deserves: How Ethics Reform Can Make a Difference* (Oxford, England: Oxford University Press, 2009).

129 Peter Overby, "Report: House Members' Ties to Defense Lobbyists are Tight," NPR, 9 September 2009, npr.org/sections/thetwo-way/2009/09/report_house_members_ties_to_d.html?sc=17&f=&utm_source=iosnewsapp&utm_medium=E-mail&utm_campaign=app (accessed 15 September 2015).

130 "Commercial Banks: Top Contributors, 2013–2014," Center for Responsive Politics, opensecrets.org/industries/indus.php?ind=F03 (accessed 9 October 2015).

131 "Securities & Investment: Top Contributors, 2013–2014," Center for Responsive Politics, opensecrets.org/industries/indus.php?ind=F07 (accessed 9 October 2015).

when it became clear that a new national health insurance plan, and the regulation that would come with it, was on the table.[132]

Despite populist sentiment against cozy relationships between regulated industries and politicians, these contributions don't result in less regulation overall. Of course there are waves of deregulation such as the extensive deregulation of the financial services industry during the Clinton administration when the largest banks were generous contributors to both political parties and sent some of their own leaders to Washington (Clinton's Treasury Secretary Robert Rubin was the former chairman of Goldman Sachs). But much of this deregulation is short-lived—Congress responded to Worldcom and Enron with extensive regulation of public company governance and disclosure in the Sarbanes–Oxley Act of 2002. After the 2008 financial crisis, the 2010 Dodd–Frank Act imposed almost 1,000 pages of new statutes, and thousands of pages of new regulations, on the financial services industry. There are arguments for and against each of these regulations on the merits, but the trajectory for most industries is clear: more regulation, not less. And the trajectory for campaign contributions from regulated industry has moved upward as well.

One reason there is so much regulation may be that politicians can create mutual dependency relationships with particular companies or entire industries by enacting regulation—especially complex regulations such as the Dodd–Frank Act of 2010 with exceptions and exceptions to exceptions. For whatever reason, both of the sponsors of that legislation, Senator Chris Dodd and Congressman Barney Frank, received large contributions from the financial services industry.[133]

The politicians become dependent upon the industry contributors for campaign money, but the contributors depend on the politicians for regulation consistent with their business model and that advantages them vis-à-vis competitors. The mutual dependency is costly, but it protects incumbent politicians from challengers by providing an enormous financial advantage, and it protects the industry contributors from competitors that, but for the regulatory scheme, might have an opportunity to break into their market.

In other instances, regulation can even become a means of rent extraction—that is, an extortion racket—in which politicians make it clear that unless they receive campaign contributions, there will be a lot more regulation.

This is probably the rationale for corporate support of the Tillman Act of 1907, which makes it a crime for corporations to give money to

132 "Health: Top Contributors, 2013–2014," Center for Responsive Politics, opensecrets.org/industries/indus.php?Ind=H (accessed 9 October 2015).
133 See Chapter 6, pages 138–139, discussing these contributions.

candidates for federal office (PACs to which employees contribute are the modern way of getting around this restriction). Congress passed the Tillman Act because many corporations wanted it; they were tired of being hit up for money by politicians with the power to regulate them.[134]

Yet this problem is still with us because corporate PACs can easily be used to get around the Tillman Act. Harvard Law School professor Robert Sitkoff, in his analysis of the Tillman Act and modern campaign finance, quotes this insightful excerpt from an editorial by Edward Kangas, who at the time of the 2002 McCain–Feingold Act was global chairman of Deloitte Touche Tohmatsu:

> *What has been called legalized bribery looks like extortion to us. . . . I know from personal experience and from other executives that it's not easy saying no to appeals for cash from powerful members of Congress or their operatives. Congress can have a major impact on businesses. . . . The threat may be veiled, but the message is clear: failing to donate could hurt your company.*[135]

In sum, a system in which elected officials receive direct or indirect campaign contributions from regulated industry is one in which mutual dependencies evolve between government and regulated business. Politicians know that either regulation or the threat of regulation keeps this relationship going. Cutting back on regulation for reasons related to the merits, for example, because regulation is excessive, unnecessary, or too costly, might be good for the economy, but it won't be good for politicians. Unregulated industries may no longer contribute to political campaigns, whereas regulated industries understand that they must make campaign contributions to get relief. And the system only keeps on going if new regulations constantly emerge, so regulated industry is under constant pressure to provide the funds politicians need to stay in office.

Enforcing

ENFORCEMENT OF LAWS and regulations should be fair and apolitical. Under our current system of campaign finance, it isn't.

Many law enforcement decisions by regulators and prosecutors are discretionary. Individuals and businesses that have political

---

134 Robert Sitkoff, "Politics and the Business Corporation," *Regulation* 26 (2003–04): 30–36, papers.ssrn.com/sol3/papers.cfm?abstract_id=479821 (accessed 15 September 2015).
135 *Id.* at 36.

connections—often obtained through campaign contributions—are likely to get a better deal than those who do not.

At the federal level, the people making these decisions are in federal agencies such as the SEC, FTC, and EPA (with respect to regulatory enforcement) and the Department of Justice (with respect to prosecutions). Many of these people are political appointees of the president or are supervised by political appointees. Political appointees are often active in the president's political party in their "personal capacity" (the Hatch Act allows executive branch employees to do just about everything but run for office themselves and directly ask for money). They attend and speak at fundraisers, and they see who is there and who is not. They also decide or help decide who is charged with violating the law and who is not. Many civil enforcement decisions are made in agencies other than DOJ, including decisions about whether to refer a matter to DOJ (DOJ prosecutors are subject to additional restrictions on participating in "personal capacity" partisan political activity under the Hatch Act, but many of their law enforcement decisions are made in conjunction with government officials who are not subject to these restrictions).

This arrangement makes businesses that do not have friends in the executive branch—that is, in the president's political party—particularly vulnerable to abuse of discretion when enforcement decisions are made. Businesses worried about adverse enforcement action may feel that they have to make friends by making political contributions to the president's political party, attending fundraisers, or having their lobbyist do it.

For regulated business, having friends in both political parties is ideal, but supporting the party that is more ideologically inclined to support aggressive regulatory enforcement against business (usually Democrats but sometimes Republicans) is particularly important. If they win, they will be looking for someone in the business community to make an example of. Who better to pick than a business that both arguably violated laws or regulations and did not support the regulators' favored political campaigns? For at least some vulnerable businesses, making campaign contributions can provide needed protection, even if some business leaders might see the system as a protection racket.

And the situation is even worse on the state level because most state attorneys general are themselves elected officials. They depend on donors to get into office and to stay there. Some state attorneys general also look to the same donors to reach the next office they aspire to, whether it be governor or election to Congress.

In the fall of 2014 *The New York Times* ran a series of three articles documenting lobbying of state attorneys general and corporate donors' contributions to both the Democratic and Republican state attorneys general associations (these three articles were awarded the Pulitzer Prize in April 2015).[136]

In one instance, an energy drink company under investigation in several states for misleading advertising contributed to the Democratic Attorneys General Association and then sent a lawyer to a weekend retreat at a beachfront resort in Santa Monica, California, sponsored by the association for its donors. There, the lawyer found the Missouri attorney general and asked him why he was investigating her client. The attorney general said that he did not know, called his office, and told his staff to drop the investigation.[137] *The New York Times* reported several other similar examples and documented in a lengthy chart the substantial sums donated by corporation and trade associations supporting state attorneys general of both parties. State attorneys general have enormous discretion in pursing civil litigation against businesses, and because of limited budgets they often hire contingent-fee law firms (many of these law firms are themselves campaign contributors) to conduct the cases they decide to pursue. For many businesses with actual or apparent problems under consumer law, environmental law, or other areas, the choice is simple: Pay now or pay a lot more later.

And when the plaintiffs' lawyers get involved the situation gets even worse (the political fundraising of the plaintiffs' bar is discussed in detail in Chapter 6). According to one of *The New York Times* stories, plaintiffs' lawyers sometimes identify businesses they would like to sue on behalf of one or more states, prepare draft complaints, and then approach state attorneys general or their subordinates at political fundraising events where they propose bringing suits on behalf of the state for a contingent fee (many state attorneys general award contingent-fee business to private law firms; this practice became prominent in the tobacco litigation, where many states hired private lawyers, but has spread to suits against other industries as well).

Of course, no prosecutor—federal or state—should discuss particular party matters such as a pending case or investigation, or the prospect of bringing new cases, at a partisan political event, much less a political fundraiser. After reading *The New York Times* articles, the author of this book submitted to the American Bar Association a proposal that ethics

---

136 Eric Lipton, "Lawyers Create Big Paydays by Coaxing Attorneys General to Sue," *The New York Times,* 18 December 2014; Eric Lipton, "Energy Firms in Secretive Alliance with Attorneys General," *The New York Times,* 6 December 2014; and Eric Lipton, "Lobbyists, Bearing Gifts, Pursue Attorneys General," *The New York Times,* 28 October 2014.

137 Lipton, "Lobbyists, Bearing Gifts."

rules be amended to prohibit such communications. Some state legislatures are considering enacting laws that would prohibit these contacts.[138] Thus far, however, such a ban has not been implemented. After publication of these articles, several state attorneys general said that they would pull out of their party associations if reforms were not made, but it is not clear what reforms, if any, will be made.

Regardless of what is done to regulate the conduct of state attorneys general and other prosecutors, the campaign finance system lies at the heart of the problem. It will be difficult to determine when contacts made through political fundraisers are being used to influence decisions of state attorneys general or other law enforcement personnel. As long as these people, or their bosses, depend on political contributions to keep their jobs, the possibility of such influence—and thus corruption of the law enforcement process—will remain. And the best choice for businesses that do not want to be targeted by law and regulatory enforcement actions may be to pay up, regardless of whether they actually support the candidates they are paying to support.

---

138 Eric Lipton, "A Bipartisan Push to Limit Lobbyists' Sway over State Attorneys General," *The New York Times*, 27 December 2014, ("perhaps most significant, a White House ethics lawyer in the administration of George W. Bush has asked the American Bar Association [ABA] to change its national code of conduct to prohibit attorneys general from discussing continuing investigations or other official matters while participating in fundraising events at resort destinations, as they often now do. Those measures could be adopted in individual states").

Chapter 4

The Widow's Mite:
Social Conservatives and Campaign Finance

As Jesus looked up, he saw the rich putting their gifts into the temple treasury. He also saw a poor widow put in two very small copper coins. "Truly I tell you," he said, "this poor widow has put in more than all the others. All these people gave their gifts out of their wealth; but she out of her poverty put in all she had to live on."
—Luke 21:1–4

NOT MANY FEDERAL judges include quotes from the Bible in their opinions. Judge Guido Calabresi of the United States Court of Appeals for the Second Circuit, however, quoted the above passage from the Gospel of Luke verbatim at the beginning of his concurring opinion in *Ognibene v. Parkes* (2010),[139] a case reviewing the constitutionality of a New York City campaign finance law narrowly tailored to prevent pay-to-play campaign contributions by city contractors.

Judge Calabresi faced a conflict between the Supreme Court's decision in *Citizens United* and a democratic society in which everyone's voice— the poor widow as well as the rich man—counted equally. He concurred with the Second Circuit's judgment upholding the New York law and distinguishing the Supreme Court's opinion in *Citizens United*, but he focused his concurrence on a resounding criticism of *Citizens United*. He ended the concurrence by returning to the Scriptural story of the widow's mite:

What is at stake here—what everyone knows is at stake here— is what was recognized and expressed so directly, succinctly,

---

139 Ognibene v. Parkes, 671 F.3d 174, 198 (2d Cir. 2011) (Calabresi, J., concurring), cert. denied, 2012 WL 950086 (U.S. June 25, 2012).

and powerfully in the story of the widow's mite. The ability to express one's feelings with all the intensity that one has—and to be heard—is a central element of the right to speak freely. It is, I believe, something that is so fundamental that sooner or later it is going to be recognized. Whether this will happen through a constitutional amendment or through changes in Supreme Court doctrine, I do not know. But it will happen. Rejection of it is as flawed as was the rejection of the concept of one-person-one-vote. And just as constitutional law eventually came to embrace that concept, so too will it come to accept the importance of the antidistortion interest in the law of campaign finance.

It is with that faith in a better future, along with an understanding of the requirements of our flawed present, that I join the majority opinion.

Judge Calabresi's words should resonate with anyone who is concerned about the power of individual conviction, including religious conviction, losing ground in modern society to the power of money.

Compared with the enormous amount of money put into campaign treasuries by commercial interests, donors motivated by religious conviction contribute relatively little. Wealth does not determine the importance of one's convictions in the eyes of God, and neither should it in a democratic society. Jesus wanted to hear from the poor widow at least as much as he wanted to hear from the rich men, and our elected representatives should do likewise.

Unless the campaign finance system is changed soon, however, causes motivated by conviction, whether religious or other moral conviction, will likely lose out to causes motivated by money. And with respect to the issues they care about, religious conservatives are likely to lose.

Morality and Money in America: The Founders' Vision, the Cross of Gold, and the Modern Assault on Natural Law

ALTHOUGH TAXATION WITHOUT representation enraged the colonists who led the American Revolution, the revolution had a spiritual dimension as well. The leaders of the revolution were of varying degrees of religiosity, but they often spoke of natural rights of men grounded in God's law. The Declaration of Independence thus said that men were "endowed by their Creator with certain inalienable rights" that no sovereign could take away.

Freedom of conscience was one of the most important political and religious rights of Americans. They could think for themselves and vote according to their conscience just as they lived their religious lives according to individual conscience rather than the dictates of a central authority. As John Adams observed shortly before the revolution:

> We electors have an important constitutional power placed in our hands; we have a check upon two branches of the legislature . . . the power I mean of electing at stated periods [each] branch. . . . It becomes necessary to every [citizen] then, to be in some degree a statesman, and to examine and judge for himself of the tendency of political principles and measures. Let us examine, then, with a sober, a manly . . . and a Christian spirit; let us neglect all party [loyalty] and advert to facts; let us believe no man to be infallible or impeccable in government any more than in religion; take no man's word against evidence, nor implicitly adopt the sentiments of others who may be deceived themselves, or may be interested in deceiving us.[140]

When they won the revolution and drafted a constitution, Americans believed that representative democracy was not just a human invention but also a gift from God. John Jay, the first chief justice of the United States wrote, "The Americans are the first people whom Heaven has favored with an opportunity of deliberating upon and choosing the forms of government under which they should live."[141]

By the 19th century this connection between faith and the franchise—and the moral duty to use the franchise against the evil of corruption—made its way into the history books. Noah Webster wrote in his 1832 *History of the United States*:

> When you become entitled to exercise the right of voting for public officers, let it be impressed on your mind that God commands you to choose for rulers, "just men who will rule in the fear of God." The preservation of government depends on the faithful discharge of this duty; if the citizens neglect their duty and place unprincipled men in office, the government will soon

---

140 *The Papers of John Adams,* ed. Robert J. Taylor (Cambridge, MA: Belknap Press, 1977), Vol. 1, p. 81, from "'U' to the Boston Gazette," written on 29 August 1763.
141 John Jay, *The Correspondence and Public Papers of John Jay Vol. I,* Henry P. Johnston, ed. (New York: G.P. Putnams Sons, 1890), 161.

be corrupted; laws will be made, not for the public good so much as for selfish or local purposes; corrupt or incompetent men will be appointed to execute the laws; the public revenues will be squandered on unworthy men; and the rights of the citizens will be violated or disregarded. If a republican government fails to secure public prosperity and happiness, it must be because the citizens neglect the divine commands, and elect bad men to make and administer the laws.[142]

Religious principles have throughout American history informed the political views of individual voters. This phenomenon is sometimes confused with, but in fact is very different from, entanglement of church and state, where the power of government is used to give preference to a particular religious viewpoint. In our individualized concept of a faith-based political discourse, religious conviction has inspired movements for abolition of slavery, abolition of child labor, workers' rights, civil rights, pacifist opposition to wars, abolition of the death penalty, and the protection of the unborn. Believers in these and other causes have steadfastly adhered to a concept of right and wrong that transcends the influence of materialism or other more narrow and selfish motives.

As the United States grew richer, however, conflict between money and morality intensified. The most tragic conflict existed from the outset because the founders never confronted the evil of slavery. Even as Great Britain and other countries moved to abolish slavery, the United States tolerated and even welcomed the spread of slavery. The booming cotton economy of the South, driven by the invention of the cotton gin and booming textile industries in the North, made it politically difficult to reverse course. Members of Congress, some of whom depended on the status quo for their livelihood and on wealthy plantation owners for their election, refused to embrace change until the Civil War forced it on them.

After the war, religious leaders in the late 19th century turned from denouncing slavery to denouncing the influence of money—Northern industrial and financial money in particular—in American political life. Populist politicians sermonized on this topic as well. Democratic presidential candidate William Jennings Bryan's "Cross of Gold" speech in his presidential campaign of 1896 was one of the most moving, and yet ineffective, attempts to address this issue. Farmers and laborers, he claimed, were being crucified by an economic system run by powerful bankers who insisted that the currency with which they loaned money be tied to the

142 Noah Webster, *History of the United States* (New Haven, CT: Durrie & Peck, 1832), 336–337, 349.

price of gold. Bryan's economic populism was poorly thought out, and his Republican opponents consistently prevailed (he was the unsuccessful Democratic nominee for the White House again in 1900 and 1908). But Bryan's more general point—that the power of money can undermine both moral truth and representative democracy—resonated powerfully in the western and southern states (the region referred to today as the Bible Belt) where he had most of his support.

In the 21st century, Christian and other faith-based voters have complained of being used by politicians who they perceive are motivated by money more than values. Regardless of religiously motivated voters' stands on particular issues (sometimes they disagree), the common theme they keep bringing up is that moral values need to have a place in politics, a place at least as important as economic considerations.

What is at stake in this debate is the origin and nature of law, a topic that consumes jurisprudence and occasionally confirmation hearings for the Supreme Court. A concept often demonized by political liberals in recent years is the so-called natural law theory, a concept with different meanings but essentially the idea that civil law is and should be designed to reflect greater moral values. Truth, for a believer in natural law, is absolute, not something that is malleable with social mores or that can be deconstructed by academics or changed by judges according to their personal opinions.

Believers in natural law should also insist that laws from the legislature reflect fundamental moral truth and not be bought and sold. The legislative process is rarely discussed when the topic of natural law comes up in debates in Congress. The focus instead is almost always on judges interpreting the law. People who make our laws discuss the concept of natural law and absolute truth in the context of what judges are doing to interpret laws but are often unwilling to compare natural law theory to what they themselves are doing. Hypocrisy abounds.

And this hypocrisy is what Marxists, critical legal deconstructionists, and others who attack natural law—or any connection between law and morality—will feed upon. Our campaign finance system, if unchecked, will reinforce their feeble vision of law as nothing more than a product of power relationships.

Those of us who believe in a strong connection between law and moral truth—the difference between right and wrong—or at least the potential for law to make such a connection, are digging our own grave if we do not strenuously object to a system in which law is—or appears to be—bought and sold in the marketplace of campaign finance.

Religious Conservatives and Campaign Finance

IN 2002, AFTER Congress passed the McCain–Feingold Act, the most prominent organization of religious conservatives, the Christian Coalition of America, sent a petition to President George W. Bush urging him to veto the bill. Pat Robertson, Christian Coalition's founder, called the new law:

> An attack on the first amendment rights of every American. McCain–Feingold rejects the constitution, insisting that people should not be able to express their opinion except when it's convenient to the politicians and only when it's well controlled by government agencies, like the FEC (Federal Elections Commission).[143]

President Bush instead signed the bill, making clear that he was relying on the courts to strike down whatever parts of it were unconstitutional.

Robertson's views reflected those of many social conservatives who have been opposed to campaign finance reform. This may be due to the early successes of the Christian Coalition, the Moral Majority, and similar groups in the 1980s in raising money and shifting allegiances in the Republican Party away from the mainline Protestant denominations and toward their brand of Christian conservatism. It was perhaps relevant that for years, Christian conservatives did not believe that their number one issue—abortion—had large commercial interests on the other side (many abortion clinics are not-for-profit, and few doctors make much money from abortions). Even with small donations from followers, religious conservatives perhaps believed that they could out-raise and out-spend their opponents.

Times are changing.

Social conservatives and faith-based voters have a lot to worry about under our current system of campaign finance. Participation in the system is impossible for most of these voters, as it is for most other Americans. On issue after issue, they are up against the few people and organizations that do participate. Consider how well social conservatives will fare vis-à-vis well-financed opponents on each of the following issues.

---

143 Jim Burns, "McCain Challenges GOP Candidates to Support Campaign Reform," CNS News, 7 July 2008 (repost of original 2002 article), cnsnews.com/news/article/mccain-challenges-gop-candidates-support-campaign-reform (accessed 15 September 2015); quoting statement by Pat Robertson.

Abortion

Individual voters, including those with strong religious conviction, differ on abortion. Some, however, are in a stronger position to influence public policy than others.

Churches and other charitable organizations can take a position on ballot measures and legislation but are prohibited from making campaign contributions. IRS rules restrict even their endorsement of candidates in partisan elections. Business interests, on the other hand, are in a position to make large campaign contributions, and as explained more fully below, some of these business interests have a financial interest in the abortion question.

Religious organizations of all opinions on this issue are standing in the shoes of the poor widow in the Gospel of Luke. Their followers' gifts to the campaign treasury are small compared with those of corporate donors.

These corporate donors include big health insurance companies and employers that buy insurance for their employees. They save money if pregnancies that are likely to lead to serious health issues for newborns are terminated. They may save money if people have fewer children to begin with. Insurance companies might raise rates to match a higher-payout environment if there was to be a change in the societal definition of a life worth saving. President Barack Obama's health plan has made health insurance a highly regulated industry, however, and pricing power may not be easy to use. To the extent insurance companies can pass costs through to the insured, businesses that pay health insurance premiums for their employees will be affected by the high costs of aggressively protecting human life.

According to the Center for Responsive Politics, "In the 2012 election cycle, the insurance industry contributed a record $58.7 million to federal parties and candidates as well as outside spending groups."[144] Some of the businesses that buy insurance are also big campaign contributors.

Drug companies make money from drugs that terminate pregnancies. They already have Plan B, which is marketed as a contraceptive, although some people call it an abortion drug. For later in a pregnancy there will perhaps soon be a Plan C, and so forth. Drug companies will want federal government approval to market these drugs (they already have it for Plan B and similar drugs). They will want these drugs included in health insurance plans, and they will want employers to be required under federal law to buy plans that include these drugs.

---

144 Viveca Novak, "Insurance: Background," Center for Responsive Politics, August 2014, opensecrets.org/industries/background.php?cycle=2016&ind=F09 (accessed 15 September 2015).

Drug companies are also among the top campaign contributors.[145]

The health-care industry as a whole contributed over a quarter of a billion dollars to campaigns in the last election cycle. According to the Center for Responsive Politics, "Physicians and other health professionals are traditionally the largest source of federal campaign contributions in this sector, which contributed a record $260.4 million to federal candidates during the 2012 election cycle. Aside from doctors' associations, pharmaceutical companies and HMOs are consistently generous givers."[146]

And for the most part the health-care industry favors more liberal abortion laws.

Euthanasia and Physician-Assisted Suicide

The political and economic calculus here is much the same as for abortion. Health insurers and organizations that pay for health insurance for employees have a financial interest in shortening expensive critical care at the end of life. They profit if euthanasia and physician-assisted suicide are alternatives to expensive treatments. On this issue health insurance providers have an advantage because as pointed out above, they contribute substantially more to political campaigns than individuals who oppose euthanasia and physician-assisted suicide. Churches and other religious organizations that have strong views on these issues cannot contribute and cannot even endorse candidates in partisan elections.

Same-Sex Marriage

The debate over same-sex marriage is another issue where social conservatives are aligned against business interests, and it is clear that on this issue social conservatives have lost.[147]

---

145 Alex Lazar, "Pharmaceuticals/Health: Background," Center for Responsive Politics, August 2015, opensecrets.org/industries/background.php?cycle=2016&ind=H04 (accessed 15 September 2015).
146 Monica Vendituoli, "Health: Background," Center for Responsive Politics, July 2014, opensecrets.org/industries/background.php?cycle=2016&ind=H (accessed 15 September 2015).
147 This author has publicly disagreed with some social conservatives in supporting legalization of same-sex marriage. See amicus brief of Kenneth Mehlman et. al in James Obergefell v. Richard Hodges, Director Ohio Department of Health in the Supreme Court of the United States, 2015 (more than 300 former Republicans, including this author, in support of petitioner). The point being made in this chapter is not that social conservatives are right or wrong on this or any other issue, but that issues should be resolved by all three branches of government on the merits, not on the basis of which side has more money to spend on the political system.

One reason social conservatives lost this debate is a shift in public opinion in favor of lifting legal prohibitions on same-sex marriage. Polling data shows that support for same-sex marriage among Republicans alone is double what it was in 1996.[148] To the extent policy changes in this area reflect changing public opinion, our republican form of government is working the way it should.

But corporate interests, through their own advocacy, accelerated this trend by weighing in on the debate, almost always on the side of same-sex marriage. They did so by spending money on persuading the public on the issue, but they also focused on the narrower task of persuading legislators through lobbying. Much of this lobbying, like other corporate lobbying, has been backed up with campaign contributions. And it made a difference at the legislative level in almost half the states before the Supreme Court stepped in to definitively resolve the issue in 2015.

The Sunlight Foundation observed that in March 2013, when the federal Defense of Marriage Act (DOMA) was struck down by the U.S. Supreme Court:

> *Since the late 1980s, pro–gay rights Human Rights Campaign has generated more than $18 million in campaign contributions and spent more than $21 million lobbying Congress. That compares to $4.3 million in campaign contributions and $112,000 in lobbying expenditures by the National Organization for Marriage, the leading organization on the opposing side of the debate.*

Corporations and corporate executives make up a significant part of the Human Rights Campaign's donor base.

Since the Supreme Court struck down DOMA, corporate support for same-sex marriage accelerated. One reason may be the difficulties corporations face in retaining employees in, and transferring them to and from, different states with drastically different marriage laws. Another reason may be that on the whole, supporters of same-sex marriage tend to be wealthier, younger, and for many corporations a more important customer base than opponents of same-sex marriage. Support for same-sex marriage can also help corporations with recruiting employees, particularly on college campuses and in the technology area, where support for same-sex marriage is overwhelming. Also, support for same-sex marriage can be used to demonstrate corporate citizenship to constituencies

---

148 Justin McCarthy, "Same Sex Marriage Support Reaches New High at 55%: Nearly Eight in 10 Young Adults Favor Gay Marriage," Gallup, 21 May 2014, gallup.com/poll/169640/sex-marriage-support-reaches-new-high.aspx (accessed 15 September 2015).

on the left of the political spectrum that are otherwise hostile to big business. Corporations with spotty corporate citizenship records may be even more inclined to use this tactic (Goldman Sachs CEO Lloyd Blankfein publicly announced his support for same-sex marriage in 2012 in the midst of heated public debate about the role of his firm in the 2008 financial crisis).[149]

In 2015, 379 corporations, many of them among the most prominent in the country, such as Goldman Sachs, Morgan Stanley, and Coca Cola, signed an amicus brief asking the Supreme Court to strike down legal restrictions on same-sex marriage in states that had not already changed their laws to permit same-sex marriage.[150] Many of these corporations are also major campaign contributors, and some of them have also been active in promoting liberalization of marriage laws at the state level. The issue was resolved by the Supreme Court in June 2015, but as discussed below, some collateral issues remain.

Religious Freedom

In September 2015 Pope Francis I gave an address to the United States Congress. One of the urgent priorities the Pope mentioned to Congress was protection of religious freedom around the globe.

The most serious infringements of religious freedom are taking place outside the United States, particularly in the Middle East. Christians are being killed or are fleeing countries where they once lived alongside Muslims and people of other faiths. Saint Paul was converted while traveling on the road to Damascus, the capital of present-day Syria, when God called out, "Saul, Saul, why are you persecuting me?"[151] But modern-day followers of Jesus are traveling as fast as they can on roads away from Damascus, the rest of Syria, and other places where they are persecuted. These places include Iraq, where the United States has already spent hundreds of billions of dollars building what is supposed to be a representative democracy. Some of these Christians become refugees to Europe or the United States. Some never make it out alive.

---

149 "Lloyd Blankfein Supports Marriage Equality," Human Rights Campaign, 5 February 2012, hrc.org/videos/videos-lloyd-blankfein-supports-marriage-equality#1 (accessed 15 September 2015). The Human Rights Campaign announced in early 2012 that Goldman Sachs CEO Lloyd Blankfein was the first major corporate supporter of marriage equality.

150 Amicus brief in James Obergefell v. Richard Hodges, Director Ohio Department of Health in the Supreme Court of the United States (2015).

151 Acts 9:4.

Where does the protection of religious minorities stand in the order of priorities for the United States? Religious freedom is a topic of a lot of talk among US politicians, but little is being done to protect the religious freedom of Christians and other religious minorities (Jews in the Middle East outside of Israel are also extremely vulnerable to persecution). The reasons US policy in the Middle East is what it is are complicated, and direct ties to campaign contributions are difficult to prove, but it is perhaps not surprising that the United States government has not effectively stood up to regimes and terrorist groups that persecute religious minorities. Many of the largest campaign contributors are worried about something else.

Oil companies operating in the region have other priorities, including political stability and stable US diplomatic relations in the region, and oil companies contribute a lot to US political campaigns. Most of the sovereign wealth funds in the region are controlled by governments that are hostile to, and sometimes persecute, Christians and Jews. These and other foreign interests are not allowed to contribute to US political campaigns, but as explained in Chapter 5, they can easily evade that law, whether through equity ownership in United States corporations or through other means. These sovereign wealth funds also do a lot of business with US companies that do contribute. Supporters of Israel contribute substantial amounts to US political campaigns, but they are focused on Israel's precarious national security situation more than on confronting internal human rights violations in neighboring countries. In the world of campaign finance and lobbying, persecuted religious minorities may have few friends in Washington.

In the 1940s Joseph Stalin, when confronted with the displeasure of the Vatican over his oppressive politics in Eastern Europe, is said to have asked a notorious question: "How many divisions does the Pope have?" Persons and regimes questioning our commitment to religious freedom may be asking similar questions. In the US, how much clout do champions of religious freedom really have? With respect to Pope Francis's speech before Congress, how many PACs does the Pope have?

Less drastic but still significant infringements on religious freedom are at issue inside the United States. Here the Catholic Church and other denominations have been at the center of controversy, including President Barack Obama's health insurance mandate requiring employers to purchase insurance that includes birth control even if they object on religious grounds. And state antidiscrimination laws have forced Catholic adoption agencies to close rather than place children with same-sex couples.

Tensions between religious freedom and official duties of government employees have also moved to the forefront, particularly after the Supreme Court in 2015 required legal recognition of same-sex marriages nationwide. Pope Francis recognized this problem by meeting privately in September 2015 with Kim Davis, a county clerk in Kentucky who refused to issue marriage licenses to same-sex couples after the court's ruling, or to allow her name to appear on licenses issued by her subordinates. It remains to be seen how local, state, and federal government in the United States will handle situations where employees, including elected officials such as Davis, can perform the vast majority of their official functions with good conscience while objecting to some tasks on religious grounds.

Then there is the impact of antidiscrimination laws, health-care mandates and other generally applicable law in the for-profit sector. Big businesses usually have no difficulty complying with these laws with respect to employees and customers; it is their small business competitors that are most likely to be owned by people who object to a few laws on religious grounds.

For example, the same-sex marriage debate has led to another debate: Should a church-affiliated college or a business that objects to same-sex marriage on religious grounds be forced by antidiscrimination laws to provide goods and services in connection with the marriage? This could include renting out a facility for the wedding or reception, providing flowers for the wedding, catering the reception, photographing the wedding, and so on. Some small businesses run by persons of strong religious conviction against gay marriage stand on one side of this debate. Much of the big business community stands on the other side.[152]

---

152 Senator Ted Cruz, the first entrant into the 2016 Republican presidential primary, in 2015 elaborated in a speech in Iowa: "The Fortune 500 is running shamelessly to endorse the radical gay marriage agenda over religious liberty, to say: 'We will persecute a Christian pastor, a Catholic priest, a Jewish rabbi. . . . Any person of faith is subject to persecution if they dare disagree, if their religious faith parts way from their political commitment to gay marriage.'" Bloomberg Politics, "Why Ted Cruz Is Fighting 'The Fortune 500' on Gay Marriage," 3 April 2015, bloomberg.com/politics/articles/2015-04-03/why-ted-cruz-is-fighting-the-fortune-500-on-gay-marriage (accessed 15 September 2015).

There are legitimate concerns about broad religious-freedom statutes that would allow businesses to discriminate against customers, for example by saying "No Jews," "No Muslims," or "No Gays." On the other hand, there are good arguments for a narrowly drawn religious-freedom exemption that would allow a service provider objecting on religious grounds not to be personally present at a wedding or other ceremony. The relevant point here is that the deliberative process on this issue in a republican form of government should include small business as well as big business (and ordinary Americans on both sides of the issue), not just large campaign contributors.

In spring 2015 legislatures in two states, Indiana and Arkansas, passed laws that in some circumstances would exempt religious organizations and businesses from complying with generally applicable laws if doing so violated their religious principles. Many gay-rights advocates interpreted these laws as exempting such organizations and businesses from laws prohibiting discrimination on the basis of sexual orientation. Corporations and business leaders in particular were incensed, fearing boycotts of their states and other economic repercussions. Indiana passed its version of the law, but within a week, after intense lobbying by business interests, the Republican-controlled legislature, upon the urging of the Republican governor, enacted an amendment making it clear that the religious freedom law did not exempt people or organizations from compliance with antidiscrimination laws.[153] In Arkansas Walmart in particular put enormous pressure on Governor Asa Hutchison to veto the bill, pointing out the controversy that had sprung up in Indiana only a week earlier.[154] The governor vetoed the bill.

Walmart spent $2,363,829 on political contributions in 2014, $7,000,000 on lobbying in 2014, and another $7,260,000 on lobbying in 2013.[155] Voters who supported the Arkansas religious-freedom bill will perceive a fundamental unfairness in the political process if it appears that the reason the bill was vetoed was that Walmart opposed it and that the reason Walmart's voice is so important is that Walmart spends millions of dollars on politics. Even opponents of the religious-freedom law should recognize that there is something unfair about a process in which they owe victory on this issue to the political influence of Walmart.

School Choice

One cause championed by religious conservatives for years has been tax credits, vouchers, or other financial assistance for private primary and secondary education to help parents pay for religious—or

---

153 Jeff Swiatek and Tim Evans, "9 CEOs Call on Pence, Legislature to Modify 'Religious Freedom' Law," *USA Today,* 31 March 2015, usatoday.com/story/money/2015/03/30/nine-ceos-call-pence-legislature-modify-religious-freedom-law/70689924 (accessed 15 September 2015); reporting that a "who's who of top Indiana business executives called on Gov. Mike Pence and legislative leaders to reform the newly passed Religious Freedom Restoration Act, so it can't be used to 'justify discrimination based upon sexual orientation or gender identity.'"
154 Nick Gass, "Walmart Slams Arkansas 'Religious Freedom' Law," *Politico,* 1 April 2015, politico.com /story/2015/04/arkansas-hutchinson-rfra-walmart-116567.html (accessed 15 September 2015).
155 "Walmart Stores Contributions: Profile for 2014 Election Cycle," Center for Responsive Politics, March 2015, opensecrets.org/orgs/summary.php?id=d000000367 (accessed 15 September 2015).

secular—alternatives to public schools. Why should people who are taxed to pay for primary and secondary education be required to send their children to public schools to get the educational services that they have already paid for? The government subsidizes loans and scholarships to private colleges, including religious colleges. Why not primary and secondary schools? For low- and moderate-income families, whose children may never get to college if they don't get a good primary and secondary school education, this issue can be critically important.

There are constitutional issues with some school-choice proposals that would directly aid religious schools, but most of the issues are political. Teachers' unions almost always oppose school choice, arguing that the money should instead be invested in public education and teacher salaries (most private-school teachers are not unionized).

Most parents and other voters would want this and other education issues to be decided on the merits, not because of campaign contributions. Still, the dominant campaign contributors in the education field are teachers' unions, led by the NEA (as pointed out in Chapter 1, the NEA and its affiliates contributed approximately $30 million in the 2014 election cycle).[156]

While churches and other organizations that host religious schools have some political clout due to their membership, they cannot endorse candidates and they cannot make campaign contributions. Reforming the campaign finance system is, however, a cause they can endorse. They should do so emphatically if they want a fair chance to present their arguments on this or any other issue.

Gambling

For several centuries religious leaders in America have worried about gambling. The Puritans who settled Massachusetts Bay in the 1600s thought it sinful and outlawed it. Some denominations, such as the Mormons, condemn gambling entirely. In 1984 the Southern Baptist Convention passed a resolution clearly stating their opposition to legalized gambling:

> *WHEREAS, Gambling is an immoral effort that creates deliberate risks not inherent in or necessary to the functioning of society; and*
>   *WHEREAS, Aggressive actions by the gambling interests in*

---

156 "National Education Association: Profile for 2014 Election Cycle," Center for Responsive Politics, March 2015, opensecrets.org/orgs/summary.php?id=D000000064 (accessed 15 September 2015).

*recent months make abundantly clear their intention of seek-
ing to expand legalized gambling throughout the nation and
especially in the states of the South and the Southwest; and
    WHEREAS, Out-of-state corporations and businesses are
investing millions of dollars in a bold effort to change state
laws to allow casinos, lotteries, and pari-mutuel gambling; and
    WHEREAS, Legislators of many states have shown
shameful willingness to give shoddy and inadequate consideration to gambling legislation, to pass legislation out of committees without public hearings, and to
schedule votes on gambling legislation in a manner carefully
contrived to be beneficial to passage of the gambling legislation.
    Be it therefore RESOLVED, That we, the messengers of the
Southern Baptist Convention assembled in Kansas City, June
12–14, 1984, encourage Southern Baptists to work diligently with
other Christians and other responsible citizens who oppose the
spread of legalized gambling . . .*[157]

Other denominations have condemned particular forms of gambling,
for example, the church leaders who unsuccessfully lobbied against legalization of casino gambling in New Jersey in the 1970s.[158]

In the world of campaign finance, however, opponents of gambling
have a minimal role. Churches and charities are prohibited from contributing to candidates or endorsing candidates. Few if any large donors put
curtailment of gambling at the top of their list of priorities, even if some
large donors, if asked, would agree with the religious leaders who think
that permissive laws on gambling are not a good thing.

Gambling interests, on the other hand, are immersed in politics and
in campaign finance.

One of the most notorious political scandals in the early 2000s
involved casino operators and American Indian tribes who hired Jack
Abramoff, a well-connected Republican lobbyist who wielded considerable influence on Capitol Hill and in the Bush administration. Abramoff
was indicted shortly before the author of this book became the White
House ethics lawyer in early 2005 (prosecutors and Congressional

157 "Resolution on Gambling," Southern Baptist Convention, 1984, sbc.net/resolutions/564
/resolution-on-gambling (accessed 12 November 2015).
158 Episcopal Diocese of Newark, New Jersey, Resolutions on Gambling Adopted by Diocesan Conventions: Resolutions Adopted by Diocesan Conventions on Gambling (1954), Casino Gambling (1974),
and Opposition to Video Lottery Machines (1995), dioceseofnewark.org/resource/diocesan-
policy-gambling (accessed 15 September 2015).

investigators uncovered e-mails in which Abramoff's associates had schemed unsuccessfully to get the previous White House ethics lawyer, Nanette Everson, fired for trying to exclude lobbyists from meetings with American Indian tribes).[159] Abramoff was later convicted of conspiracy, fraud, and tax evasion mostly in connection with his lobbying activities on behalf of American Indian gaming interests. Ironically, most of the criminal charges were related to his having defrauded his clients, not the corrupt political system that he and his clients used to wield influence in Washington.

Redemption, however, is possible, even for a casino lobbyist who is a convicted felon. Upon release from prison Abramoff admitted that the campaign contributions, for which neither he nor anyone else was prosecuted, were de facto bribes:

> During the years I was lobbying, I purveyed millions of my own and clients' dollars to congressmen, especially at such decisive moments. I never contemplated that these payments were really just bribes, but they were. Like most dissembling Washington hacks, I viewed these payments as legitimate political contributions, expressions of my admiration of and fealty to the venerable statesman I needed to influence.
>
> Outside our capital city (and its ever-prosperous contiguous counties), the campaign contributions of special interests are rightly seen as nothing but bribes. The purposeful dissonance of the political class enables congressmen to accept donations and solemnly recite their real oath of office: My vote is not for sale for a mere contribution. They are wrong. Their votes are very much for sale, only they don't wish to admit it.[160]

Today Jack Abramoff is gone from the lobbying and campaign finance scene, but casino operators and lobbyists are still there. Sheldon Adelson, the owner of Sands Casinos, is one of the biggest individual donors to the Republican Party. His Las Vegas Sands casinos have contributed close to $600,000, all to Republicans (Adelson spends millions more out

---

159 H. R. Committee on Government Reform, 109th Congress Staff Report 50–51, 29 September 2006, (contains e-mails from Abramoff and his associates concerning, among other things, White House ethics advisor Nanette Everson's trying to prevent lobbyists from attending meetings and a suggestion by one of Abramoff's associates that someone contact a high-level White House official to get her fired).
160 Jack Abramoff, "I Know the Congressional Culture of Corruption," The Atlantic, 24 July 2012, theatlantic.com/politics/archive/2012/07/i-know-the-congressional-culture-of-corruption/260081 (accessed 15 September 2015).

of his personal fortune on electioneering communications, much of it not reported). The gaming industry as a whole has contributed millions of dollars more to both parties.[161]

And the situation is only likely to get worse. For over a decade, promoters have been seeking to expand gambling on the Internet. These promoters will no doubt also become active in the campaign finance system.

On any issue that concerns gambling, will politicians listen to casino magnates and their lobbyists, or to religious organizations and citizens who worry that gambling brings harm to too many families and communities? Does every American get a voice, or is the deck stacked against us?

The Entertainment Industry: Violent and Sexually Explicit Movies, Video Games, Social Media, and More

The entertainment industry has traditionally been a major campaign contributor—mostly to Democrats, although sometimes to Republicans. Entertainers helped support the election of one of their own, Ronald Reagan, to the presidency in 1980. Electronic entertainment—video games and social media—much of it marketed to minors, is now a quickly growing industry.

Social conservatives' many concerns with the entertainment industry will not be reiterated here. While some of those concerns—about movies, television, and video games—have been aired for decades, the Internet and social media are giving rise to new issues. And groups other than religious conservatives—including parents and women's rights advocates—are worried as well.

But none of this may matter if those who are concerned about the entertainment industry—and particularly about its venture into the Internet—cannot put money where their worries are. And they are up against a lot. According to the Center for Responsive Politics, the TV/movies/music industries contributed more than $25 million in the 2014 election cycle, with Walt Disney alone contributing more than $1.5 million.[162]

It is often said that critics of the entertainment industry who want to protect children from obscenity and violence are up against the First Amendment. There are First Amendment issues, but the courts would

---

161 Alex Lazar, "Casinos/Gambling: Top Contributors," Center for Responsive Politics, August 2015, opensecrets.org/industries/background.php?cycle=2016&ind=N07 (accessed 15 September 2015).
162 Emily Kopp, "TV/Movies/Music: Top Contributors," Center for Responsive Politics, April 2014, opensecrets.org/industries/indus.php?ind=B02 (accessed 15 September 2015).

allow legislatures to do a lot more to regulate the delivery, if not the content, of entertainment. The real problem is that these entertainment companies have the same First Amendment right as individuals to throw money around in the political process. And the entertainment companies have a lot more money.

Marijuana and Other Recreational Drugs

The marijuana industry was launched in Colorado and Washington, followed by Alaska and Oregon. So-called medical marijuana is sold in many other states. Marijuana is already a nearly billion-dollar industry (in 2014 legal marijuana was a $700 million industry in Colorado alone).[163] Recreational drugs will be an important new segment of the American economy.

Profits from marijuana sales will likely be invested in campaign contributions to secure legalization in other states as well as federal law facilitating transportation of the drug across state lines. This change in federal law is necessary for many banks and other lenders who otherwise will not lend to marijuana companies.

Recreational drug companies will also want minimal regulation of sales. They will likely oppose laws that restrict advertising, sales of marijuana near schools, or putting the drug in candy and other food; that require warning labels; or that regulate either the quality or quantity sold. Finally, recreational drug companies will probably seek to legalize, and profit from, other recreational drugs. For many illegal drug dealers, marijuana is an entry-level drug for new customers who can then be lured to more expensive and more addictive products, and legal recreational drug companies are likely to view their business model the same way.

This agenda will require considerable investment in the campaign finance system, but that is probably something that recreational drug companies are willing to do. Indeed, the fundraising juggernaut is well under way. In later October 2014, shortly before voters in Oregon and Alaska voted on legalization, *The New York Times* reported that "[t]he old antidrug coalition has struggled to find traction and money. Supporters of legalization have outdone opponents' fund-raising in Oregon by more than 25 to 1, and in Alaska by about 9 to 1."[164]

---

163 Sarah LeTrent, "Is America Ready for Marijuana Moguls?" CNN, 20 April 2015, cnn.com/2015/04/15 /living/high-profits-breckenridge-cannabis-club-intro (accessed 15 September 2015).
164 Kirk Johnson, "For Marijuana, a Second Wave of Votes to Legalize," *The New York Times*, 28 October 2014, nytimes.com/2014/10/29/us/for-marijuana-a-second-wave-of-votes-to-legalize.html?_r=0 (accessed 15 September 2015).

In 2014 voters in Alaska and Oregon voted to legalize recreational pot, raising the total number of states where it is legal to four. A pot PAC may be in the not-so-distant future, with a coke PAC, a speed PAC, an LSD PAC, and others soon to follow.

Thus far, social conservatives have not devoted a lot of their efforts to combating drugs. When, however, children are affected by this marketing campaign and drug use and addiction increases, this complacency is likely to change. But by then, it could be too late. The campaign finance system will have given the recreational drug industry an insurmountable lead in the federal and state legislatures, if not in the court of public opinion.

Driving the Money Changers from the Temples of Our Democracy

THE STORY OF the widow's mite reveals Jesus's response to a society, including a religious hierarchy, that prioritized money over people. Another passage in the Gospels, Matthew 21:12–13, tells about one of the few times when Jesus becomes angry, and it was when he saw commerce intrude upon a place where higher principles were supposed to prevail: "Jesus entered the temple courts and drove out all who were buying and selling there. He overturned the tables of the money changers and the benches of those selling doves."

Many of our government buildings are built to resemble ancient Greek and Roman temples. Our government buildings are secular, but they house a republican form of government that many citizens believe is a divine right. Our Declaration of Independence said so, and our money bears the words "In God We Trust." Those who still believe that our republican form of government is a blessing from God must ask whether we are taking care of it. Or are we allowing modern-day money changers to work the halls of Congress and state legislatures?

Driving the money changers from the temples of American democracy will not be easy, but it is critically important if values other than money are to have any weight in public discourse. So-called values-based voters—voters who prioritize things other than financial gain—have the most to lose. As discussed above, preserving human life is sometimes costly and can easily be compromised for the sake of material gain. Discouraging children and young adults from indulging in and eventually becoming addicted to—gambling, pornography, and drugs—means curtailing new avenues of commerce that allow some people to make money.

When government makes decisions about these and other issues, values-based voters in our current system of campaign finance are in the position of the poor widow with her mite compared with the many millions poured into politics by the commercial interests that oppose them. Churches are barred by law from participating in partisan politics or they lose their tax-exempt status. Furthermore, like the widow of Jesus's day, many devoutly religious people are people of modest means. As discussed in Chapter 2, the participation problem created by our system of campaign finance is probably felt most strongly in the states with lower per capita income, states where a large number of voters who care about moral and social issues happen to live.

The money that influences lawmakers' decisions takes on a life of its own, just as the commercial dealing in the temple courts did in Jesus's day. Waiting for Jesus to come again to drive the money changers out of our political system is one approach; another is to do what we can either to drive the money changers out or to counter their influence.

Chapter 5

Foreign Campaign Money, US Sovereignty, and National Security Risk

IN APRIL 2015 Fabian Thylmann, the German founder of an international pornography distribution company, was indicted in Cologne, Germany, on charges that he had not paid taxes on $100 million in profits. Meanwhile in the United States, also in April 2015, the FEC declined to pursue an investigation of Thylmann's funding of a political campaign to defeat a Los Angeles County ballot measure that required adult film stars to wear condoms while making movies. Despite Thylmann's efforts, the ballot measure passed. A California AIDS advocacy group then filed a complaint with the FEC charging that $327,000 in donations made by companies tied to Thylmann's pornography business violated Federal Election Campaign Act prohibitions on foreign nationals contributing to US campaigns. The FEC's three Democratic commissioners voted to investigate the source of the contributions and the California committee that opposed the ballot measure and accepted the funds, but the FEC's three Republican commissioners voted not to pursue an investigation. This deadlock prevented the FEC from going forward. The FEC's Office of the General Counsel has also opined that the act's ban on foreign contributions does not apply to such ballot initiatives.[165]

---

165 For a more detailed discussion of this case, see Michelle Conlin and Lucas Iberico Lozada, "FEC Decision May Allow More Foreign Money in U.S. Votes, Critics Say," Reuters, 24 April 2015, reuters.com /article/2015/04/24/us-usa-election-fec-idUSKBN0NF1V420150424 (accessed 15 September 2015).

Thylmann had apparently found a loophole through which he could inject profits from his German pornography business into American politics. In a global economy in which wealth is increasingly dispersed, Thylmann's efforts likely are only the beginning of a push by foreign nationals—ordinary businesspeople but also pornographers, organized criminals, dictators, and even terrorists—to use their money to control our government.

Any political conservative who is at all committed to the founders' vision of the United States as a republic independent of foreign influence would have to be disgusted—and alarmed—by this situation.

From the beginnings of our republic, the founders were concerned about foreign influences over our government. Our Constitution was specifically designed to withstand the inevitable pressures in a world where other countries are as rich, if not richer, than we are. Regardless of the magnitude and concentrations of wealth and political influence abroad, the United States government would be independent of that influence. The Emoluments Clause of the Constitution (Article I, Section 9, Clause 8) provides:

> No Title of Nobility shall be granted by the United States: And no Person holding any Office of Profit or Trust under them, shall, without the Consent of the Congress, accept of any present, Emolument, Office, or Title, of any kind whatever, from any King, Prince, or foreign State.

The Emoluments Clause has been enforced over our 240-year history, with Congress passing specific legislation authorizing certain foreign gifts but not others. Under it, employees of the United States government are prohibited from a wide range of involvements with foreign governments, including some posts at foreign universities and board memberships for corporations controlled by foreign governments. One well-known Harvard Law professor—Mary Ann Glendon—was allowed an appointment on a presidential advisory committee in 2005 only after the Department of Justice Office of Legal Counsel opined that her position on another advisory committee for the Vatican did not violate the Emoluments Clause.

The Emoluments Clause does curtail some avenues of foreign influence, but its reach is limited. It says nothing, for example, about foreign governments' efforts to influence the United States government through persons who are not employed by the United States government but instead lobby the government. By the 1930s Germany and Italy were employing lobbyists and other intermediaries to influence the United States, primarily to support the already strong movement in the United States to keep us out of any future European wars. While Congress had no appetite for pitting the United States against the growth of fascism in Europe (the Senate had refused to ratify the Treaty of Versailles in the 1920s and continued to show lack of interest in foreign affairs during the Great Depression), Congress was concerned about other countries—particularly nondemocratic countries—trying to influence decisions of the United States government.

The Foreign Agents Registration Act of 1938 (FARA) was aimed at exposing German, Italian, and Japanese activities in the United States. The act requires persons who are agents of foreign principals in a political or quasi-political capacity to publicly disclose their relationship with the foreign principal, as well as their activities, receipts of payment, and disbursements. The FARA Registration Unit of the Counterespionage Section (CES) in the National Security Division (NSD) is responsible for the administration and enforcement of FARA.

In 1966 Congress took another step to curb foreign influence when it prohibited campaign contributions from foreign governments and from foreign nationals, a provision that was later incorporated into the Federal Election Campaign Act.[166] As explained below, this provision is relatively easy to circumvent, and at times it is flatly violated. But perhaps back then it did not matter that much—our principal adversary on the world stage was the Soviet Union, which, despite its immense arsenal of nuclear weapons, had relatively little private sector wealth. Incidents of Soviet money finding its way into American companies—particularly those wealthy enough to influence American politics—were few. The countries that had most of the world's corporate wealth were for the most part our allies, although by 1973 Americans were reminded by the Arab oil embargo that the West's domination of economic wealth would not be permanent.

There is now more accumulation of wealth outside of the United States, some of it in the hands of people who because of their proximity to the United States want to influence decisions in our government.

In 2014 the Justice Department accused a Mexican businessman of funneling more than $500,000 through shell companies and super PACs into US elections. José Susumo Azano Matsura, the owner of several construction companies in Mexico, allegedly bankrolled several Southern California candidates because he wanted to develop the San Diego waterfront. In order to buy political support for the project, he allegedly

166 2 U.S.C. § 431 *et. seq.*

funneled money through a super PAC (this is a fundraising vehicle that, as pointed out in Chapter 1, emerged after the Supreme Court's 2010 *Citizens United* decision, which allowed organizations to spend unlimited amounts of money on electioneering communications for or against candidates). According to the criminal complaint, Azano's money was funneled through a US shell company before being contributed to the super PAC. The super PAC was only required to disclose the name of the US shell company, so the contributions appeared to come from within the United States.[167]

This incident is not an aberration; the influence of foreign money in US political campaigns will likely increase. The world's total wealth is more dispersed than it was in the few decades after World War II. The United States is no longer the sole economic superpower but one of many economic powers in the world. Although economic growth in the United States has been strong, some other parts of the world are growing even faster. Furthermore, the world's economies are more integrated. Trade barriers have come down. Americans invest abroad, but foreigners invest here as well.

According to the Organization of International Investment, foreign direct investment in the United States (FDIUS) has increased sharply in recent years. Despite the 2008–2010 recession, FDIUS reached $2.65 trillion in 2013, up from $2.05 trillion in 2008.[168] Foreign nationals own American hotels, office buildings, and businesses—as well as an increasing percentage of our enormous national debt. Furthermore, some countries have substantially more government involvement in corporate decision-making, and in private-sector investing through sovereign wealth funds, than does the United States, which traditionally has kept public and private sectors separate. This means that some foreign investments in the United States are being made directly or indirectly by foreign governments.

For example, China is now the world's largest or second-largest economic power, depending upon the measure. With over three times as many people as the United States, it will likely grow its economy faster than the United States in the next few decades. Its foreign exchange reserves approached $4 trillion in 2014. China is also the largest corporate borrower on world credit markets. Home to many wealthy

---

167 John Hudson, "Feds: Mexican Tycoon Exploited Super PACs to Influence US Elections," *Foreign Policy*, 11 February 2014, foreignpolicy.com/2014/02/11/feds-mexican-tycoon-exploited-super-pacs-to-influence-u-s-elections (accessed 15 September 2015).

168 Organization of International Investment, *Foreign Direct Investment in the United States, 2013 Report*, ofii.org/sites/default/files/FDIUS_2013_Report.pdf (accessed 15 September 2015).

businesspeople, the country has also recently liberalized its restrictions on currency conversion and Chinese nationals investing their money abroad. Furthermore, there is abundant evidence that powerful government officials in China, and families of those officials, have substantial investments in and influence over Chinese companies. When *The New York Times* published a detailed account of the connections between Chinese industry and powerful Chinese political families, its website was inaccessible in China for weeks. Most Chinese businesspeople, however, already know of the government's role in their companies, and in their own professional lives. And the government will use its power to integrate Chinese capitalism with the agenda of the Communist Party in the manner that it sees fit.

Chinese businesses have expansion plans in the United States. Shuanghui, the largest Chinese meat processing company, in 2013 took over Smithfield, one of the largest US meat processing companies, for a total purchase price of $4.7 billion. Cementing political alliances in Virginia, Smithfield's home state, was important to the transaction's success, as was establishing good relations in Congress (a 2005 proposed takeover of Unocal by the Chinese state-owned CNOOC oil company failed in large part due to Congressional objections). Chinese companies also want to do business with the US government and state and local governments. Two Chinese railcar manufacturing firms, CSR and CNR Corp., are proposing to merge into a new company called China Railway Transportation, which will have a combined market capitalization of $26 billion. The new company plans to actively seek contracts building railway systems in the United States—contracts which would most likely come from state and local governments and that could very well involve federal subsidies. In October 2014 CNR received a $566 million contract with the Massachusetts Department of Transportation to build 284 train cars for Boston's subway, with an option to provide up to 58 more, and the company views this as a beachhead to win more public transportation contracts in the United States.[169]

Two conservative think tanks, the Heritage Foundation and American Enterprise Institute, are sufficiently concerned about Chinese global

---

169 Jad Mouawad, "Chinese Rail Firm Makes Inroads with U.S. Factory and Boston Transit Deal," *The New York Times*, 3 September 2015, nytimes.com/2015/09/04/business/china-railway-crrc-boston-transit.html (accessed 15 September 2015); Sophia Yan, "China Wants to Build a Train System Near You," CNN Money, 3 December 2014, money.cnn.com/2014/12/03/news/china-rail-system/index.html?hpt=hp_t2 (accessed 15 September 2015); Jad Mouawad, "A Rail Firm from China Puts a Toe into the US," *The New York Times*, 4 September 2015 (discusses the contract and the company breaking ground on a $60 million plant in Springfield, Massachusetts, that will assemble the new cars for the Boston subway system).

investments that they set up an online database called China Investment Tracker, which reports that, excluding bond purchases, Chinese investments in the United States exceeded $14 billion in 2013, a 50% increase from 2012. Whether or not one has suspicions of Chinese investments and motives, it is obvious that corporate America is very different with the present level of Chinese investment. Corporate wealth may be in America, but it is not necessarily American wealth. Equating corporate political speech with individual political speech, as the United States Supreme Court does for purposes of First Amendment protection in *Citizens United*, creates the possibility if not the likelihood that political speech will be allocated in proportion to the ownership of corporate wealth in our country. As foreign ownership of corporate wealth increases, an increasing amount of political speech in the United States will be funded directly or indirectly from abroad. Sometimes foreign corporations will be behind these expenditures, sometimes individuals, and sometimes governments. We may never know, but if these expenditures can be made, they most likely will be made.

It is also clear that at least some foreign governments are already going beyond traditional avenues of diplomacy and are using private institutions in the United States to influence US government policy. An important avenue of influence is private foundations and charities that can receive contributions from foreign as well as domestic donors. Saddam Hussein's government in Iraq, for example, contributed two million barrels of oil to a charity set up by a covert Iraqi agent in Michigan, which then paid for members of Congress to travel to Iraq in 2002.[170]

One of the most politically connected foundations—the Bill, Hillary & Chelsea Clinton Foundation—refused contributions from foreign governments while Hillary Clinton was secretary of state but lifted that ban after she left office. *The New York Times* in 2015 called upon the foundation to ban donations from all foreign sources while Hillary Clinton runs for president.[171]

In 2014 *The New York Times* documented substantial evidence that foreign governments were directly influencing major Washington think tanks through direct contributions.[172] These think tanks are an important

---

170 Philip Shenon, "U.S. Says Hussein Spy Agency and Iraqi-American Arranged '02 Trip by Lawmakers," *The New York Times*, 27 March 2008.

171 "Separate Philanthropy from Political Clout: Hillary Clinton Should Ban Foreign Donors to the Clinton Global Initiative," *The New York Times Editorial*, 20 February 2015 ("donors have included the United Arab Emirates, Germany, Saudi Arabia, Australia, Oman, and a Canadian government agency reported to be involved in promoting the Keystone XL pipeline").

172 Eric Lipton, Brooke Williams, and Nicholas Confessore, "Foreign Powers Buy Influence at Think Tanks," *The New York Times*, 6 September 2014.

part of the Washington policy-making establishment. Policy ideas from think tanks are often promoted by people and organizations that make campaign contributions and electioneering communications, even if think tanks and other 501(c)(3) groups cannot directly participate in politics. This author previously discussed the interrelationship between think tanks, 501(c)(4) organizations, and political campaigns in a 2009 book on government ethics, and these relationships persist to this day.[173]

Members of Congress have condemned the think tanks, demanding that they stop taking foreign government money for studies on US domestic or foreign policy. They have a point. But members of Congress should do likewise. They should not tolerate a campaign finance system in which foreign governments can use corporate wealth to influence our government or voters' decisions about who runs our government.

As pointed out above, Congress gave some thought to this problem in federal legislation back in the 1960s, an age when campaign finance was much cheaper and simpler than it is today. Congress made it illegal for foreign governments, foreign nationals, or companies controlled by foreign nationals to contribute money to US political campaigns and for campaigns to accept their money.

Making something illegal, and making it not happen, are two separate things.

Given the current state of campaign finance in the United States, getting foreign money into US political campaigns is about as easy as getting illegal alcohol into the freshman yard of a typical college campus. Corporations, labor unions, and a few individual donors are throwing an enormous party for US politicians. Money keeps the party going and anybody who brings money to the party is welcome. The Supreme Court has in several instances told Congress that it cannot force people to take their money away from this party even if Congress, while enjoying the party immensely, wants to cool it down.

Foreign nationals keep a low profile at the political money party. They—like underage drinkers—know that they are not supposed to be at the party. They will also devise strategies for getting in. Even if direct contributions by foreign nationals to US political campaigns are illegal, there are plenty of ways to make indirect campaign contributions, create electioneering communications, and otherwise provide support or opposition to US political candidates.

---

173 Richard W. Painter, *Getting the Government America Deserves: How Ethics Reform Can Make a Difference* (Oxford, England: Oxford University Press, 2009), "Chapter 9: Off-the-Books Lobbying, Electioneering, and the Special Purpose Entities That Do It."

First, many foreign governments have supporters who are American citizens and who contribute to political campaigns. The American Israel Political Action Committee (AIPAC) is the most-talked-about example and spends a lot on political campaigns to influence American foreign policy. Other groups of Americans, however, have also formed political action committees that support foreign governments or opposition groups against foreign governments.

Second, as pointed out in Chapter 1, an enormous amount of political advertising and other messaging is paid for through dark pools of funds controlled by 501(c)(4) tax-exempt organizations and similar groups that do not disclose their donors. It is easy for foreign corporations, including corporations controlled by foreign governments, and sovereign wealth funds to channel money through these organizations to help the candidates they like and—with negative advertising—take down candidates they don't like. And nobody—except perhaps the candidates—may know who did it.

Third, American businesses are increasingly entangled with, and in some cases, dependent on foreign businesses and foreign investors. Keeping the two separate for purposes of political expenditures is virtually impossible.

- While foreign-controlled companies and foreign nationals cannot legally contribute to US political campaigns, the American subsidiaries of foreign companies can legally form PACs and collect contributions from their American employees. There are already a lot of such PACs, and they raised a total of $14.1 million in the 2014 election cycle by October.[174]

- These American subsidiaries can also contribute to super PACs and other organizations that make independent expenditures. As more American corporations are acquired by companies in China, Japan, the Middle East, and Europe, among other places, more American employees will be asked to give to political campaigns favored by their bosses, who report to other bosses outside the United States.

- Many investment funds, including private equity funds, do not disclose the identities of their investors, even if these funds make substantial investments in US corporations that enable them to effectively control corporate decision-making.

174 "Foreign-connected PACs: Election Cycle 2014," Center for Responsive Politics, March 2015, opensecrets.org/pacs/foreign.php?cycle=2014 (accessed 15 September 2015).

Restrictions on campaign contributions by foreign-controlled companies are difficult to enforce when nobody knows who the investors in a corporation really are.

- Foreign companies, including companies controlled by foreign governments, engage in joint ventures with US businesses. The foreign company can give favorable terms in the venture to the US business, which then has money left over for political expenditures. The US business makes the political expenditures but the message that goes along with the money comes from abroad.

- US businesses—including lobbyists and others—can anticipate foreign governments' and foreign companies' desire to influence our political system and make contributions needed to get access to public officials. Once they have this access, they will attract business relationships with foreign nationals who view this access as part of the package.

- Foreign investors can easily influence decision-making by US corporations without falling under the legal definition of foreign "control" of the corporation that triggers a ban on political contributions. Influence over a US corporation's foreign office; a joint venture agreement; a supplier or customer agreement; control of a line of credit the corporation needs or a substantial holding of its debt securities; a dominant role in a multinational trade association; or just about any relationship can be sufficient for a foreign person, company, or government to get what it wants from a US company in the US political arena, including lobbying and campaign contributions.

Fourth and finally, the decades-old legal restrictions on foreign campaign contributions are not only impossible to enforce; they are logically inconsistent with the Supreme Court's more recent holdings that domestic campaign contributions and electioneering communications are a protected form of free speech. The only way the court can uphold restrictions on foreign contributions is to conclude that the First Amendment does not apply in the same way to protect speech by a foreign national. Corporations thus can be "persons" under the law, but presumably not corporations controlled by foreign investors, even if they have their headquarters and their employees inside the US. Thus far, the courts have upheld such logic. *Bluman v. FEC* upheld the foreign campaign contribution ban, distinguishing *Citizens United*.[175] But this result is on its face at least inconsistent with Fourteenth Amendment equal protection as well as the First Amendment itself (the Supreme Court in *Bluman* took the rare step of affirming the lower court's ruling without writing an opinion). Regardless of what our laws say, foreign nationals will expect that when they arrive in the United States, they have the same First Amendment rights as Americans do. Foreign investors will expect that if money has constitutional rights, their money does as well, and they will probably act accordingly.

Sovereign wealth funds, billionaires, and others allied with governments in Russia, China, the Middle East, and elsewhere, are pouring money into the United States. Foreign investment funds (private equity funds, sovereign wealth funds) hold securities in many US companies. Foreign companies are buying US companies that they operate as wholly owned subsidiaries. Do we really think we can tell them that they can't pay to play under federal law even if that is part of corporate personhood blessed by our Supreme Court? As discussed above, they might even have a constitutional challenge to laws barring foreign-controlled companies from contributing, and meanwhile they can easily evade the rules, using the many strategies, most of which are perfectly legal, also discussed above.

National Security Risk

NATIONAL SECURITY IS a serious concern. Many decisions made by elected officials in Congress as well as political appointees in the executive branch who work for the president involve some aspect of national security, including the general levels of funding for the armed forces, particular weapons programs, troop deployments, intelligence operations, homeland security, technology export, efforts to combat computer hacking, economic sanctions, and a wide range of other issues. Foreign nationals and their allies in the United States who can influence US elections and who can create dependency relationships between elected officials and themselves are likely to influence how these decisions are made. They are also likely to have access to information about those decisions that could in turn be conveyed to foreign governments or to terrorist organizations.

---

175 Bluman v. FEC, 800 F.Supp.2d 281 (D.D.C. 2011) (three-judge court, per Judge Brett Kavanaugh of the D.C. Cir.), aff'd without op., 132 S.Ct. 1087 (2012).

Economic Risk

HOW FOREIGN COMPANIES—AND FOREIGN GOVERNMENTS that directly or indirectly control foreign companies—will use their power to influence US politics has yet to be seen. Companies in some countries will use it differently than others. Some will combine a geopolitical agenda with their economic agenda, and some will not. But this power to use corporate wealth to influence our political system will be used if we allow corporate wealth to influence American politics. If we choose not to counterbalance this influence by injecting more American money into American political campaigns—for example, by empowering ordinary American citizens to fund political campaigns of their choice from tax receipts—we leave the playing field to be dominated by whomever controls whatever wealth is present in the United States.

But perhaps this is nothing to worry about because US companies also buy companies overseas, and do business and invest overseas; the political influence is symmetrical, at least as long as we remain a major economic power.

Perhaps not. The political influence of US companies over foreign governments is not symmetrical with influence foreigners potentially have over the US government. Most other political systems are not as open as the United States to influence by corporate campaign contributions. Direct bribery still works in some countries, but the Foreign Corrupt Practices Act has for decades prohibited American companies from influencing foreign governments in this more conventional manner. The act has been interpreted strictly to go well beyond conventional bribery, for example, to prohibit a US corporation from giving a hiring preference to children and other relatives of high-ranking government officials (JPMorgan and other US banks doing business in China have been investigated by US authorities for this practice). In other words, our laws are highly protective of other countries' political systems against corruption by US companies but relatively ineffective at protecting our own system from corruption, including corruption by foreign nationals, foreign companies, and even foreign governments.

This asymmetry of political influence over each other's political systems will likely put American businesses at a disadvantage vis-à-vis foreign companies with respect to many concrete issues that affect both competitiveness and profits: trade, taxes, environmental and labor standards, currency regulation, technology export, and more. With respect to many of these issues foreign governments may be more responsive to domestic concerns, and less open to foreign influence, than our own government. If so, American businesses will likely lose their competitive edge. As American businesses lose economic power, foreign businesses will become even more powerful, and support their agenda through even larger campaign contributions. And if this trend continues for long the United States could quickly become a second-rate economic power.

There was a time when asymmetry of political influence favored American companies doing business abroad. Companies such as the United Fruit Company in the early 20th century conducted operations in so-called banana republics that could easily be bribed to do what the American company wanted, for example to provide cheap bananas for the American market. Today business leaders and political leaders in other countries may be looking at our campaign finance system and thinking about how they could control much of what happens in what was once the richest country in the world. We may not provide them with cheap bananas, but we may end up giving them whatever it is they want on whatever terms they want. Our government—responsive only to those who have the money to influence it—may do little or nothing to protect us.

Sovereignty Risk

NATION-STATES HAVE SOVEREIGNTY, but they can also lose it. They can lose it in war if they are weaker than an opponent who invades and occupies. Much of Eastern Europe experienced that from 1939 to the late 1980s. They can also lose sovereignty if their government can be infiltrated by foreign agents or is beholden to foreign agents.

The territory that is now the United States was at various times ruled by officials appointed by England, France, or Spain. The Netherlands also at one point controlled the territory that is New York City. Locally elected legislatures were controlled by directions coming from these foreign governments. Americans did not have control over our own government until the War of Independence.

In the late 19th century, portions of China—which had a disorganized and poorly functioning government—were carved up into spheres of influence by other world powers.

Local governments were also manipulated by foreign powers in much of the Middle East and Latin America during the same time frame.

Our sovereignty may be lost, not from military invasion but from corruption of our government from within. If corporations and other organizations have a dominant role in electing government officials, and if elected officials have a dependency relationship with those organizations, then sovereignty rests not with the people of the United States, but with the people who control the organizations that influence elections. Whoever has enough money can obtain control of many American corporations, and increasingly these people are foreigners.

For many Americans, global business is a good thing, creating wealth and lifting millions out of poverty. But global business should not be allowed to impose global government—so-called world government—on the United States. This risk is particularly pernicious when other countries may do a better job of protecting their sovereignty from external influence than we do. The United States in this scenario is subjected to world government while much of the rest of the world is not.

Political Risk

EVEN IF THE United States does not lose its sovereignty, our corrupt system of campaign finance puts us at a political disadvantage in the world compared with countries that do a better job combating corruption.

As discussed in Chapter 1, representative democracy has many advantages over oligarchy and other forms of government, but representative democracy is a relative newcomer in human history (oligarchy and monarchy have dominated most of the past several thousand years). Representative democracy clearly will not thrive if it is corrupt. If important parts of our government can easily be influenced and diverted from the national interest, but other countries' governments are less easy to influence, our political system is worse. It does not matter if other countries also have elements of corruption. If our government is more corrupt—and because of that corruption makes decisions that diverge further from the national interest—our comparative political disadvantage is substantial.

Conflict of Commitment as a National Security Risk

THERE IS ONE more reason our present system of campaign finance is a grave national security risk: the time commitment it demands from all elected officials, including the president, as well as senior White House and executive branch officials who engage in "personal capacity" political work, much of which involves attending and speaking at fundraisers. This time should be spent on their jobs, which include keeping close track of emerging threats to our national security around the globe, such as terrorism and support for terrorism, cyberterrorism, political instability abroad, economic disruption, threats to the energy supply, espionage, and much more.

In October 2014 Senator Kay Hagan (D-NC) missed a Senate Armed Services Committee meeting to attend a fundraiser. The meeting was a classified briefing on ISIS and other national security threats with James Clapper, the director of national intelligence. Apparently for this senator, talking with donors was more important than hearing what Clapper had to say about an organization that has terrorized Syria and Iraq, ruthlessly beheaded several American hostages, and dragged the United States once more into an Iraq engagement that many Democrats steadfastly opposed, at least when President George W. Bush was in office.

In the executive branch, there is no accessible record of who does and does not attend briefings, including briefings with the president. What we do know is that President Barack Obama participated in 228 fund-raisers while in office, compared with 8 for Ronald Reagan.[176] Regarding our adversaries abroad—and other threats to our national security— President Obama is at an enormous disadvantage compared with his predecessors. To some extent this is a voluntarily imposed disadvantage (he does not have to attend these fundraisers), but he apparently has to choose between devoting full time to the presidency and doing what is necessary to raise money for Democrats in Congress. During his first term, he apparently had to raise money, a lot of money, to keep his own job. A second-term president does not have to worry about reelection but is under enormous pressure to fundraise for members of his own party, knowing that electoral losses are likely to be blamed on him. The president's refusal to show up at fundraisers could create serious political problems in Congress, making it difficult for the president to advance legislation and even his own nominations of judges and senior executive branch officials.

How can the president stay on top of important national secu-rity issues—and stay informed about potential threats—when he is

---

176 Jonathan Fleet, "Lawrence Lessig compares the number of fundraisers between Presidents Reagan and Obama," Politifact New Hampshire, 20 January 2015, politifact.com/new-hampshire /statements/2015/jan/20/lawrence-lessig/lawrence-lessig-compares-number-fundraisers-betwee (accessed 12 November 2015).

preoccupied with fundraising for himself or his party? He can't, and our potential adversaries around the world know this. They know that senior advisers to the president and members of Congress and their staff will be similarly preoccupied, particularly in the six to eight months before an election. And they will plan accordingly.

In sum, the current campaign finance system is a grave economic risk and a national security risk. As more assets in the United States are sold to foreign buyers and global business deals increase in magnitude, it must be clear that our government is not for sale. Otherwise, America could eventually revert to the status we had in colonial days when foreign powers not only owned considerable assets in America but controlled our government. Our founding fathers were aware of the risk that foreign powers could try to buy our government when they drafted the Emoluments Clause of the Constitution, which prohibits any officeholder in the United States government from accepting honors or gifts from foreign governments except as Congress expressly permits. The Emoluments Clause has served us well for over 200 years, but what is the point of that provision anymore if a foreign government can channel money into the political campaigns on which elected officials in the United States depend to remain in office?

And if that happens, the spirit of the Boston Tea Party will have had a good run—more than 200 years—but it will be finished.

Chapter 6

Disenfranchisement
at the Top:
Why Campaign Finance Hurts the
Rich as well as the Poor

AS POINTED OUT in Chapter 2, the founders envisioned a participatory democracy that would include all Americans, not just a governing class. Some of the founders embraced an egalitarian vision that would put the common man on equal footing with the aristocrat. Others—perhaps even most of the men who helped draft the Constitution—believed to some extent that prosperous citizens such as themselves should participate in government more often, and in more prominent positions, than people of more modest means.

The egalitarian vision of participatory democracy is undermined by our system of campaign finance for the reasons discussed in Chapters 1 and 2. The more elitist vision of participatory democracy, however, is also undermined by our current system of campaign finance. This chapter explains why that is the case.

As discussed more extensively below, disgust with the campaign finance system extends into the upper echelons of American society.

The top 10% or even the top 5% of income earners cannot get much from the campaign finance system (a $500 or $1,000 donation does not make a big difference except perhaps in a small-scale local election). Upper-middle-class voters—professionals, private sector white-collar workers, and small-business owners—are an important constituency. Most of these voters are respected members in their communities, well educated, and inclined to be interested in politics. Increasingly these voters know that they are marginalized in the campaign finance system by

donors who have a lot more money than they do. When they lose interest
in the political process the candidates they tend to support are likely to
lose as well. Exclusion of these relatively prosperous but not superrich citizens from the political process is particularly worrisome for pro-business
candidates who need their support.

The top 1% of income earners don't fare much better. This is important
because the people who make large individual campaign contributions
are almost all among the top 1%, even if most of the top 1% don't make
large contributions. High income earners also have the resources to invest
in changing the campaign finance system, although, as explained more
fully below, the 1% are not a cohesive group. Collective action problems
make it difficult for even this group of voters to effect change.

A critical first step to overcoming these collective action problems
is for financially successful Americans—the top 1% and even the top
0.01%—to realize that the campaign finance system is as much a problem
for them as for everyone else. This can be difficult when public discourse
so often treats campaign finance as just another "equity" issue in which
rich people benefit at the expense of others. Progressive politicians sometimes encourage this view because combining the cause of campaign
finance reform with the age-old politics of class envy can be an effective
way to win elections. Many in the top 1% resent this and react by tun-
ing out the debate over money in politics—they don't like the campaign
finance system, but they don't like the way many reformers talk about
it. Others become hostile to reform ideas, discouraged by the suspicion
that reformers want government to take away their free speech along with
their money.

This assumption that the top 1% benefit from the current campaign
finance system is premised upon other assumptions: that the top 1% care
mostly about making more money even if they don't need it; that they
care about making money from particular types of businesses that benefit
from government favoritism rather than from diversified portfolio investments that benefit from a generally strong economy; that they find it easy
to use campaign contributions to manipulate the political system to get
what they want for a particular business interest; and that they care about
these priorities more than they do about other priorities.

These assumptions are wrong on multiple levels.

As explained more fully below, the current system does substantial
harm to everyone, including financially successful Americans in the top
income bracket. The system is not an oligopoly of the top 1% or even the
top 0.01% because most high income earners do not contribute substantial

amounts to political campaigns, and even extremely rich people for the most part do not bother to contribute the maximum amount they are allowed by law. With some notable exceptions, even the highest levels of society respond to the campaign finance system with a polite "thanks, but no thanks."

The Real Interests of the Top 1%

Financial Priorities

Getting government to grant favors to a particular industry is only important if one is disproportionately invested in that industry. Many financially successful people make money in particular industries, but as they get older some of them shift their focus toward diversified investments. Some second- or third-generation members of wealthy families start out with a diversified portfolio. The rich also have to worry about whether government will protect them from people who want to take their money by theft or fraud (most of Ponzi schemer Bernie Madoff's victims were millionaires).

For example, an investment banker might favor loose regulation of financial markets so he can maximize profits in his particular industry, but his priorities could change once he retires and his role in financial markets is principally as an investor. His children are in an even more precarious position if they lack their father's investment sophistication. Their view of investor protection laws could be very different from that of the investment bank their father worked for.

Most rich people derive a substantial portion of their income from investments. Investors as a group should worry about the fact that in 2014 the financial services industry spent an enormous amount on political contributions (see Chapter 3), whereas organizations representing investors spent virtually nothing. The financial services industry is right on some issues but not others. Rational investors should prefer that government make decisions about financial market regulation on the merits, not because of campaign contributions.

Investors also care about the overall condition of the economy and the fiscal condition of government. Will there be continued economic growth? Is federal and state government debt out of control? Is there too much consumer and business debt in the economy as a whole? Will inflation similar to that of the 1970s come back? Is there so much corruption that Congress cannot take decisive action on these and other important issues? If bad decisions are made about government expenditures, trade policy, financial regulation, monetary policy, or other areas of economic management because of campaign contributions from special interests, investors have a lot to lose. A corrupt government destroys wealth, and financially successful Americans know that much of the lost wealth is likely to be theirs.

Nonfinancial Priorities

The argument that rich people don't care about things other than money fuels class-war rhetoric but is counterintuitive. Economists recognize that money and material goods have diminishing marginal utility as people acquire more of them (how many fancy sports cars does a rich man really want in the garage?).[177] For the rich, things other than money are likely to increase happiness more than having even more money. These are the same things that increase other people's happiness, but a person who is free of worries about money may rank them even higher in the order of priorities.

Rich people, like other people, are concerned about broader social issues. For example, a PNC Bank survey of millionaires published in 2014 revealed that two-thirds (64%) of millionaires are concerned about economic inequality in America. And the solutions financially successful people talk and disagree about are many of the same solutions that other Americans talk and disagree about. Forty-nine percent of the millionaires surveyed by PNC Bank supported raising the minimum wage, whereas 38% opposed, while 44% supported raising taxes on top income earners, with 41% opposed.[178]

Good health is likely to be as much a priority for the rich as it is for other people. Although health does vary with income, there is only so much good health that money alone can buy. Rich people don't need to worry about paying for their health care, but they do need to worry about whether good health is a priority for society overall. Laws that allow a particular company to sell a product at the expense of public health do not help the rich man unless he has a financial interest in that particular

177 George Joseph Stigler, "The Development of Utility Theory, I and II," *The Journal of Political Economy* 58, no. 5 (October 1950), 373.
—, "The Adoption of Marginal Utility Theory," *History of Political Economy* 4, no. 2 (1972), 571.
178 "For America's Millionaires, Social Issues Beat Politics in an Election Year," PNC Wealth Management, last modified October 2014, pnc.com/content/dam/pnc-com/pdf/aboutpnc/PressKits/Wealth%20 %26%20Values%20Survey/2014_1027_WV_Social_Issues_Newsletter.pdf (accessed 15 September 2015).

company. And the product can harm the rich man if he or his family members or his employees are exposed to it. A few people might want an exception to public health rules to benefit a particular company in which they have a financial interest, but the majority of people, including the rich, have little to gain from such an exemption and a lot to lose.

In his book *Republic, Lost,* Lawrence Lessig expresses doubt about whether the chemical bisphenol A (BPA) is safe.[179] The vast majority of soft plastic children's products contain BPA in the United States, but not in Europe, a fact that may or may not be due in part to industry influence in US elections. Lessig does not prove that BPA is unsafe, although he exposes a curious divergence between industry-funded studies finding no harm and non–industry-funded studies more likely to find harm.

People, including people in the top 1%, may debate the evidence and the costs and benefits of regulating or banning BPA in children's products, but the rich person's child is just as exposed to this risk as any other child. As Lessig points out, people generally assume that a product is safe if the government allows it to be sold in the United States. The rich are no exception. They have better things to do with their time than research scientific studies that are supposed to be reviewed carefully by federal regulators who approve products for the market. They rely on government to inform them about product safety and are hurt like everyone else if, because of campaign contributions or for any other reason, the government gets the answer wrong.

Of course the CEO or major stockholder in a company that manufactures products containing BPA might have a different view. But most rich people have no such connection with BPA—indeed even fewer than have a connection with the financial services industry in the previous example. Most rich people don't have any connection with the manufacture or sale of products for children. They have views on children's product safety issues similar to the views of other Americans, with one exception—they are probably less likely to be convinced by the argument that a product should be allowed because it is cheaper than alternative products manufactured in other ways. The person who could afford to make an informed choice has a lot to lose if a manufacturer uses campaign contributions to keep a cheap but questionably unsafe product on the market without even a warning that there are legitimate questions about its safety.

This does not mean that rich people who are not invested in a regulated company will always support aggressive product safety regulations. Many people draw upon their business experience to raise legitimate questions about the practicality of a regulation and its costs and benefits.

179 Lessig, 21–22.

Some regulations are a bad idea on the merits (one very rich man, Michael Bloomberg, believes that large-size sugary drinks should be banned, but many people disagree on the merits even if they don't own stock in soda companies). Political conservatives have a long history of raising concerns about excessive and inefficient regulation. But this is about the merits, something very different from a regime in which the content of public safety regulations is influenced by campaign contributions coming mostly from a particular industry. That regime hurts the rich along with everyone else.

Rich people are also concerned about the environment. Populists often repeat the mantra that rich people don't care about the environment because they are too busy making money by destroying the environment. Not true. While top officers of companies that pollute the environment are usually rich (there are fewer such companies than one might think), it does not follow that rich people in general have a substantial financial interest in such companies, much less favor polluting the environment. Indeed, concern about environmental issues has traditionally been strong among Americans who have the time and resources to enjoy the outdoors.

Worries among the top 1% about the environment are likely to accelerate with the changing nature of pollution. In an earlier era, the rich could localize some environmental problems in areas populated by the poor, but global warming by definition is not local (some rich Americans already show less interest in paying millions of dollars for oceanfront properties that could someday be underwater). Water pollution and air pollution are hard to localize as well.

Once again, people disagree about how to solve environmental problems. We are all harmed by environmental problems, and we are all also harmed by lost jobs and lost economic growth from overregulation or unintelligent regulation. Rich people, like the rest of us, want the government to get the answer right. They may question policymakers who lack experience or who attack environmental problems from an ideological perspective or with antibusiness rhetoric. But this is about the merits and is different from the outlier views of the person who makes so much money destroying the environment that he does not care how it affects him and his family.

Global conflict is another worry for the wealthy. Going back to the days of King John, wars have meant high taxes. The older generation recalls that in the years after World War II, and at the beginning of the Cold

War, the highest marginal tax rate rose as high at 90%. They also recall that Republican President and former General Dwight D. Eisenhower, in his farewell address to the nation in 1961, warned against a "military industrial complex" that could unjustifiably drive up military spending and perhaps the likelihood of war.

War also brings rapid growth of government, which is unlikely to shrink once the war is finished. Wars sometimes trigger social upheavals that undermine whatever establishment is in place, whether the decimation of England's upper class in World War I or the American establishment's troubles with its own younger generation in the Vietnam era. A few of the people in the top 1% may benefit from the defense industry and increased military spending regardless of its utility, but most of the top 1% end up paying for it. According to the 2014 PNC Bank survey of millionaires, nearly half of the respondents were extremely concerned about US military involvement in global conflicts.[180]

Many rich people, like other people, support a strong defense, and in some situations they may support imposing economic sanctions or even military action on a global troublemaker. But they do so because they believe these actions are necessary to keep the peace in the long term. In other situations they might favor reductions in military spending or the lifting of economic sanctions to reduce the cost of government. But it is not true that rich people on the whole benefit from big defense spending or war.

Terrorism is another threat to the rich as well as other Americans. Cyberterrorism often targets corporate interests. A few rich people are connected with companies doing business with, or laundering money for, countries that support terrorism. These people and their companies may use whatever strategies are available to them, including campaign contributions and lobbying, to undermine economic sanctions, restrictions on technology export, and other measures. Most rich people, like most other people, however, will see these special interests as a national security threat and will rely on their government to prevent them.

Government's decisions about war and peace, and national security, are too big for any rational person to want them to be decided based on who set up a super PAC or funded a 501(c)(4) organization. This is particularly true when, as pointed out in Chapter 5, much corporate wealth originates outside the United States.

The point here is that people in the top 1% are not remarkably different from everybody else in their views on many issues. Research that

180 "For America's Millionaires, Social Issues Beat Politics in an Election Year," PNC Wealth Management.

has shown a difference in policy preferences between rich people and the general population has focused almost exclusively on questions weighted toward an express or implied emphasis on taxes, government spending, and income redistribution.[181] These are, however, only a subset of the important issues facing the government, and even on those issues some of the richest Americans, such as Warren Buffett, have argued for higher taxes and a more, not less, prominent role for government. On a wide range of other issues, rich people disagree with each other as much as they do with the rest of us.

To the extent they are different, rich people usually benefit from a conservative approach to public policy that avoids big systemic risks: excessive government spending and taxation, excessive government debt, inflation, financial instability, financial fraud (another form of wealth redistribution), environmental destruction, dangerous consumer products, and ineffective and wasteful military and foreign policy. Even if increasing one or more of these systemic risks benefits particular industries in which a few people in the top 1% have a vested interest (companies that pollute, sell the government products it doesn't need, sell unsafe products, sell bad investments, or sell dangerous technology to unfriendly foreign governments), most rich people want to avoid the consequences of these behaviors. They don't want to see more such behaviors simply because campaign contributions are used to facilitate them.

Politics vs. Charity

One of the starkest findings of the PNC Bank survey of millionaires was how little interest they have in donating money to political parties and candidates to achieve their priorities.

Only 3 in 10 donated to a political party or candidate within the past year. Among those who made political donations, 4 in 10 gave under $500, 2 in 10 gave $500 to $1,000, and just over 3 in 10 gave $1,000 or more. This meant that only 30% of 30%, or approximately 10%, of the surveyed millionaires were giving more than $1,000. This is less than half the maximum allowable amount for a single candidate per cycle and barely the ticket price in many wealthy communities for two people to attend a single political fundraiser (some fundraisers charge $2,500 or more per

---

181 Benjamin I. Page et. al, Democracy and Policy Preferences of Wealthy Americans, Perspectives on Politics (2013), faculty.wcas.northwestern.edu/~jnd260/cab/CAB2012%20-%20Page1.pdfwhen (accessed 15 September 2015).

attendee). Ninety percent of the millionaires were not even participating at this relatively modest level.[182]

The millionaires preferred charities to political contributions. According to the PNC survey, 965 had donated money, goods, or time to a nonprofit organization in the past year, and two-thirds had encouraged their children to do to the same. The National Philanthropic Trust (NPT) reports in a separate survey that 95% of high-net-worth households contributed to charity in 2013, almost the exact percentage of households overall that contributed to charity.[183]

According to the NPT poll, Americans gave $335.17 billion to charity in 2013, with corporate giving at $16.76 billion. By contrast the total amount spent on federal elections in 2012 was $6.3 billion.[184] These statistics suggest that a lot of people don't want to participate in our campaign finance system even if they do want to give money to causes they believe in.

Charitable giving poses many of the same collective action problems that political giving does ("if I contribute, will others do likewise or just get a free ride off of my donation?"). Nonetheless, charitable giving is noticeably different from political giving in that the vast majority of people of all levels participate, and they give a lot more—almost 50 times as much—money to charities as they give to politics. One system has the public's confidence as a way to change the world for the better. The other does not. Even though government has a big role in both creating and solving social problems, few Americans believe that political donations are an effective way to get the government to do the right thing. Even Americans who can afford to make big political contributions, for the most part don't.

Even the Forbes 400—the very richest citizens and all billionaires—are only about 50% engaged with the campaign finance system. As of October 17, 2012, in the 2012 presidential race, about half of the Forbes 400—the country's richest citizens—had contributed to President Barack Obama or to his opponent, Governor Mitt Romney. Romney had received a total of $3.4 million for his campaign and the Republican National Committee (RNC) from 158 of the Forbes 400 through October 17. Obama and the

182 "For America's Millionaires, Social Issues Beat Politics in an Election Year," PNC Wealth Management, last modified October 2014, pnc.com/content/dam/pnc-com/pdf/aboutpnc/PressKits/Wealth%20 %26%20Values%20Survey/2014_1027_WV_Social_Issues_Newsletter.pdf (accessed 15 September 2015).
183 "Charitable Giving Statistics (2013)," National Philanthropic Trust, nptrust.org/philanthropic-resources/charitable-giving-statistics (accessed 7 October 2015).
184 Russ Choma, "The 2012 Election: Our Price Tag (Finally) for the Whole Ball of Wax," Center for Responsive Politics, 13 March 2013, opensecrets.org/news/2013/03/the-2012-election-our-price-tag-fin (accessed 15 September 2015).

Democratic National Committee (DNC) had raised $1.7 million from 62 of the Forbes 400.[185] This may seem like a lot of money, but it comes from a group of people with a combined net worth of $1.7 trillion. The average amount given was around $22,000 (the median was probably far lower). Most important, most people in the Forbes 400 are not spending on 501(c)(4) and similar groups the amount of money they could, and presumably would, spend if they believed they could accomplish something. Just 1% of this group's total assets would be $17 billion. Fundraising and expenditures for 501(c)(4) organizations are growing, but they do not appear to be anywhere near that amount, and much of that money comes from corporations rather than individuals. The bottom line is that a group of people who could have a massive impact on elections if they wanted to by spending only 1% of their total net worth, is not making that investment. These financial titans may want to change the world in many different ways—but in most cases political expenditures do not appear to be the way they choose.

Campaign Finance as a War of Attrition: Trial Lawyers vs. Business and Other Endless Contests among the Rich

SOME RICH PEOPLE make campaign contributions—personally or through corporations—to get specific economic benefits in return, even if the direct link between contribution and benefit is hard to prove. Some of these benefits come at the expense of society as a whole, but in many situations the cost of these political favors is disproportionately borne by other wealthy individuals and businesses. After all, that is where the money is.

Sometimes these people fight back with political expenditures of their own. When opposing sides play, campaign finance can resemble an auction where bids keep going up; each side may raise the ante, making it uncertain who will prevail in the end. In some of these scenarios, campaign contributions cancel each other out, and both sides are worse off than if neither had made contributions. In other scenarios the contributions change outcomes, but the biggest losers are other people who have money to begin with.

---

185 Paul Blumenthal, "Forbes 400 Contribute Record Amount to Presidential Campaigns, Super PACs," *The Huffington Post*, 5 November 2012, huffingtonpost.com/2012/11/05/forbes-400-campaign-contributions_n_2047750.html (accessed 15 September 2015).

For example, when a government contract goes to a campaign contributor, some other business owner does not get the contract. An unnecessary or excessively expensive government contract is paid for by taxpayers, and disproportionately by upper-income taxpayers. Drug companies may use campaign contributions to persuade the government to allow them to charge higher prices, but this comes at the expense of businesses that buy health insurance for their employees. Copyright owners contributed millions in campaign contributions to get the 1998 Sonny Bono Copyright Term Extension Act, a 20-year extension on copyrights from Congress, but businesses that want to use copyrighted material have to pay more for the material or not use it (the latter is a loss to the economy as a whole). Wealthy real estate developers may make political contributions and lobby government at the local level to get zoning variances in wealthy neighborhoods (the residents may then make campaign contributions to counter the developers' efforts and keep the zoning ordinances intact). A polluter may lobby for federal and state regulations that help its business but decimate the tourist industry in surrounding areas.

The battle between plaintiffs' lawyers and the business community is an example of how such a war of attrition in campaign finance can play itself out.

The plaintiffs' litigation industry in the United States by far exceeds its counterparts anywhere else in the world. The United States is unique in allowing lawyers to charge contingent fees, meaning plaintiffs themselves do not have to invest in their cases and the lawyers who do invest in cases can carry a diversified portfolio of cases. The United States is also among the very few countries that do not require the loser in litigation to pay the winner's legal fees (the so-called English rule that is used in many other parts of the world). Rather, plaintiffs' lawyers' gains come at the expense of the businesses they sue.

One would think that the business community as a whole—given its enormous campaign contributions—would have the political influence to bring the litigation industry to heel, or at least to bring the amount and cost of litigation in the United States in line with the rest of the world. But the United States, the country with the highest level of corporate political spending, is the country with the most plaintiffs' litigation. For the observer who believes that money buys influence, and that more money buys more influence, this result does not make sense. The business community as a whole must spend more money on politics than plaintiffs' lawyers. So why doesn't business win?

But for the observer who understands the strategic impact of targeted political spending by cohesive groups to obtain single objectives, and the collective action problems of dispersed people and organizations with numerous objectives, the resilience of the American litigation system against withering attacks by industry makes a lot of sense. The business community spends a lot of money on politics, as discussed in the context of corporate contributions in the next section, but the business community has a lot of issues to contend with, not just the litigation system. Plaintiffs' lawyers by contrast have a much narrower agenda, and they know how to make political expenditures to accomplish it.

According to the Center for Responsive Politics:

> Contributions to federal candidates and political committees by lawyers have increased during the past 10 years, and collectively, they are consistently larger during presidential election years. Each cycle, the contributions significantly favor Democrats. In the 2008 election cycle, the industry contributed a massive $234 million to federal political candidates and interests, 76 percent of which went to Democratic candidates and committees.[186]

Many officeholders thus know that they will have a powerful enemy if they suggest changing the litigation system in a way that plaintiffs' lawyers don't like. Of course even more money is spent on political campaigns by business interests that for the most part presumably don't like plaintiffs' lawyers, but there are plenty of other ways to help business contributors—such as by listening to their preferences on spending on government contracts and regulatory policy. Savvy politicians will avoid feuding with a well-organized special interest lobby such as trial lawyers that would likely retaliate by giving money to an opponent.

For Democrats in particular, supporting tort reform could be political suicide. The plaintiffs' bar in many districts has the political connections and money to launch a serious primary challenge. Republicans are sometimes more vocal about tort reform, but they also do not want to see trial lawyer money going to their opponents. Often they too stand down. And the state of our legal system shows it.

One could argue that American legislatures make rules governing our litigation system on the merits (in other words, most of the rest of the world is wrong about the costs and benefits of litigation) and that campaign contributions have nothing to do with it. Good lawyers can

186 "Lawyers and Law Firms: Top Contributors, 2013–2014," Center for Responsive Politics, opensecrets.org/industries/indus.php?ind=K01 (accessed 7 October 2015).

argue any position. But trial lawyers continue to make campaign contributions. Presumably they do so for a reason. That reason is probably that trial lawyers are getting a good return on their investment in campaign finance.

Although both trial lawyers and businesses spend a lot of money in the battle over legal reform, a phenomenon discussed later in this chapter in more detail is that the narrow interest (here the trial lawyer industry) often prevails over broader interests (here those of the business community as a whole in avoiding excessive litigation). The larger, more dispersed group has collective action problems that are probably greater than the smaller, more coherent group. Which businesses will fund the fight against excessive litigation, and which will free ride off of the efforts of others? Which businesses should invest in the fight because they know ahead of time that they are likely to be subjected to massive unfair plaintiffs' litigation? Which businesses will be taken by surprise when a class action suit is filed?

The Chamber of Commerce and other groups try to overcome this collective action problem by educating businesses in many different industries about the broad systemic risks of excessive litigation and then encouraging businesses to invest in political and public education efforts to counter the efforts of trial lawyers. These expenditures include campaign contributions, but many of the contributions come from corporate PACs and organizations, including the Chamber itself, that have a broad range of issues to deal with. Their political agenda includes taxes, trade, burdensome federal and state regulation, employment law, and more. Excessive and costly litigation is not their only issue. Elected officials know how broad the business community's agenda is and, when they give the business community something in return for campaign contributions, they will often look for a way of doing so without offending the litigation industry. For example, it is probably more advantageous for elected officials to oppose tightening regulation of product safety than it would be for them to support making it more difficult for plaintiffs' lawyers to sue companies for unsafe products. There are relatively few campaign contributions backing prophylactic regulatory measures to promote consumer product safety, so many politicians won't back them. Manufacturers thus can be given at least some of what they want, even if helping them escape the clutches of plaintiffs' lawyers is a more costly political decision that many elected officials will not make.

In recent years American trial lawyers, like other industries, have sought to export their business model to the rest of the world. They have had limited success (some European countries are experimenting with litigation formats that resemble class actions) but overall these efforts have not prevailed. Most countries want no part of the American litigation system, and many countries believe they can solve problems ranging from financial services fraud to unsafe consumer products by other means. There could be many explanations for this, but one may be that political systems in some countries are not as easy to influence with campaign contributions as ours is. Could other countries be making decisions about their civil litigation system on the merits, while the United States is basing its decisions on the political clout manifested in campaign contributions?

The purpose of this discussion is not to demonize plaintiffs' lawyers, but to show how one group of wealthy individuals can benefit at the expense of other wealthy individuals and businesses. Political expenditures by plaintiffs' lawyers and their corporate opponents are a good example of the war of attrition that can erupt when political contributions coupled with an agenda antagonize a well-organized opponent. Another important point illustrated by this example is that the campaign finance game gives some advantage to concentrated special interests—such as trial lawyers—over those that are more dispersed—such as the business community in general. The views of those who give the most money don't necessarily prevail; the relevant consideration is how strongly contributors hold certain views and where those views rank compared to other priorities.

Politics as Spectator Sport: The Players and Those Who Watch

BARRY GOLDWATER CLEARLY stated in *The Conscience of a Conservative* his view that both corporations and unions should keep their money out of politics:

> *In order to achieve the widest possible distribution of political power, financial contributions to political campaigns should be made by individuals and individuals alone. I see no reason for labor unions—or corporations—to participate in politics. Both were created for economic purposes, and their activities should be restricted accordingly.*[187]

---

187 Goldwater, *The Conscience of a Conservative*, 49.

Due to developments discussed in Chapter 1, with which Goldwater strongly disagreed, it has not turned out that way. Some corporations, unions, and individuals are big-time players in the game of campaign finance. Some of these participants are happier playing the game than others.

Corporations

Some corporations make more political contributions than others. According to *Business Insider*, the biggest corporate donors in the 2012 election cycle were:[188]

The 10 Companies Making the Biggest Political Donations					
Company	Total Contributions (mid-2012)	To Democrats	To Republicans	Spending on Lobbying (mid-2012)	Industry
Las Vegas Sands Corp.	$11,738,600	0%	100%	$300,000	Resorts and Casinos
Goldman Sachs Group, Inc.	$4,769,994	29%	71%	$1,380,000	Diversified Investments
Comcast Corp.	$2,774,151	64%	36%	$4,600,000	Cable TV
AT&T, Inc.	$2,504,219	35%	65%	$7,050,000	Telecom Services
Dreamworks Animation SKG, Inc.	$2,370,150	99%	1%	n/a	Movie Production
Microsoft Corp.	$2,253,565	68%	32%	$1,790,000	Software
Huntsman Corp.	$2,250,389	0%	100%	$100,000	Specialty Chemicals
Honeywell International, Inc.	$2,222,605	37%	63%	$1,750,000	Aerospace/Defense Products and Services
Bank of America Corp.	$2,125,513	26%	74%	$870,000	International, Money Center Bank
Lockheed Martin Corp.	$1,927,900	38%	62%	$3,979,250	Aerospace/Defense Products and Services

These 10 companies are in gambling (1); financial services, which in its modern state arguably has some of the characteristics of gambling (2); communications (2); movies (1); computer software (1); chemicals (1); and defense (2). All of these businesses are heavily regulated (some with issues under the antitrust laws) and/or do a lot of business with the government.

Whether on balance these and other corporations get a lot of bang for their buck is debatable, but the money is spent anyway.

It is also true that many corporations opt out of the system—they do not want to donate and are willing to accept the consequence of having

188 "The Ten Companies Making the Biggest Political Donations," *Business Insider*, 4 July 2012.

less influence with the government. Other corporations may selectively engage only in a few local races or other contests in which they believe they can have a genuine impact and perhaps get something in return.

It is doubtful that many corporate leaders like the current campaign finance system the way it is.

A July 2013 survey by the Committee for Economic Development (CED), called the Money in Politics Project, confirmed this deep-rooted antipathy corporate America has for the system.[189] According to the CED survey:

> *American business executives—from both political parties—have deep concerns about how U.S. elections are funded, according to CED's latest survey. Business executives also overwhelmingly agree that the campaign finance system is "pay-to-play" and in need of major reforms.*
>
> *"Results from our survey show that business leaders believe that the campaign finance system needs reform, and disclosure is the answer," said Steve Odland, CEO of the Committee for Economic Development (CED). "CED continues to encourage robust discussion around these issues. CED urges members of the business and labor communities, civic leaders, and public officials to promote full participation by all parties in the campaign process, and bring increased transparency to campaign finance disclosure."*
>
> *Top-level findings show the level of frustration with large donors and hidden money in campaigns:*
>
> * *85% of business executives say the campaign finance [system] is in poor shape or broken;*
> * *87% say that the campaign finance system needs major reforms or a complete overhaul;*
> * *64% of executives say that the U.S. campaign finance system is pay-to-play and it is a serious problem;*

189 "Perspectives from Business on Campaign Finance Reform," Committee for Economic Development, 31 July 2013, ced.org/events/single/perspectives-from-business-on-campaign-finance-reform (accessed 13 November 2015); Hart Research and American Viewpoint, "Survey: American Business Leaders On Campaign Finance," Committee for Economic Development, 24 July 2013, ced.org/reports /single/survey-american-business-leaders-on-campaign-finance (accessed 13 November 2015). The bipartisan research team conducted an online nationwide survey among 302 business executives for the CED. The results of the survey, along with a new CED report, "Hiding in Plain Sight: The Problem of Transparency in Political Finance," were released at a Washington, D.C., event hosted by CED and The Conference Board Governance Center. The event featured former Chairman of the Federal Election Commission Trevor Potter and a wide range of corporate executives.

- *71% say that major contributors have too much influence on politicians;*

- *The majority of those surveyed agreed that the solution to these problems is campaign finance disclosure;*

- *Nine out of ten business leaders surveyed support reforms that disclose all individual, corporate and labor contributions to political committees;*

- *89% support limits on how much money individuals, corporations and labor organizations can give to political candidates and how much they can spend for political purposes during an election.*[190]

The CED polling data confirms that corporate leaders, even if some of them give money to support candidates, are not happy with the current system of campaign finance for much the same reasons as other people are not happy.

This disillusionment is also explained by the fact that corporations are not very effective filters for the broader political views of any of their constituencies, whether directors, officers, or shareholders. Corporations are not natural persons, even if they are fictional persons in the eyes of the law, and the Supreme Court in *Citizens United* gave corporations free speech rights similar to those of natural persons. Corporate political giving is for the most part associated with narrow business objectives and often is not guided by any broader political agenda or vision of who is a better candidate for public office.

First, key corporate constituencies may disagree even if the corporation appears to speak with one voice. Corporations are controlled by directors and officers, not by their shareholders. Shareholders, unless they have a control block of shares, have a role in corporate governance that is mostly limited to selecting directors annually in an election that is usually uncontested. The directors and officers make decisions about electioneering communications, establishment of PACs, and contributions to politically active trade associations. These corporate officers and directors are mostly high-income earners, but so are many of the shareholders whose money is used for these expenditures without their consent.

Second, not all of the individuals involved with corporations—shareholders, directors, or officers—are Americans, meaning foreign nationals can use corporations to influence American political campaigns,

---

190 *Ibid.*

reducing the impact of American individuals. As explained more fully in Chapter 5, in a global economy no longer dominated by the United States, foreign nationals and sometimes foreign governments have an increasingly important role in the ownership and management of many US corporations. Foreign interests are legally prohibited from contributing directly to US political campaigns, creating an incentive for them to filter their influence through investments in, management of, or joint ventures with US corporations. To the extent corporations represent the interests of an elite on the political stage, it may be a global elite, not the richest Americans.

Third, political expenditures are almost always directly linked to the business objectives of the corporation—supporting candidates who are perceived to support those objectives. Corporate managers who stray and support controversial candidates without a clearly stated business objective get in trouble with customers and shareholders (this happened to Target Corporation when it supported a controversial candidate for governor of Minnesota in the 2010 election cycle). This means that corporate managers who make decisions about corporate political expenditures are not considering many of the factors they would consider in spending their own money.

Fourth, at least some corporate expenditures are made not because the corporation's managers support a candidate but because they fear the consequences for the corporation if the corporation does not contribute. The banking industry, for example, is likely to give to incumbent congressmen who have a significant impact on banking regulation, whether or not they agree with those congressmen. A look at the top 20 contributions to former Congressman Barney Frank (D-MA) and Senator Chris Dodd (D-CT), whose names are on the 2010 Dodd–Frank Act, is illustrative.

According to the Center for Responsive Politics, the top eight contributors to Congressman Barney Frank's campaign in 2008 were six individual banks, one accounting firm that audits financial services firms, and one trade association of bankers: Brown Brothers Harriman, UBS, JPMorgan Chase, Bank of America, Manulife Financial, Royal Bank of Scotland, Deloitte LLP, and the American Bankers Association (the rest of the top 20 were also mostly in the financial services industry).[191] In 2010—the year the Dodd–Frank Act was passed—Congressman Frank's top eight contributors were all firms in the financial services industry: FMR Corp., Bank of New York Mellon, State Street Corporation, Bank of America, New York Life Insurance Company, Liberty Mutual,

---

191 "Barney Frank: Top 20 Contributors, 2007–2008," Center for Responsive Politics, opensecrets.org /politicians/contrib.php?cid=N00000275&cycle=2008 (accessed 17 November 2015).

Promontory Financial, and Weiss Capital (once again the rest of the top 20 were mostly in the financial services industry).[192]

Between 2003 and 2008, Senator Chris Dodd's top 20 contributors were mostly in the insurance and banking industries, including American International Group (AIG), Royal Bank of Scotland, Credit Suisse, UBS, Citigroup, JPMorgan Chase, Morgan Stanley, Goldman Sachs, Lehman Brothers, Bear Stearns, and Merrill Lynch.[193] AIG contributed a total of $128,278 to his campaign (AIG became insolvent and was rescued by a federal bailout in 2008). This list of contributors also includes five of the largest US investment banks, three of which failed in the 2008 financial crisis in part due to lax federal regulatory oversight (the other two probably would have failed as well if it had not been for the 2008 federal bailouts). Three of these top 20 contributors to Senator Dodd's campaign were large foreign banks (see Chapter 5 for a general discussion of foreign influence on US political campaigns). A calculation of the top contributors to Senator Dodd's campaign from 2005 to 2010 reveals many of the same names,[194] though by the middle of that period, many if not most of these entities were on the brink of insolvency.

Some business leaders might describe a situation where they contribute to politicians who regulate them as "extortion" or a "protection racket," but many contribute anyway. The connection between this phenomenon and the ever-growing body of government regulation of business is described more fully in Chapter 3. Business leaders need to recognize that by making these types of contributions they may be encouraging big government rather than diminishing it.

This problem is even worse if competitors contribute to a politician who has the power to revamp the competitive landscape in an industry through regulation. Corporations that do not set up a PAC or do something else to back powerful politicians can be at a big disadvantage vis-à-vis competitors, particularly when new regulation is enacted. The Dodd–Frank Act of 2010 had almost a thousand pages of legislation and led to thousands more pages in agency regulation aimed at the financial services industry, including sweeping mandates, exceptions to those mandates, and exceptions to the exceptions. This regulation arguably

---

192 "Barney Frank: Top 20 Contributors, 2009–2010," Center for Responsive Politics, opensecrets.org /politicians/contrib.php?cycle=2010&type=I&cid=N00000275&newMem=N&recs=20 (accessed 17 November 2015).
193 "Chris Dodd: Top 20 Contributors, 2007–2008," Center for Responsive Politics, opensecrets.org /politicians/contrib.php?cycle=2008&cid=N00000581&type=I&newmem=N (accessed 17 November 2015).
194 "Chris Dodd: Top 20 Contributors, 2009–2010," Center for Responsive Politics, opensecrets.org /politicians/contrib.php?cycle=2010&type=I&cid=N00000581&newMem=N&recs=20 (accessed 17 November 2015).

favored the largest financial institutions, which can afford the high cost of compliance and also spend the most on political contributions and other expenditures.

Yet another problem is that, as explained in Chapter 1, labor unions make enormous political contributions despite their representation of an ever-shrinking percentage of the American workforce. Corporations that don't contribute risk being outgunned in the contentious policy debates with labor, even if labor unions are able to bring fewer voters to the polls than ever before.

In sum, corporate managers don't always contribute, don't always want to contribute, and are not always backing the elected officials they want in office. They are spending this money because they believe that without the spending, legislative results would be even worse or because they believe rivals and unions will outspend them.

Fifth, corporations are legally restricted from making some types of campaign contributions, for example, direct contributions from the corporate treasury to a candidate's campaign. They also may fear customer or employee backlash. Corporate managers thus often make their political expenditures through trade associations such as the several securities industry groups or even larger groups such as state and national chambers of commerce. There the money is commingled with money from other corporations that may or may not have similar objectives. Another group of decision-makers at the trade association level decides how political expenditures are made, removing the decision-making yet another level from the people who pay for them (the corporations and ultimately the shareholders). Earmarking by a corporation of money for a particular political campaign (for example, telling the chamber of commerce that the money is to be spent on a particular campaign) is also likely to be a straw donor arrangement that violates federal and state election laws. The trade association managers may listen to the general concerns of corporate managers who send money to their associations, but may not always do what they want, particularly if they have conflicting views.

All of this means that corporate political expenditures are a relatively weak mechanism for getting the political system to respond to the interests of corporations, and particularly the shareholders who own corporations. Despite all the political rhetoric on the left about campaign finance and capitalism reinforcing each other, corporate campaign contributions overall probably don't benefit capitalism any more than the labor union contributions discussed in Chapter 1 benefit workers overall.

The top 1% of Americans, particularly those whose principal interest is that of shareholders, would probably be better off if political expenditures were voluntarily curtailed by all corporations. But it is difficult for share-holders to act collectively to stop the practice. Corporate officers and directors may feel compelled to continue. Pay to play will sometimes be a necessary business strategy, particularly when competitors—and labor unions—are free to spend whatever they want to get what they want.

Individual Donors

Goldwater envisioned a robust role for individuals in campaign finance, but one that would "achieve the widest possible distribution of political power."[195] He envisioned lots of individuals contributing relatively modest amounts to support candidates of their choice and enjoying the political power that comes with that support.

Unfortunately even the individual side of campaign finance has not turned out that way. A very few individuals contribute massive amounts of money. In fact they are spending so much money that *The New York Times* observed in 2014 that oligarchs in some races are becoming their own political parties—picking and financing the nominees—with the Democratic and Republican Parties themselves receding into the background.[196]

Most other individuals, including wealthy individuals, are disengaged. As pointed out earlier in this chapter, most millionaires don't even make a $1,000 political donation (according to the PNC survey 10% of millionaires did so in 2013). Most people either watch on the sidelines or contribute such comparatively small amounts that candidates, political parties, and political strategists treat them as if they were irrelevant.

Even those who contribute $1,000 or more usually don't get much for it. The individual $1,000 to $2,500 donors may attend a cocktail party or dinner where they will have five minutes or so to chat with the candidate, if they are lucky, but that is about it. Individuals donating $5,000 or more may get somewhat more time, but candidates go to so many such fundraisers that they probably don't remember, must less seriously consider, much of what is said to them, unless of course it echoes something that is said by a lot of donors or by the coordinator of a PAC or some other larger financial backer. Many of these individual contributions are made in a social context similar to the much more common charitable fundraising

---

195 Goldwater, *The Conscience of a Conservative*, 49.
196 Jim Rotenberg, "How Billionaire Oligarchs Are Becoming Their Own Political Parties," *The New York Times Magazine*, 17 October 2014, nytimes.com/2014/10/19/magazine/how-billionaire-oligarchs-are-becoming-their-own-political-parties.html?_r=1 (accessed 15 September 2015); reporting on the 2014 governor's race in Florida and other races where opposing candidates are supported by billionaire Tom Steyer's NextGen super PAC and the billionaire Koch brothers' Americans for Prosperity.

event—a friend organizes the event and asks friends to attend. Sometimes the donors know the candidate already from previous social or business relationships. Very few Americans in the top 1% of income earners make political expenditures beyond a single $1,000 to $2,000 donation per election cycle.

A few enormously wealthy donors, such as Tom Steyer and the Koch brothers, by contrast make headlines with their political activity—much of it through donations to political campaigns, parties, and PACs. Some of it is through 501(c)(4) tax-exempt organizations that can receive unlimited contributions from corporations as well as individuals—and that can make unrestricted electioneering communications after the Supreme Court's decision in *Citizens United*. These individual donors have different motives for these expenditures, but for some of them politics is a passion because they are genuinely committed to particular causes such as free enterprise (the Koch brothers), the environment (Tom Steyer), the United States' relationship with Israel (Sheldon Adelson, also a supporter of free enterprise), or enhancing the role of government in society (George Soros).

Some of these individuals' political activities are tied to selfish motives (the Koch brothers emphasize deregulation of the energy industry, Adelson advances the interests of his global gambling empire, and Soros probably won't support candidates who would crack down on currency speculation). Still, these very wealthy individuals are probably making these expenditures not principally with the objective of making yet more money from government decisions but rather because politics is their passion. Just as art collecting, horse racing, yacht racing, or other passions captivate other rich people, their obsession is politics. Some rich people can boast a Warhol painting in their living room; others, a presidential candidate or better yet a president in their living room. Political power and the ability to shape public policy to conform to one's views are as captivating as any other passion of the rich, and some superrich people choose to spend their money in this way.

The activities of these few individuals, along with corporations, labor unions, and other organizations (discussed above) make politics a sport in which a few superrich Americans and other people, such as corporate officers and labor bosses who can spend other people's money, indulge themselves. The rest of the country stays on the sidelines.

Most people who contribute large amounts of money to political candidates are rich (the exception is people such as labor bosses who donate other people's money). But, as pointed out by the PNC poll discussed above, most rich people do not contribute large amounts to political campaigns. By way of analogy, most Americans who own polo ponies and play polo are rich but still most rich Americans do not own polo ponies or play polo. Collecting art, yachting, owning sports franchises, and other activities are also dominated by the rich. Still, relatively few rich people engage in any one of these activities. Contributing to political campaigns is yet one more activity that a few rich people find satisfying and perhaps even financially rewarding if they get something in return, but it's also an activity in which most rich Americans do not participate. Some rhetoric around campaign finance reform makes it sound as if rich Americans as a class are using campaign contributions to make sure that society's rules benefit them. But the facts show otherwise: Most rich people, like other people, do not participate in the campaign finance system.

To the extent money drives politics—particularly decisions about who wins primaries in the two major political parties—for most Americans of all income levels our system of democracy is a spectator sport. Most Americans, including rich Americans, aren't in a position to benefit personally from political contributions even if they can afford to make those contributions. Almost all Americans watch while very few play.

This is the situation we are in, a situation that would have alarmed even the most elitist of our country's founders if they had known that this is where the government they created would end up.

WHY IS IT that so many people, including rich people, entirely opt out of participating in the campaign finance system or spend a lot less money on politics than they could afford to spend? Why is it that people who want their money to have an impact on the world overwhelmingly choose to give to charity instead?

The remainder of this chapter explains why for so many the game of campaign finance is a losing proposition even if a few can benefit from it.

The Collective Action Problem

IMAGINE A GAME in which 10 players are each given $100 and the same list of 10 political issues numbered 1 to 10. Each player is assigned one of the issues and that issue is different from each other player's issue. Each player will get another $50 if he or she "wins" on his or her issue. For the other 9 issues, however, the player loses $10 if the player who has that issue wins. With these payoffs each issue benefits the player who has that issue in the amount of $50 if he wins but costs the other players collectively $90. The other players thus have a collective interest in making sure he does not win on that issue. But each player also has his or her own $50 issue in which winning will come at the expense of the other players, each losing $10.

In order to win on his or her designated issue, a player must spend more money lobbying for that issue than all the other players combined spend lobbying against that issue. If, for example, player 1 spends $20 on his issue (deregulation of derivative securities), the other players can defeat him by collectively spending $20 or more against that issue. If they do, nobody gains or loses money. Otherwise player 1 wins on his issue and gets $50, while each other player loses $10. Same for player 2, whose issue is increase government subsidies of for-profit educational institutions. If the other players collectively spend at least as much money on that issue as he does, nobody pays or gets anything. If they spend less than player 2 on this issue, each player loses $10 and player 2 gets $50.

The game could be played sequentially, with each player making irrevocable decisions on spending money for or against issues, starting with player 1. Alternatively, the players could be allowed to change their minds when they see what other players are doing.

How will the players play the game? There are various scenarios, but they may realize that it is difficult to spread their money around to defeat the other players who want to win and get $50 on their special issue, that other players may not join them in this effort to say no to special interests, and that it might be better to accept these losses as inevitable and at least try to get $50 for their issue. No matter how the game is played a lot of the players end up losing, because each player loses not only the money spent to secure victory on his or her issue, but the money—$10 per player per time—that is lost whenever another player wins on his or her issue.

Most of the players will realize that they would have been better off collectively not spending any money for or against any issue, if they had a choice. A binding agreement not to spend money at all on issues and keep their $100 would maximize their collective welfare, but how could the players make such an agreement enforceable?

When rich people play the campaign finance game against other rich people—whether it be trial lawyers vs. industry, investment promoters vs. investors, or other rival interests—this game may be a helpful analogy for where they are likely to end up. In the end, most players will be losers.

The Donor's Dilemma

MANY DONORS SEEK solely to advance a political viewpoint, to help a friend's political career, to support a candidate they like, or to attain the personal satisfaction of being close to people with political power. They don't want anything specific in return. Some donors do have something personal they want, such as an ambassadorship or some other political appointment or admission of a relative to a military academy. Yet other donors, particularly corporate donors, seek to advance the agenda of a specific business enterprise. They donate money so someone in power will help them have a better chance of making more money. Sometimes competitors are doing the same thing, in which case it can be difficult to unilaterally stand down from campaign contributions even if one detests the campaign finance system.

In some of these situations there could be an implicit quid pro quo (the more express the arrangement is, however, the more likely it will be prosecuted as bribery). More probable than a quid pro quo is a dependency relationship in which holders of public office believe that they need the donor, alone or combined with other donors, to pay for their reelection campaigns. If so, the donor may get what he wants from the elected official—or so he hopes.

This strategy usually only works, however, if the contributor knows specifically what he wants from government (an earmark for a contract, a regulatory loophole, a particular industry tax credit, etc.), the contributor identifies a time frame to lobby elected officials before a discretionary decision is made about what he wants, and the contributor's lobbying is effective because he has created a dependency relationship with office-holders who are in a position to influence the decision. Usually these plans must be well laid and executed before the decision. This pay-to-play strategy can work, particularly if the contributor works with other similarly situated contributors to put together a large campaign war chest, but a lot can go wrong.

The more politically controversial the contributor's request is, the more costly it usually is for the politician to grant the favor, meaning it may not be granted at all or the contributor will have to contribute more to get it. When consent from a legislature or other group of officehold-ers is required to obtain the favor, the contributor may have to find a way to influence all of them, which further elevates the controversy and costs (disclosure of campaign contributions and lobbying contacts may give persons opposing the contributor a chance to generate controversy before the discretionary decision is made, further reducing the contributor's chances for a good return on investment).

The point here is not that this strategy is ineffective or too costly—it sometimes does work. If the strategy works, the return on investment for the contributor can be hundreds or even thousands of times the cost of the campaign contributions. The point is that this pay-to-play strategy is cost effective for obtaining some favors, usually relatively discrete favors such as inserting a particular spending earmark or regulatory loophole in a bill, or orchestrating Congressional interference with a particular agency regulation. The strategy is less likely to be effective for obtaining a high-profile political victory or a broad-based favor such as a widely applicable tax cut.

A collective action problem for campaign contributors is rooted in the fact that the bigger and more public the benefit they want from government, the more costly the campaign contributions that are likely required to get it. The more broadly dispersed the benefits are from the desired action, the more contributors will have to participate in the political fundraising effort for it to succeed.

Industry associations are formed to help overcome this collective action problem in certain industry groups—for example, the Securities Industry Association and the American Trial Lawyers Association. But putting together the necessary funds and discouraging free riders— people and companies that benefit from others' campaign contributions without themselves contributing—becomes more difficult as the group of beneficiaries grows. The strategy becomes much more difficult when one moves beyond particular industry segments to try to organize on behalf of the interests of the wealthy as a whole. How many large PACs for example, are dedicated specifically to broad-based tax cuts and cutting government spending as their principal issue and how much do these PACs raise compared with industry-specific PACs, including defense industry PACs, that encourage more government spending, which brings higher deficits, higher taxes, or both? Defendants in lawsuits have powerful organizational allies—such as the U.S. Chamber of Commerce—but even those organizations can only make limited headway against the more concentrated political influence of the plaintiffs' bar.

If one particular interest group is pitted against another, even if both interest groups are dominated by the very rich, the smaller and more cohesive interest group with more narrowly targeted interests usually has an advantage. For example, as mentioned earlier in this chapter, rich people almost all invest in financial markets and would presumably want securities and banking laws that favored investors. Yet apart from some limited political activity by institutional investors, there are no high-profile efforts to coordinate campaign contributions and lobbying efforts on behalf of investor protection. A smaller subset of rich people also work in the financial services industry and want investor protection laws that allow them more flexibility and higher fees—and less liability exposure—when selling financial products and providing services to investors. As discussed earlier in this chapter, this subset of rich people in the financial services industry has injected massive amounts into both campaign contributions and lobbying. The narrower, more focused group prevails over the more dispersed group, even if most rich people are investors.

The campaign finance system presents even bigger collective action problems for people—including the top 1% of income earners—when it comes to issues that affect society as a whole, such as excessive government spending, unsafe consumer products, and environmental damage. These problems affect *almost everyone,* including rich people, yet most people who are affected by these issues cannot afford to contribute to political campaigns. Rich people who contribute to influence government on these issues are subsidizing the vast majority of both rich people and other people who do not contribute. A few rich people become engaged politically because they worry about an issue such as the environment (billionaire hedge fund manager Tom Steyer has set up a PAC focused on environmental issues, although his support almost exclusively for Democrats and minimal efforts to support pro-environment Republicans suggests that he also has some more-partisan priorities). But most rich people are likely to view such big picture efforts as futile. "Why should I," they ask, "pay to take on dozens of different special interests when many other people with just as much money as I have don't contribute anything?" With respect to the broader issues in which government affects their lives, the rich will likely be in a position that is not that much better than anyone else.

This dilemma forces potential donors either to abandon the campaign finance system entirely (many do) or focus their attention back on their own more discrete special interests where they face less opposition and fewer free riders and can more effectively influence government with campaign contributions. A manufacturing company CEO may be an environmentalist on big picture issues (perhaps CO_2 emissions) that do not relate to his business any more or less than to other businesses, but he knows that he can do little to stop the many other people and organizations that contribute to the problem and contribute to politicians so they can continue to do so. He does know that he can, through campaign contributions, get federal or state regulators to ease up on a narrow provision of the law that affects his own company's contribution to water pollution in a particular location, and he is tempted to do just that. He knows that pay to play won't help solve the big problems, and in fact makes those problems worse, but he also knows that it is possible to successfully pay to play with respect to his own particular issue.

The term *special interest* is often used to describe supporters of these positions, and there are many of them, whether it be a company making a chemical that is dangerous when discharged into the environment, a financial services firm that wants to sell a certain product to investors, or a financial institution that wants to circumvent sanctions against a foreign dictator. Some people in the top 1% have ties to one or more of these special interests and benefit from that special interest financially. Some will make contributions to get what they want on one or two discrete issues, even if many of these same people would prefer to live in a system where their own broader concerns, the concerns of other rich people like them, and those of the majority of the population were given priority over special interests. People in the top 1% in this scenario find themselves playing a game that they may detest, but by playing the game they get at least something from the political system, whereas the alternative is to get nothing at all.

The dilemma for the person who can afford campaign contributions is that much of what he wants for himself, his family, and his country cannot be obtained by participating in the campaign finance system. He knows that campaign contributions are unlikely to address his concerns about a wide range of issues, such as government fiscal policy, public health, the environment, and war and peace, when special interests can all too easily make targeted campaign contributions to further a different agenda. But from time to time he might also face circumstances where he has his own targeted agenda and some of what he wants can be obtained if he makes political contributions. He is tempted to participate in the campaign finance system even if the big-picture consequence of his participation and participation of others is that a lot more of what they want in general will be taken away.

Still, the fact that the majority of rich people make only modest campaign contributions, particularly from their own money (most rich people don't max out on contributions), suggests a widespread lack of confidence even among the richest Americans that campaign contributors in most situations realize a reasonable return on their investment.

The "tragedy of the commons" (the ancient collective action problem of overgrazing and destruction in a common pasture that could be solved if the livestock keepers all agreed to reasonable limits on use of the pasture)[197] is the tragedy of the less than 1% of Americans who fund a corrupt campaign finance system. The system in which contributors pay a comparatively low fee to feed off of our government undermines their own collective self-interest, not to mention that of the rest of the country. If they could only get others to stand down from pay to play, it would be in their collective interest to do so. But nobody seems to be able to reach a consensus on how to fix campaign finance, and when consensus is reached on even a partial solution such as the disclosure regime or the McCain–Feingold Act, it is ineffective because people cheat (collective action is made even more difficult when the Supreme Court rules that part of an agreed-upon solution is unconstitutional).

A person in this position has limited options. He could stay away from the campaign finance system (this is the choice that most people make), or he could try to find an opportunity to increase his wealth by making his own targeted campaign contribution to get a government contract at taxpayer expense, more lenient regulation of a particular business enterprise, or something else, even if in doing so he worsens the dilemma for other people in a similar situation. The short-term play for some financial gain may be the best he can do in a system that will not allow him to address the broader concerns that he worries about. This dilemma presents many of the richest Americans with an end result similar to that of Americans of modest means who do not face the dilemma because they don't have the money to make choices about campaign finance at all.

Overcoming the Donor's Dilemma

COULD THE COLLECTIVE action problem be solved if the top 1% or even the top 0.01% had a chance to vote collectively—perhaps online—on specific issues and candidates and then agree to pool everyone's political

---

197 W. F. Lloyd, *Two Lectures on the Checks to Population* (Oxford, England: Oxford University Press, 1833) (explaining the overgrazing problem). See also G. Hardin, "The Tragedy of the Commons," *Science* 162 (1968). Subsequently, the term has been used by many commentators to describe a wide range of collective action problems.

expenditures to support the decision of the majority (this would be an arrangement similar to a shareholders' voting trust in corporate governance)? In such an arrangement, even if the oil company CEO wanted looser environmental regulations on a particular type of oil production, he would have to convince the rest of the group that the looser environmental regulations were in the group's collective interest. Some in the group, perhaps a majority, might vote in the national or global interest, particularly when they had no immediate financial stake in a particular issue.

As undemocratic as it is, it could be argued that such a direct democracy of the top 1% or even top 0.01%—a modern rendition of what England had before the Reform Acts—might yield better decisions for the entire country than a republican form of government in which government is driven in different and sometimes incoherent directions by a relative few contributors who play the campaign finance system for whatever they can get.

Such a "voting trust" for campaign contributors is interesting to imagine but would be very difficult to implement. The contributions would have to be made ahead of time and then subject to a majority vote. The closest arrangement we have to date is trade organizations and chambers of commerce, which are hardly direct democracies for their members. Many wealthy individuals and companies have no connection to these organizations. Managers of these organizations, not members, make decisions about how political expenditures are made, and they take into consideration a range of factors, including the intensity with which particular members want particular results, rather than the will of the whole.

The option of collective governance through campaign finance—oligarchy—thus is not realistically available to the 1% even if they wanted it. An enforceable "voting trust" to which all or even most rich people committed all of their political expenditures is unlikely to evolve. Most rich people would not subscribe. Some would correctly view such an effort as undemocratic and un-American even though our current system has enormous problems. They would share Barry Goldwater's view that concentrated power is antithetical to individual freedom. Overcoming their own collective action problems would not be worth it to them if the cost was even more concentration of power, not less.

More realistically, rich people could help themselves, and the rest of us, overcome these collective action problems by contributing their time and money to the cause of campaign finance reform. There are a range of solutions, including reform PACs such as Mayday PAC, that are discussed in Chapter 9, the private sector democracy dollars program also discussed in Chapter 9, and the Taxation Only with Representation Act that would make every American a small donor, discussed in Chapter 8.

Campaign finance reform thus far, however, has for the most part failed to get backing from rich Americans, in part because reform has been identified rightly or wrongly with political interests hostile to the top 1%. For example, a 2014 *New Yorker* article on Mayday PAC was captioned with a cartoon drawing of one of its cofounders, Lawrence Lessig, facing off against a fat man in black tails and top hat with a cigar resembling the character on a Monopoly game board. Ironically the article noted that Lessig was working with rich donors to put together Mayday PAC and even said in the article's title that the PAC needed fifty billionaires to fund it.[198] Lessig in 2015 ran for president, this time with the support mostly of small donors, but the reality is that his efforts and those of other reformers likely will also need the support of rich Americans in order to succeed.

Demonization of the top 1% by some campaign finance reformers or by the journalists who write about reform has contributed to the agnostic and sometimes hostile position that many of America's more prosperous citizens have toward reforming the system. Hopefully some will see through the rhetoric and recognize that they, along with the rest of us, are being hurt by the system, and that they should invest some of their wealth in fixing it. The alternative is to continue subjecting the entire country to the "tragedy of the commons" by allowing people who can afford the price of admission to continue feeding off of our government, while at the same time destroying it.

The "Democracy Participation Tax"— a Poll Tax for the Rich

DISILLUSION WITH OUR system is widespread not only with the general public but also, as the CED poll of business leaders shows, in the upper echelons of society where people have the money to play the game—whether it be funding a super PAC, starting a 501(c)(4) organization to make electioneering communications, funding a trade association that gives to campaigns or makes electioneering communications, or some other strategy. Not everybody wants to play this game even if they can afford it. Not everybody wants to pay to play with politicians any more

---

198 Evan Osnos, "Embrace the Irony," *The New Yorker,* 13 October 2014.

than they want to pay taxes in excess of what the government really needs. Some corporations would rather focus on investing in their core business, and some rich people would rather devote their time and their fortune to investments, the arts, education, or other causes. To the extent they get involved with government and politics, many business leaders and other successful people want to be respected for their ideas (some of these ideas could help government), and they resent being asked to pay money to get their ideas across.

Having to shell out money to meaningfully participate in government is for corporations and rich individuals nothing more than another tax. It is a type of poll tax—a "democracy participation tax." They can afford to pay it, whereas others cannot, leading to much resentment being directed at them by people who believe that corporations and rich individuals pay the tax and control our government in return. But the truth is that many rich people and even corporations refuse to pay this tax—they refuse to give politicians yet more of their wealth in return for dubious benefits and the risk of further damage to donors' reputations with the general public. They have paid enough for this government, and they don't expect any special treatment other than what is owed to every American: a meaningful role in electing leaders who will be free of dependency relationships with special interests.

Campaign Finance and the Politics of Class Envy

FINALLY, THE CAMPAIGN finance system causes the richest Americans to lose in another way: They have to live with being demonized in the press, by politicians and others who mix the campaign finance issue up with the politics of class envy. Instead of being admired for their success (many rich people worked hard to get where they are), they are relentlessly attacked for having an unfair advantage. Ostentatious display of political spending by Soros, Adelson, the Koch brothers, and a few others feeds the misconception that most rich people are playing the same game. Politicians and other agitators who hate the rich—and our economic system that allows people to become rich—use this situation to their advantage.

Sometimes, political attacks on the rich, and on the private sector in general, lead to punitive measures by government toward a particular industry (excessive regulation, etc.) or against rich people as a whole (big tax increases). Politicians who play the class warfare game will jump on the bandwagon to distract public attention from their own relationships with campaign contributors. Although the campaign finance problem is a problem with government, it is instead blamed on the private sector. This becomes an excuse for politicians to grow the size of government further as a counterweight to a private sector presumed to have too much influence, and the bigger more powerful government only makes the campaign finance problem worse (see Chapter 3 explaining how government grows in size and power as more and more money is raised for political campaigns). For Americans concerned about our country sliding toward socialism, the politics of class envy is one of the most pernicious consequences of our campaign finance problem.

Chapter 7

The Basic Parameters of a Conservative Agenda for Campaign Finance Reform

WHAT ARE WE to do to restore the representative democracy envisioned by our founders?

First, what not to do. We should not get caught up in a class war over this issue. Despite all the rhetoric about the top 1% or top 0.05% using the campaign finance system to control the country, no cohesive group of people is in control. Incumbent politicians have power, but they depend on, and must bend to, special interests. There are different special interests depending on the issue at stake. But most people, including the rich, have general interests (health, financial security, and national security among others) that are more important than their unique special interests. And the government's ability to protect these general interests, for rich and poor alike, is almost always undermined by our system of campaign finance.

When the big picture, rather than a discrete part of it, is considered, it is clear that nobody is in control. The system is out of control. And the worst thing that citizens—rich, middle class, and poor—can do is to waste their time fighting with each other about who benefits more from this corrupt system and at whose expense. If you look at the big picture, everyone is getting a bad deal.

Second, playing the game won't help much. A wealthy donor might be able to contribute to political campaigns to get a government contract or to get a particular regulatory loophole for his business, but he probably cannot address most of his problems with government that way. And many of those problems are created by the fact that other wealthy donors are getting what they want on discrete issues—for example, their own government contracts and regulatory loopholes.

So how can we solve this problem?

Efforts to Regulate Political Expenditures Are Probably Futile, and May Be Unconstitutional, but That Is Also Not an Issue Worth Fighting Over

ONE APPROACH THAT has been tried and probably won't work is legal restrictions on campaign spending, contributions to campaigns, and electioneering communications by corporations, individuals, and labor unions.

First, electioneering communications in particular are difficult to regulate because they are made all the time in a country with a free press. As discussed in Chapter 1, control of newspapers was an important way of influencing elections through much of the 19th and 20th centuries. By the mid-20th century, control over radio and television stations was added to the mix, and now in the 21st century, Internet sites and other media outlets are important as well. Media magnates continue to play an important role in politics. Rupert Murdoch's media empire includes both Fox News and *The Wall Street Journal*. The late Richard Mellon Scaife owned the *Pittsburgh Tribune-Review*, which was among the first newspapers to publish news about President Bill Clinton's sexual indiscretions in the 1990s. Negative movies about presidential candidates did not start with the Hillary Clinton movie that was the subject of the *Citizens United* case; only a few years earlier director Michael Moore, with financial support from the Hollywood film industry, made scathing movies about President George W. Bush, including the infamous *Fahrenheit 9/11*, which was released in the middle of the 2004 presidential campaign.

If the definition of a campaign contribution covers more than direct monetary contributions to a political campaign to include expenditures on electioneering communications that further a campaign, a comprehensive definition would include investment in media outlets that support or oppose candidates for political office. These media outlets—newspapers, magazines, websites, radio and TV stations, movies, and much more—are bought and sold in private markets. Only a small fraction of the population can afford to invest in one. And electioneering communications in these outlets are unquestionably covered by the First Amendment protection of freedom of speech and of the press.

Second, even legal rules that fall short of directly regulating media outlets have run into constitutional problems with the US Supreme Court, most recently in the *Citizens United* and *McCutcheon* decisions. These problems could take years to resolve through a change in the court's composition, enactment of new legislation to attempt to get around the constitutional problems, or an amendment to the Constitution.

Third, efforts to restrict speech also run into enormous practical problems. An often repeated—and true—phrase is that keeping money out of politics is like trying to keep water inside a leaking faucet. It just does not work, even if the restrictions are constitutional. Whatever the restrictions are, people find a way around them. For example, as pointed out in Chapter 5, even laws barring political contributions from foreign nationals and companies controlled by foreign nationals are difficult if not impossible to enforce.

This author has already written in his book *Getting the Government America Deserves*[199] about the many practical loopholes in campaign finance legislation that existed before the Supreme Court decided *Citizens United* in 2010. This author also saw that system in place while he was the chief White House ethics officer from 2005 to 2007. There were almost as many worries about money in politics then as there are now. *Citizens United* may be a poorly reasoned decision, and the concept of corporate personhood for First Amendment purposes may be strange at best, but the issue at hand is whether fighting to reverse that decision is worth it. It is not.

Reform proponents who demonize the Supreme Court and call for constitutional amendments to reverse its decisions thus hold out false hope for an end to corruption in politics. A constitutional amendment that would merely return to the status quo of 2009 is not worth it, and the process of passing it could be highly disruptive. Reform discussions that

---

199 Richard W. Painter, "Chapter 7: Campaign Finance—The Elephant and Donkey in the Room," *Getting the Government America Deserves: How Ethics Reform Can Make a Difference* (Oxford, England: Oxford University Press, 2009).

obsess over the Supreme Court's convoluted interpretation of the First Amendment may impress constitutional law scholars and score political points with a broader audience of activists but will not change anything.

Conservatives, however, walk right into a political trap when they obsess over campaign finance being a free speech issue and only a free speech issue. By arguing that spending money is a form of free speech they imply that rich people's speech and corporate speech is what they care about and want to protect. This alienates most voters. Conservatives who get caught up in such discussions also sometimes appear as if they don't recognize that the current relationship between money and politics is a problem or as if they don't care. Once again, this gives an advantage to their opponents. It would be much better for conservatives, at least conservative elected officials, to leave the First Amendment issues to be resolved by the courts—including the Supreme Court's unpopular conclusion that corporations are "persons" under the Constitution. Conservatives need to focus their attention on solutions to the campaign finance problem that are both constitutional and that will work. What they don't need to do is deny that there is a problem.

The Liberal Agenda: POTUS + SCOTUS = Reform

LIBERAL REFORMERS RECOGNIZE that our current system of campaign finance is a problem and have a "solution" to the problem. The solution may not solve the problem, but it gives the liberal reformers so many other political, legal, and policy benefits that they may not care.

The teaser in their plan is a constitutional amendment to overturn *Citizens United* and other Supreme Court decisions that purportedly stand in the way of reform. This amendment is highly unlikely to ever pass, but it puts the issue on the table and makes the Supreme Court central to the purported solution.

The more achievable objective—and the one many liberals really want—is a change in the composition of the Supreme Court. Unless the court were to weigh heavily the value of precedent (stare decisis), the court could rule 5-4 the other way if one more liberal justice were appointed in place of a conservative justice, or at least liberals can hope so. Accomplishing this objective requires election of a liberal president to nominate the liberal justice and a Senate, probably with a Democratic majority, willing to confirm a new liberal justice.

For all of the reasons explained above, a change in the composition of the Supreme Court, even if it led to new rulings reversing *Citizens United* and other cases, probably would not do much more than return us to the status quo of the early 2000s shortly after McCain–Feingold was enacted and the pervasive pattern of legislatures enacting reforms and political operatives and election lawyers figuring a way around those reforms. But for the left, this may not matter because their plan of action—electing a liberal president and then changing the composition of the Supreme Court—has so many other advantages for them and their supporters.

Conservatives of course do not want this "POTUS + SCOTUS plan" to succeed. It means liberals using the campaign finance issue to gain the upper hand in all three branches of government. But will conservatives recognize that there is a problem and offer a solution of their own?

Conservatives Will Lose Without a Strategy on Campaign Finance Reform

POLITICIANS WHO CRITICIZE the Supreme Court and call for constitutional amendments know that they can demonize the very system that puts them in office and keeps them there without suggesting any reform that will change things within their lifetime. And conservatives who support the Supreme Court's unpopular vision of corporate personhood under the First Amendment, without suggesting any alternative approach to the problem of money in politics, are these politicians' easy prey. Given a choice between a candidate who acknowledges that there is a problem but who supports an unlikely solution to the problem, and a politician who will not even acknowledge that there is a problem, voters are likely to choose the former. The campaign contributors know this and are likely to send their money to the candidates who will win, even if those candidates demonize contributors publicly while doing whatever is necessary to get the contributions privately.

Conservatives are getting checkmated in the debate over campaign finance—by liberals who in fact will do little or nothing to fix the system because their proposals either won't work or won't be implemented anytime soon. But that does not matter because they look good when compared to those who won't even acknowledge that there is a problem.

Transparency about Government— Including Campaign Finance— Is a Conservative Agenda

CITIZENS SHOULD KNOW as much specific information as possible about the influence of money on the people who run our government. Conservatives who believe in limited government should support citizens' right to know. It is difficult if not impossible to limit the cost and power of government if we don't know what government is doing and why, as well as who is seeking to influence government and how.

The private sector—particularly businesses that do not make substantial political expenditures while competitors and labor unions do—should support the right to know. Believers in free enterprise should want to know more about a public sector that regulates, and sometimes competes with, the private sector without being subject to the discipline of markets. Taxpayers should want to know how their money is being spent and why.

For example, why did the government choose to support a particular renewable energy company, such as a solar panel manufacturer, as opposed to other companies? How much money are elected judges and legislators getting from plaintiffs' lawyers? How much money is a competitor for a government contract donating and to whom? How much money is coming into US political campaigns from foreign commercial interests that want a certain result in a trade negotiation?

Designing a disclosure regime that will expose most political expenditures—including funding 501(c)(4) electioneering communications—is a complex task beyond the scope of this book. Transparency will not be complete because there is no way to ferret out all of the ways people can support or channel money into political campaigns. But there could also be a lot more transparency than there is now.

Shareholders furthermore could insist on greater transparency in their corporations.[200] The free speech rights that corporations have under *Citizens United* don't include the right not to tell their owners (shareholders) what management is doing with shareholders' money. Also, these issues are directly relevant to stock price because political expenditures favored by corporate managers can backfire if they antagonize regulators or other government officials or alienate consumers. Shareholders have a right to know and perhaps should also have a right to prior approval by

---

200 Committee on Disclosure of Corporate Political Spending, "Petition for Rulemaking," SEC file no. 4-637, 3 August 2011, sec.gov/rules/petitions/2011/petn4-637.pdf (accessed 13 November 2015). The SEC is currently considering rules but has not moved forward.

shareholder vote before such political expenditures are made (this latter change could be effected through amendments to articles of incorporation or changes to state corporate law).

Finally, reform proposals that require political donations to be anonymous—on the theory that anonymous donations cannot buy influence—go in the wrong direction.[201] First, it would be difficult to enforce anonymity across the spectrum of donors, and large donors would find a way of making sure that elected officials know who they are. The antidote of making all donations revocable assumes that all donors can be required to donate through a portal or other system that allows for anonymity and that giving donors the option to revoke the donation preserves anonymity. Given the broad range of ways money can be channeled to political campaigns—PACs, 501(c)(4) organizations, or simply making constitutionally protected electioneering communications on one's own—this is virtually impossible. In sum, anonymous voting may work, but anonymous donating probably would not work in the situations where we worry about the donor's influence the most. There is great risk that in an anonymous donation regime for large donations, the donor, the donor's friends, and the officeholder would know who gave the money while everyone else did not. That is what we have today in the case of 501(c)(4) organizations that don't disclose their donors, and we need to change that regime instead of expanding it.

An important exception to the transparency norm should be individuals who make medium-size donations that cannot alone significantly impact an election, but that collectively are important. Anonymity might encourage more such donors. Donors of up to $1,000 per campaign and up to $5,000 in total per election cycle should be permitted to keep their donations private from neighbors, employers, and work colleagues. Raising the threshold for public disclosure from the current $200 would likely increase the number of these medium-size donations and broaden elected officials' base of financial support.

America Needs More Speech and More Money in Politics, Not Less

IN 2003 STEPHEN ANSOLABEHERE, a political science professor; John De Figueiredo, a business school professor; and James Snyder, an

---

201 Bruce Ackerman and Ian Ayres, *Voting with Dollars: A New Paradigm for Campaign Finance* (New Haven, CT: Yale University Press, 2004) (proposing such an anonymous donor regime).

economics professor, all at the Massachusetts Institute of Technology, published a paper titled "Why Is There So Little Money in U.S. Politics?"[202] They argued that most people and corporations view giving money to political campaigns as an ineffective way of influencing government and therefore don't contribute. Campaign contributions—at least through the date of their paper—were relatively modest in aggregate amounts and were coming from relatively few people. Some of these observations about overall spending have changed in the years since the 2010 *Citizens United* decision and subsequent massive increase in spending on electioneering communications, but the observation about low individual participation in campaign finance—the fact that only a small percentage of the population contributes—is still true.

Expanding upon this analysis, the problem is not that there is too much money in politics, but that there is not enough money in politics from a wider range of contributors. More Americans need to participate in the system of campaign finance. It will take more public participation, and more money from more people, to drown out the impact of post–*Citizens United* electioneering communications that are paid for by a very few people and organizations.

The public gets bombarded with information about candidates for public office from advertisements, newspapers, TV, talk radio, and the Internet. Much of this information is inaccurate (there is no legal sanction for untrue speech in the political context—by contrast, civil and potentially criminal penalties apply to untrue statements in a proxy contest for shareholder votes in a public company). Some candidates are able to give the public more information about themselves—and their opponents—than other candidates. Attempts to regulate the accuracy of political speech, like attempts to regulate the amount of money spent on political speech, are nonetheless unlikely to succeed. The First Amendment and the practical impossibility of regulating speech work together to make such limitations unworkable. What can be done is to provide more resources for candidates, and people who support candidates, to respond to what others say.

The adage "fight speech with more speech" is directly on point.

---

202 Stephen Ansolabehere, John M. De Figueiredo, and James M. Snyder, "Why is There so Little Money in US Politics," *Journal of Economic Perspectives* 17 (2003), 105, papers.ssrn.com/sol3/papers.cfm? abstract_id=366446 (accessed 15 September 2015).

The Supply Side: We Need to Create More Outlets for Electioneering Communications

POLITICAL SPEECH IS a growing industry in which providers of communication outlets both make money and serve the public interest by giving candidates, as well as candidates' supporters and opponents, a public forum. Market solutions need to focus on expanding rather than contracting the market for political speech, which means increasing the supply of media outlets for political speech as well as the demand for them by empowering a broader segment of the public to pay for political speech.

By way of analogy, the automobile was a hundred years ago a luxury for the rich. Henry Ford figured out a way to make it available to middle-class Americans. People following his footsteps in the automobile industry have made the automobile available today to almost every American. We need to do the same thing with respect to electioneering communications. In a representative democracy, widespread public participation in selecting and influencing candidates, and in helping pay for campaigns, is critical to our political success. We need technological and other innovations that make meaningful participation in government available to at least as many Americans as can afford to drive on our highways.

This book will not discuss specifically what those innovations are, and might be in the future, except to note that the Internet and social media have enormous potential. Regulators should not stand in the way of innovation with regulations that increase rather than decrease the cost of electioneering communications.

Some parts of the media market are regulated—particularly radio and broadcast television—and it is the government that limits the number of stations that can broadcast on particular frequencies (to some extent the government has to do this or radio and broadcast television would not work). People and companies that hold these licenses then provide free content, as well as paid advertising, including political advertising, to listeners and viewers. Cable television and subscription radio services are regulated differently. The point here is not that government regulation of these media outlets is undesirable—some of this regulation is probably necessary—but that costs of political advertising are likely to be higher in media markets that are heavily regulated and have high barriers to entry.

Alternative media markets are being developed—some relatively free of government regulation and associated costs. These alternative media outlets could lower costs of communication, including the cost of campaigning. More spending by campaigns on different media outlets also would make it harder for any one ad campaign—or any one source of campaign funds used to pay for it—to influence an election. The relative dominance of radio and television advertising also may recede as more voters spend more time on the Internet, social media, and other outlets. Finally, there is a saturation point for political messaging in which messages start to cancel each other out and there is less value from an incremental increase in advertising for any one political campaign.

The fact that campaigns are still paying top dollar for ads in certain media (still generally TV and radio) on the eve of elections, however, suggests that we are still far from saturating the market. As tired as we are of political ads every election season, the public seems to have an appetite for more—or campaigns would not be buying them. And electronic media outlets other than TV and radio are not yet being used to their full potential. If more small donors can be brought into the campaign finance system (the demand side of the equation that is the focus of Chapter 8 and part of Chapter 9), supply-side innovators should be encouraged to meet this demand by using underexploited media outlets more effectively and by creating new ones.

As with the old media outlets of newspapers, radio, and television, there is the risk that private actors can sometimes monopolize or limit access to some media outlets, for example, access to the Internet, which could drive costs up. The cost of political campaigns is intertwined with issues in the media as a whole: net neutrality (whether a search engine can steer traffic more quickly to websites that pay more to be in the "fast lane"), public access to the Internet, media concentration of ownership, and other issues. This book will not discuss these issues in detail, or take sides on any of them, except to note that these issues are important to a robust supply side for electioneering communications. This supply side in turn affects campaign costs and whether meaningful participation in campaign finance is possible for the general public.

The Demand Side: More Americans Need to Participate in Making and Paying for Electioneering Communications

THE POLITICAL SYSTEM also needs to get the money that is spent on political campaigns from a much broader range of people. This includes the 99% who cannot afford meaningful participation in campaign finance as well as the many among the top 1% of income earners who don't partic-ipate in campaign finance. A much broader segment of the public needs to be brought in to participate in making small donations that collectively can have a substantial impact.

This increase in participation would make elected officials less depen-dent on the small fraction of the population that contributes—or controls corporations, unions, or other organizations that contribute—substantial amounts to campaigns.

As discussed earlier in this book, those who pay for electioneering communications have a lot of control over their content and sometimes have the leverage to get what they want from public officials who are elected because of these communications. There is a dependency rela-tionship. A broader spectrum of the public—a much broader spectrum—needs to have a chance to participate in both making and paying for electioneering communications. The Internet has helped in the first respect—individuals, for example, can tweet to their followers their views about candidates (some individuals of course have more followers than others, and business entities may have even more followers than the candidates themselves). But individual access to social media is not enough; individuals also need to participate in the funding of political campaigns that, along with organizations that support or oppose polit-ical campaigns, have a dominant position on the Internet, social media, and other media outlets.

Inducing more Americans to pay for electioneering communications is difficult because of the high marginal utility of money spent on other things (housing, food, education, etc.) for individuals outside the top 1% or 0.5% of income earners as well as collective action problems ("why should I contribute?"). Paying for electioneering communications—via campaign contributions or otherwise—also is in most instances an ineffective way of getting what one wants from elected officials except with respect to a very discrete issue. Rational people who weigh the costs and benefits to themselves personally from campaign contributions may not contribute, and most don't. Some solution to this collective action problem—such as the tax-rebate-funded campaign contributions discussed in Chapter 8—is needed unless we are to tolerate a system in which demand to participate in campaign finance for almost all Americans is close to zero.

Taxation Should Be Conditioned upon a Solution to the Campaign Finance Problem

AS POINTED OUT in Chapter 6, even the richest Americans are for the most part disenfranchised by the current system of campaign finance. Other Americans are as well. A government that operates without accountability to anyone, much less to the public as a whole, has no business imposing taxes that in some cases approach half of a person's earnings. As the noblemen told King John in 1215 and the Americans told the British colonial rulers when they tossed tea into Boston Harbor in 1773, people who have no meaningful say over their government should not have to pay for it.

This concept is discussed more extensively in Chapter 8—including a proposed "Taxation Only with Representation" constitutional amendment or statute at the federal or state level.

Chapter 8

Taxation Only with Representation

PUBLIC FINANCING OF political campaigns has been talked about for a long time. President Theodore Roosevelt suggested it more than 100 years ago.[203] The federal government provides some financing (not enough) to campaigns that agree to abide by certain limits on fundraising. Still, public financing needs to be substantial—a lot more than we have today—to make a real difference in reducing the dependence of elected officials on special interest funding sources that dominate campaigns.

Some states allow tax credits or refunds for political contributions. Minnesota, for example, allows taxpayers to request a political contribution refund if they contribute money to qualified candidates for the Minnesota legislature; candidates for Minnesota governor, lieutenant governor, or attorney general; candidates for Minnesota secretary of state; candidates for Minnesota state auditor; or Minnesota political parties. Contributions to candidates for federal office do not qualify for the refund. Taxpayers can request only one refund for each calendar year in which they made contributions, but the request can include contributions made to more than one candidate or party. The maximum annual

---

203 "There is a very radical measure which would, I believe, work a substantial improvement in our system of conducting a campaign, although I am well aware that it will take some time for people so to familiarize themselves with such a proposal as to be willing to consider its adoption. The need for collecting large campaign funds would vanish if Congress provided an appropriation for the proper and legitimate expenses of each of the great national parties, an appropriation ample enough to meet the necessity for thorough organization and machinery, which requires a large expenditure of money. Then the stipulation should be made that no party receiving campaign funds from the Treasury should accept more than a fixed amount from any individual subscriber or donor; and the necessary publicity for receipts and expenditures could without difficulty be provided."
Theodore Roosevelt, "State of the Union Address 1907," speech, US Capitol, Washington, D.C., 3 December 1907, infoplease.com/t/hist/state-of-the-union/119.html (accessed 13 November 2015).

refund is $50 for an individual or $100 for a married couple. (The program has been temporarily suspended due to budget constraints.) [204]

Oregon allows a tax credit for political contributions but refuses to give this credit to the taxpayers who pay the highest taxes. Taxpayers whose federal adjusted gross income exceeds $200,000 on a jointly filed return, or $100,000 on all other returns, cannot claim the credit. The credit is equal to the monetary political contribution of up to $100 on a joint return or $50 on a single or separate return. Qualifying contributions are made to a candidate for federal, state, or local elective office, or to the candidate's principal campaign committee, provided at least one of the following occurs in Oregon during the same calendar year as the contribution: The candidate's name must be listed on a primary, general, or special election ballot; a prospective petition of nomination must be filed by or for the candidate; a declaration of candidacy must be filed by or for the candidate; a certificate of nomination must be filed by or for the candidate; or a designation of a principal campaign committee must be filed with the Oregon Secretary of State's Office. Oregon taxpayers can also claim a credit for contributions to qualifying political action committees. Contributions can also be made to national, state, or local committees of major political parties. Oregon also allows a tax credit for contributions made to minor political parties that qualify under state law.[205]

In November 2013 Representative Thomas Petri (R-WI) introduced the Citizens Involvement in Campaigns (CIVIC) Act, which would provide tax credits for individual political contributions up to $200 and a deduction for contributions up to $600.

Reformers in the legal academy have also joined the fray, including Bruce Ackerman and Ian Ayres, who suggested that $50 in Democracy Dollars or Patriot Dollars be given to each voter to contribute to the

---

204 "Political Contribution Refund," Minnesota Department of Revenue, revenue.state.mn.us /individuals/individ_income/Pages/Refund_for_Political_Contribution.aspx (accessed 7 October 2015); describes the refund in plain language. Minnesota's political contribution refund program was suspended for two years at the urging of Republicans in the state legislature. "This year, it was House Republicans that pushed the proposition and the maneuver is somewhat ironic: The state's Republican party and local units routinely get more money from the program than Democrats do. For instance, the latest round of data from 2013 shows that Republican party units raised nearly $900,000 from the program to the DFL's roughly $500,000." Catharine Richert, "Parties launch last-minute fundraising plea," MPR News, 17 June 2015, blogs.mprnews.org/capitol-view/2015/06/parties-launch-last-minute-fundraising-plea (accessed 10 December 2015).

205 Under the Oregon law, partners in partnerships and shareholders in privately held corporations that are taxed as partnerships can claim a credit for their share of political contributions made by the partnership or S corporation. There is no tax credit for public corporations. See "316.102, Credit for Political Contributions," WebLaws.org, oregonlaws.org/ors/316.102 (accessed 10 December 2015).

candidate of his choice. Lawrence Lessig, in his book *Republic, Lost,* made a compelling case for vouchers along similar lines.

Too often, these initiatives are discussed as if they were yet one more government expenditure program. Advocates of small government attack government "handouts" to political campaigns in an era of trillion-dollar deficits. A voucher can be likened to food stamps or some other coupon program.

These arguments miss the point. Taxpayer money originally belonged to taxpayers, not to the government, and a portion of it should be spent in a way that ensures that taxpayers have a meaningful voice in choosing the people who spend the rest. Shouldn't taxpayers whose money is used to pay for the government have a meaningful say in who runs the government? And as pointed out in the rest of this book, simply having a choice on Election Day between candidates preselected by the major parties—and their big donors—is not a real say.

Another problematic term is the tax credit, which is the mechanism that some states now use to help taxpayers contribute to political campaigns of their choice. Unfortunately, there are many other tax credits that are inefficient and designed to induce taxpayers to make choices they would not otherwise make. Many conservatives object to the notion that government raises taxes and then gives credits to people who do what government wants them to do. Is there that much difference between awarding tax credits for doing something the government wants and imposing a tax penalty on a taxpayer who does not do what the government wants, such as purchase health insurance? Should the government use the tax code to tell people what to do with their money? These are legitimate questions. Alternatively, tax credits are sometimes seen as yet another subsidy or entitlement in which government picks up part of the cost of someone doing something they would do anyway, for example, the energy-conscious or environmentally minded homeowner who installs solar energy panels on his roof. Many conservatives would like to see all tax credits abolished and are reluctant to sponsor a new one.

The tax rebate discussed here is very different from other tax credits. First, government is only broadly telling people what to do with the money—to use it to support a political campaign of their choice. Much of the money will be spent on campaigns that oppose each other and draw upon vastly different ideological perspectives. There is no government policy determining which campaigns are worthy of receiving the money, the type of determination that is made when taxpayers are told they can have a tax credit for heating their house using one method (solar energy) but not another (electricity, oil, or natural gas). If the tax credit analogy is at all appropriate, this credit is similar to the few tax credits that expand citizens' choices, for example, a tax credit that many conservatives support to cover part of the costs of educating the taxpayer's children at the primary or secondary school of choice. Rather than being stuck with schools—or elected officials—chosen by other people, citizens should have the right to make these choices for themselves.

The tax rebate discussed here could be characterized as an entitlement, but unlike many other tax credits, it is something to which all citizens are rightly entitled. A homeowner is not entitled to a government subsidy for solar energy panels on his house; how he heats his house is his business and should be his expense. But a voter is entitled to a meaningful voice in choosing candidates in primaries and general elections. A citizen is also entitled to be represented by public officials that do not depend on a very few other persons or entities to get reelected. This tax rebate allows the taxpayer to decide what to do with his own money in the political arena.

This rebate also gives taxpayers a real voice in deciding what is done with the rest of their tax money by choosing who gets to spend it. In addition to voting on the ballot, each taxpayer would be able to use the money to "vote," which is necessary because money, as well as ballots, chooses who wins. Politicians depend on both money and votes, and they will never be fully accountable to the public unless the public has the power to give or withhold both money and votes.

This tax rebate should be for everyone. Neither upper-income nor lower-income taxpayers should be excluded. Oregon's approach of denying the credit to taxpayers making more than $100,000 suggests an attempt to generate contributions only from lower- and middle-income taxpayers. This is not an acceptable approach for people who genuinely believe that an important rationale for this rebate is that it is the taxpayers' money to begin with and taxpayers should have a right to vote with a portion of their tax money.

The rebate, however, should also be available to people who make too little money to pay income taxes. Every citizen—even a homeless person—pays some taxes (state income tax, social security tax, sales tax, gas tax, etc.) and probably pays taxes that total over $200 per year. If the federal government gives people who don't pay federal taxes a rebate for campaign contributions, it could compensate itself by subtracting these amounts from federal revenue sharing with states in which those people live and pay taxes, but it is important that every American be given a chance to participate in funding elections as well as voting.

Every citizen over age 18 thus should get a $200 tax rebate for this purpose—by check or electronically. The point would be that every citizen is entitled to use some of his or her tax money ($200) to help choose the people who decide how the rest of the tax money is spent, and it would be up to the individual citizen to decide whether and how to "vote" with her $200 in federal, state, or local elections. People could increase the size of their monetary vote by also using after-tax money on political expenditures. But *everybody* would get to spend $200 of their tax money to help choose their government before being required to pay *any* additional taxes to support their government.

Taxation should be conditioned upon this fundamental right to meaningful representation. State constitutions and the federal Constitution thus could include an amendment providing for taxation only with representation, with language along the following lines:

> *Neither the government of the United States nor any state or subdivision thereof shall levy an income tax, sales tax, property tax, inheritance tax, or any other tax upon any natural person over 18 years of age who is a citizen of the United States or upon his or her estate unless the United States government or the state levying said taxes pays an amount totaling at least two hundred dollars within the same calendar year or within the immediately following calendar year to the campaign of one or more candidates for elected federal, state, or local office chosen by such citizen [for whom such citizen is also eligible to vote]. A citizen's right to designate taxpayer-funded political contributions pursuant to this amendment is waived in any year in which the citizen fails to designate a recipient of such payment or dies before designating a recipient of such payment. Every five years after adoption of this amendment, Congress shall by statute or, in the event Congress shall not enact such a statute, the United States Treasury shall by regulation, adjust the taxpayer-funded political contribution amount to be more or less than two hundred dollars to reflect changes in the purchasing power of the United States dollar within the preceding five years.*

Alternatively, federal or state statutes could be enacted providing taxpayers with similar rights with respect to the first $200 of tax receipts. Suggested language for both constitutional amendments and statutes is provided in Appendix A.

The money could be contributed to any bona fide political campaign of the taxpayer's choice. There would be no restrictions turning on how much money the campaign also spent from other sources or how much other independent expenditures were made on behalf of the candidate. This would avoid the problems that concerned the Supreme Court in *Arizona Free Enterprise Club's Freedom Club PAC v. Bennett*,[206] where the court struck down a provision of the Arizona Citizens Clean Elections Act that provided public financing designed to offset campaign spending and independent expenditures by opponents.

The only restriction on taxpayer choice might be—as reflected in the bracketed language above—that the taxpayer must be eligible to vote for the candidate receiving the taxpayer's money. If out-of-district donations were allowed with tax rebate money, there is some risk that taxpayers in some districts (particularly "safe" districts where election outcomes are virtually assured with or without campaign funding) might direct their rebate money to races in other districts, perhaps even in other states. New York, Massachusetts, and California Republicans, for example, might ignore races at home if they think Democrats are likely to win, and divert their tax rebate money to primaries and general elections in the South and West. In some cases, these donations could overwhelm donations from voters inside the district, distorting campaigns and making officeholders more beholden to out-of-district donors. For this reason, it is probably advisable to restrict donations funded with tax rebates to candidates for whom the taxpayer is eligible to cast a vote in a caucus or election. The downside of this limitation is that it could narrow some voters' choices considerably—for example, Republicans who live in Chicago might face the prospect of only having a realistic impact with donations to candidates in races for governor, the US Senate, and president and would not have an opportunity to use tax rebate money for out-of-district races that affect the composition of the Illinois congressional delegation or the composition of the Illinois legislature. Limiting tax rebate contributions to candidates in the same state as the taxpayer is another alternative.

Some commentators might object that such a tax rebate program puts more money into politics when the objective should be to get money out of politics. As discussed earlier in this book, however, getting money out of politics, or even reducing the amount of money in politics, is probably impossible. There are too many ways of making political expenditures, ranging from direct contributions to funding 501(c)(4) organizations that run issue ads; funding charitable foundations such as the Clinton Foundation that promote the image of a candidate; making a movie about a candidate (as happened in the *Citizens United* case); owning a newspaper

---

206 131 S.Ct. 2806 (2011).

that publishes positive or negative stories about candidates; and many more (as discussed in the Epilogue, more unusual strategies include funding a sexual harassment suit against a sitting president and paying a married presidential candidate's pregnant mistress to keep quiet). Even the most narrow construction of the First Amendment would put some of these strategies beyond the reach of campaign finance law, and a broad interpretation of First Amendment, such as that in *McCutcheon* and *Citizens United,* makes most of these strategies virtually impossible to regulate.

Furthermore, as discussed above, Americans probably do not spend enough money on the process of choosing their government. Campaign money could be better spent—perhaps on issue-oriented ads rather than attack ads. But the amount of money spent—around $8 billion, or less than $25 per citizen, is relatively small compared with the enormous size of our economy, the size of the federal budget, and the responsibilities of the public servants Americans choose on Election Day. The problem is not the amount of money. It is the fact that election campaigns are not funded with $25 from each citizen, but instead with far fewer contributions in much larger increments, sometimes tens of millions of dollars, coming from a very small segment of the population. The problem is that public servants depend on this money and the people who spend it to get elected, pushing the concerns of other Americans much lower down the government's list of priorities. Giving each taxpayer $200 to contribute would make a big difference even if other private money from a very few donors were there as well. Indeed, a large influx of taxpayer money into political campaigns at the direction of thousands and perhaps millions of individual taxpayers might discourage some larger donors from contributing substantial amounts to political candidates who are less likely to be beholden to them.

A final objection to taxpayer-funded campaign contributions is that they will decrease tax revenues and either drive up deficit spending or require offsetting tax increases. As pointed out in Chapter 3, however, government spending is already driven up by expenditures made at the behest of big campaign contributors. Whether dysfunctional solar energy companies, construction companies building bridges to nowhere, superfluous defense contracts, or educational institutions seeking to qualify their students for federally subsidized loans, too many campaign contributors get what they want at taxpayer expense. The cost of not doing something about our campaign finance system is too high.

Assuming 40 million taxpayers participate and designate a recipient for their $200, the cost of the taxpayer-funded campaign contributions would be $8 billion, a tiny fraction of the federal budget of approximately $3.5 trillion. A program of that magnitude would presently match or exceed all other expenditures on federal elections combined, making politicians much less dependent on contributors who demand government contracts or other expensive favors in return. Although there is no way of predicting the exact reduction in expenditures because of this diminished influence, it would not have to be very much to make up for the $8 billion. And that would be in addition to the other benefits to national security and economic competitiveness if the United States were to have a government less prone to external influence.

Another way of looking at it is that the United States spends approximately $500 billion every year on the defense budget. It must be worth allowing taxpayers to spend $8 billion to make the government that oversees our military, our foreign policy, and our domestic policy less dependent on special interests. This is particularly true when—as pointed out in Chapter 5—corporations and other business entities funding elections in the United States are increasingly likely to be controlled by forces outside the United States.

Taxation Only with Representation as a Conservative Approach to Campaign Finance

CONSERVATIVE ACTIVISTS ARE embracing the concept of tax rebates for small-dollar donors. John Pudner was the campaign manager for David Brat when he toppled Representative Eric Cantor (R-VA), a top GOP House fundraiser, in the 2014 primary (Brat went on to win the House seat in the general election against a well-funded Democrat). Pudner, now executive director of the conservative reform group Take Back Our Republic, has endorsed the tax rebate concept, comparing it favorably with business tax deductions and credits already available for big political contributors.

> *I think it is pretty clear that most Americans would choose to help everyday people, not multi-millionaires. And there's an easy way to do it: Getting more taxpaying citizens involved in their*

government by offering a tax credit for donating to political can-
didates. Conservatives like the Take Back Our Republic Action
Fund and liberals like Common Cause agree that Congress' deci-
sion to give mega donors a tax benefit for the millions of dollars
they inject into U.S. elections was wrong.[207]

Jay Cost, writing an article called *Every Man a Political Donor* for the *Weekly Standard* in June 2015, lauded Pudner's promotion of the tax rebate:

If our ultimate goal is to restore citizens' faith in their govern-
ment, shouldn't we also do what we can to make it easier for those
same citizens to give a small contribution to the candidates of
their choice? Citizens who write the small checks tend also to
start talking to their friends, go knock on doors, or share infor-
mation via social media. And when citizens get involved, the out-
comes are better.

The nonpartisan group Represent.Us has endorsed a similar
tax credit, which is worth considering. It might be a way to reduce
the bad effects of money in politics without trampling on the First
Amendment or doubling down on the failed campaign finance
reforms of the last century.[208]

Conservative activists clearly see the need for reform. And as pointed out in the discussion of the 2015 *New York Times*/CBS News poll at the beginning of this book, conservative voters overwhelmingly want to see

---

207 John Pudner, "The Tea Party Case Against Mega Donor," *The Daily Beast,* 26 May 2015, thedailybeast.com /articles/2015/05/26/the-tea-party-case-against-mega-donors.html (accessed 15 September 2015).
208 Jay Cost, "Every Man a Political Donor," *Weekly Standard,* 15 June 2015. Cost goes on to compare the tax rebate approach with failed efforts to keep corporate and union money out of political campaigns:

This is an embarrassment to our republic. Occasionally, some outrageous scandal manages to shame even our impudent Congress, which hastily passes some campaign finance "reform" to deflect public outrage. . . . They outlaw certain financing practices without providing alternative ways to raise funds. Thus, progressives outlawed business contributions with the Tillman Act of 1907; many businesses ignored it, and presidents enforced it poorly. Conservatives outlawed labor contributions with the Taft– Hartley Act of 1947; labor responded by creating the first political action committee (PAC), an artifice to circumvent the law. When a federal court ruled that labor's PAC was illegal, the unions leaned on Congress to pass the Federal Elections Campaign Act (FECA) of 1971, with various amendments to fol- low in the course of the decade. In total, FECA eliminated whatever limits Tillman and Taft–Hartley had maintained; business and labor PACs proliferated, while interest groups found all sorts of workarounds to the restrictions that it imposed. Most recently, the Bipartisan Campaign Reform Act of 2002 was so draconian that the Supreme Court invalidated swaths of it on First Amendment grounds.

The verdict of a century's worth of failed reform is that it is not enough to limit the flow of money. Campaign finance, after all, is essential to democratic politics. Money in politics is like water flowing downhill. It cannot be stopped; rather, it must be redirected in a socially beneficial way.

a solution to the campaign finance problem. What remains to be seen is whether conservative officeholders will follow public opinion on this issue or just continue to follow the money.

Implementation of Taxation Only with Representation

THE PRACTICAL ASPECTS of a plan for taxation only with representation would be very similar to the voucher plan suggested by professor Lessig.

There are a few potential pitfalls, but those should be relatively easy to resolve.

First, there is the risk that candidates or their supporters could pay voters for their $200. A related risk is that employers could pressure employees to give their $200 to candidates favored by the employer. This problem is best resolved by making it easy for everyone to confidentially change the recipient of his or her $200 from one campaign to another either online or through paper submission. Also, each person's online account should be protected by a password, and it could be made a criminal offense to access another person's account, for an employer to apply any sort of pressure to get access to an employee's account, or to pay anyone in exchange for designation of their $200 to a particular campaign. Because of the relatively small amount of money to be gained from any single violation of these rules, and the potential for severe penalties, such laws should protect individual voters from outside pressure to designate their taxpayer campaign contributions in a particular way.

Second, there is the risk of abuse by some minor candidates who start campaigns with no genuine interest in winning an election but only in obtaining taxpayer funds to pay friends or relatives on their campaign staff. For example, a local preacher could pressure members of his congregation to give their $200 to his "campaign" for Congress that employs his wife as campaign manager at a substantial salary. This type of abuse could be curtailed by imposing a small restriction on recipient campaigns: They could be denied taxpayer contributions through the Taxation Only with Representation Act if they fail to meet certain indicia of legitimacy, such as raising $X in campaign contributions from other donations, raising small donations from a certain number of people paying with after-tax funds, spending only a certain portion of their budget on salaries, etc. The few campaigns that were funded only or principally with Taxation Only with Representation Act money might be required to avoid nepotism in hiring and agree to audits and other antiabuse measures. As a general matter, taxpayers should not be restricted in their choice of campaigns, but in the very rare cases where a campaign could not meet basic indicia of being a bona fide campaign, the taxpayer would be told that he or she would have to designate another campaign to receive the money.

Third, and the biggest potential pitfall, is that campaigns could take both the taxpayer-funded contributions and donations from PACs and other large donors that create dependency relationships. The dark pools of 501(c)(4) money used for electioneering communications would continue to operate regardless of what taxpayers did with their taxpayer-funded contributions. One way of dealing with this problem is to limit recipients of the taxpayer-funded contributions to those campaigns that do *not* receive PAC money and certain other larger donations. This is the approach favored by professor Lessig in his voucher proposal.[209] The problem with this approach is that it can never be comprehensive: PAC money can probably be traced, and a total spent on each candidate calculated, but it is very difficult to measure the extent of 501(c)(4) expenditures as well as other political spending (for example, the amount of money spent keeping a money-losing newspaper or website afloat while it supports or opposes candidates). Furthermore, conservatives in particular might rebel against such a restriction on which campaigns they can select to receive *their* money. If the objective of a Taxation Only with Representation law is to give money back to taxpayers to support candidates, the money isn't really theirs if the government restricts which candidates they can give it to.

On balance it would probably be better to address this problem through less restrictive means. One approach is to make sure the amount of taxpayer-funded contributions is high enough to drown out or at least reduce the significance of other contributions. The statute establishing the tax refund could provide for an automatic increase in the amount of the contribution allowed to each taxpayer if total campaign expenditures reported to the FEC exceed certain thresholds. (An upward adjustment to a particular candidate's receipt of taxpayer-funded contributions that is tied to a particular opponent's contributions or expenditures would run into the constitutional problem identified by the Supreme Court in *Arizona Free Enterprise Club's Freedom Club PAC v. Bennett,* but an across-the-board increase in the total amount of taxpayer-funded contributions

---

209 Lessig, *Republic, Lost.*

could constitutionally be tied to the total amount the FEC reports being spent on campaigns in the aggregate.)[210]

Furthermore, taxpayer-funded contributions to candidates who also receive PAC money and other large contributions would still probably help them become less dependent on the PACs and big donors, provided the taxpayer-funded contributions were generous enough to become a significant part of a campaign's budget. The big money would still have an influence in some campaigns, but less influence than it has now, and because the big money has less influence, some donors might choose not to provide it.

The Taxation Only with Representation provision could also be strengthened with other measures that would inject more small-donor funding into campaigns and further dilute the influence of big donors. One approach would be to supplement the program with a tax deduction or other incentive for other smaller donations from personal funds, as Representative Petri's bill did for donations up to $600. Finally, an aggressive disclosure regime for both larger donations and 501(c)(4) contributions and expenditures would help taxpayers choose who should, and should not, receive their money. Voters who use an online program to designate recipients of their taxpayer-funded contributions could be given information about PAC contributions to, as well as some identified 501(c)(4) expenditures on behalf of, campaigns they consider designating as recipients of their taxpayer funds. The web page could include an official message that "It is the intent of Congress that taxpayer-funded donations support campaigns that do not receive substantial support from PACs and other large contributors, but you are free to give your money to the campaign of your choice."

The goal once again is not to drive big money out of politics, an approach that has been tried and has failed as a practical matter and has run into serious constitutional problems. The objective is to get enough other money into politics that candidates do not depend on big money to get elected. A Taxation Only with Representation regime of sufficient magnitude should accomplish that objective.

---

210 This number would, of course, be less than the total amount spent on campaigns because it would not include 501(c)(4) spending and some other independent expenditures.

Chapter 9

Market Solutions to the Dependency Problem:
The Reform Super PAC, Democracy Dollars, Deal with the District, and Other Innovations

TODAY MANY ELECTED officials are addicted to special interest money—they believe they need it to get reelected. Freeing politicians from this type of dependency does not require the 12-step program that managing an alcohol addiction might require, but it will require multiple steps to be taken by concerned citizens in both the public and the private sectors.

The previous chapter is about what citizens should demand from their government: the right to use a small portion of their tax dollars to get a meaningful voice in choosing and helping pay for candidates for public office. This chapter explores what the private sector can do to expand voters' role in the campaign finance system and to free elected officials from dependency relationships created by campaign contributions.

The Reform Super PAC

PRIVATE ACTORS CAN use a key component of the campaign finance system—the political action committee, or PAC—to change the system. As explained more fully in Chapter 6, high-income individuals have a lot to gain from reform, perhaps even more than the rest of us. High-income individuals, like the rest of us, also have big collective action problems when countering well-organized special interests with a narrow political agenda. A reform PAC could give the broader population, including high-income individuals, the ability to overcome collective action problems and fix our system of campaign finance.

One major reform PAC has already been established, the Mayday PAC, which raised approximately $10 million for the 2014 election cycle.[211] Unfortunately Mayday PAC confronted so many Republicans and conservatives who had a recalcitrant attitude toward campaign finance reform—an attitude that this book is intended to change—that Mayday PAC had few Republican recipients to choose from in the 2014 general election (Mayday PAC did spend a considerable amount on the New Hampshire Republican primary for US Senate, but its candidate lost). Mayday then spent much, although not all, of its money in the general election supporting Democrats who support campaign finance reform. And in 2014, when Democrats in general suffered big losses, most of these candidates also lost. Nonetheless, given the potential for a change in attitude among Republicans and conservatives about campaign finance, and given the likely fluctuations in the two political parties' relative performance, observers who write off the Mayday PAC idea based on its performance in a single election cycle are making their judgment too soon. And they are probably wrong.

The principal objective of a reform PAC should be discouraging candidates from accepting campaign funds likely to create a dependency relationship with narrow special interests such as a few fabulously wealthy individuals, unions, trade associations, or businesses. At present, most such dependency relationships are created through PACs and super PACs, although there could be yet more corrupting dependency relationships if the Supreme Court were to strike down limits on individual contributions to particular campaigns. The objective of the reform PAC is to promise its support to candidates who in turn promise to refuse contributions that create these dependency relationships.

The first step is for a reform PAC to raise from private donors a considerable amount of money to distribute to eligible candidates—a category described in more detail below. To raise sufficient funds, the PAC needs to convince upper-income Americans in particular that reform is in their interest—an argument laid out in Chapter 6. One of the problems the reform PAC will face is the popular characterization of the campaign finance problem that depicts rich people manipulating the political system with contributions, as if most rich people make big

211 "Mayday PAC: Outside Spending Summary 2014," Center for Responsive Politics, opensecrets.org /outsidespending/detail.php?cmte=C00562587&cycle=2014 (accessed 13 November 2015).

campaign contributions (they don't). This characterization is not just inaccurate; it is likely to alienate the very people who could do the most to help solve the problem by contributing to the reform PAC. Mayday PAC tried to convey to its wealthy donors—many from Silicon Valley—the message that reform was in everyone's interests,[212] but to raise more money in the future, even more effort may be needed to distance the campaign finance debate from debates over income inequality and other class issues. These two sets of issues—campaign finance and income inequality—may or may not be related, but that link is only harmful to the fundraising process for a reform PAC, and as pointed out in Chapter 6, there are many reasons why a person who is financially successful would want campaign finance reform and thus should want to donate to a reform PAC. To raise money from these people, the reform PAC should use those arguments and avoid arguments likely to alienate the donors.

Furthermore, fundraising efforts for a reform PAC need to be broad-based. Mayday PAC had a broad base of donors but also brought in a considerable portion of its funds from a single region of the country—Silicon Valley. Too much concentration of donors to a reform PAC can undermine its purpose and potentially alienate other donors.

Another approach is to conduct fundraising for a reform PAC on a state-by-state basis, where donors know that contributions go to support dependency-free candidates close to home. For Mayday PAC, or any other reform PAC, to have independent branches in each state might help it raise more money overall.

On the other hand, the donor pool should not be too small. If candidates know who the donors to the reform PAC are, and only one or two candidates in a particular state are eligible to receive its support, it could become yet another vehicle for establishing a dependency relationship between candidates and donors to the PAC. To avoid this problem a reform PAC could distribute its funds to at least three candidates and no more than a third of the money to each candidate; leftover funds would be designated for eligible candidates in neighboring states. At the beginning of this initiative the reform PAC might have to be regional—involving donors and candidates in several states—until there are enough eligible candidates in a single state to justify a separate PAC. Another approach is to try to construct a regime whereby donors to the reform PAC would be anonymous, but this involves legal and practical complications as well as a compromise of an important principle, that the campaign finance system needs more transparency, not less. Reformers cannot ask for more transparency in some areas while promoting anonymity in others.

---

212 Evan Osnos, "Embrace the Irony," *The New Yorker,* 13 October 2014.

Once the money is raised the next step is for the reform PAC to make funds available on a nondiscriminatory basis—for example, without regard to party affiliation or positions on particular issues—to eligible candidates, which would be any candidates who refuse to accept other PAC money or other types of campaign contributions that the reform PAC determines create dependency relationships. The categories of contributions deemed to create dependency relationships should be set by the reform PAC in advance so both its donors and candidates know what the rules are for eligibility. The reform PAC could also require that eligible candidates support one or more particular measures that would facilitate campaign finance reform, a requirement that Mayday PAC has and that is reasonable if the acceptable measures are sufficiently diverse and candidates do not need to support all of them (for example, public financing of campaigns, the Taxation Only with Representation Act discussed above, enhanced disclosure of PAC money and 501(c)(4) funding sources, etc.).

Mayday PAC is somewhat different from the above model in that its managers also have considerable discretion in deciding which races to enter and how much to spend, rather than committing themselves ex-ante to set formulas and criteria for distribution of funds. This approach has some advantages in that it allows the reform PAC's managers to do the same strategizing that other PACs do, spending their money where it is most likely to be effective. One disadvantage is that, if the funding is not automatic and equal for all eligible candidates, the reform PAC's managers can be accused of playing favorites, and perhaps of favoring one party over the other.

As pointed out above, almost all of the candidates backed by Mayday PAC in the 2014 election cycle lost, and most of these were Democrats, a situation created by the fact that most Republican candidates resisted initiatives for campaign finance reform. On the other hand, it is difficult for Mayday PAC or any other PAC to claim to be bipartisan if a lot of its money is given to candidates in one party (the one Republican race Mayday spent a lot of money on was the New Hampshire primary for a Senate seat where Mayday's support for Jim Rubens, who challenged Scott Brown for the Republican nomination, weakened Brown considerably and may have cost him and the Republicans the seat in the general election). As more Republican voters and candidates realize that campaign finance reform is their issue too, it should be easier for reform PACs to find eligible Republican candidates, as well as Democrats, and reform PACs should support them.

Finally, reform PACs confront collective action problems in that many people support campaign finance reform but may also want to rely on others to support the cause financially. Reform PACs can overcome part of the collective action problem by accepting contributions that are not binding unless a certain amount of money is raised. The money would be put into escrow until a certain goal is reached (the Mayday PAC has already used an arrangement of this sort). PAC donors in this scenario would have some assurance that they were not donating to a hopeless cause.

One even more aggressive strategy would be for the reform PAC to pick four or five Senate races and announce that unless the incumbent senator votes for a meaningful campaign finance bill before a certain deadline, the PAC will release a very large amount of money to support an opponent in a primary or a general election. This strategy might be effective in getting legislation passed—for example, the Taxation Only with Representation law suggested in the previous chapter. The downside of this approach is that for the threat to be credible the opponent has to receive the reform PAC's support, and the opponent might be only marginally better on campaign finance reform and might even accept support from other PACs working against reform.

Whatever strategy the reform PAC uses, it will be more likely to succeed if it chooses a particular strategy and sticks with it. That strategy could be supporting candidates who do not take PAC money or instead putting all of the PAC's resources into trying to force particular campaign finance reform legislation by doing whatever is necessary to get it passed. A reform PAC that tries to do both—for example, only supporting candidates who refuse to take any PAC money and who back reform legislation—may accomplish less because it can't find enough candidates to support in races where those candidates can win. The requirement that a candidate not take any other PAC money may be particularly debilitating in a race where the opponent has a lot of it and the reform PAC does not have enough to make up the difference. The reform PAC's emphasis needs to be not on ideological purity but on getting the job done.

Private Sector Democracy Dollars

THE TAXATION ONLY with Representation statute or constitutional amendment discussed in the previous chapter is an important first step toward increasing public participation in campaign finance. The state government and the federal government should allow taxpayers the right to help choose the people who spend the rest of their tax dollars.

The private sector can also help channel a small portion of consumer spending into small political contributions, thereby widening the base of financial support for officeholders and candidates.

The Democracy Dollars concept that Bruce Ackerman and Ian Ayres proposed in 2004 for the public sector was a government-run voucher system similar in some respects to the voucher system proposed by Lawrence Lessig in 2011. That same concept, however, could be taken into the private sector as a promotion device similar to frequent-flier miles, credit card points, loyal-customer points, and in an earlier era Green Stamps.

The administrator of a private Democracy Dollars program would be a company or other organization (it could even be a for-profit company if it charged modest fees to its users or had advertising on its website). Retailers and other businesses could then distribute Democracy Dollars instead of frequent-customer points or other promotion giveaways. Democracy Dollar accounts should probably be limited to a total inflow of $200 per person per year, a maximum balance of $200 per person, and donations limited to $200 per candidate per election cycle, to keep participants under the threshold for FEC reporting. The administrator of the program should also probably prohibit distributions of Democracy Dollars from employers to their employees, universities to their students, religious organizations to their members, or similar arrangements where the entity distributing the Democracy Dollars arguably has some influence over contribution decisions by the recipient (such distributions could be seen as contributions to political campaigns by the original distributor of the Democracy Dollars, in violation of federal election law). Use of Democracy Dollars in ordinary consumer transactions, however, could not be fairly characterized as a political contribution by anyone other than the consumer, who alone has the right to decide how they are spent.

The key requirement for the program would be that Democracy Dollars have to be distributed on a nondiscriminatory basis in connection with ordinary commercial transactions. Businesses would distribute Democracy Dollars to customers for the same promotional reasons many businesses now offer to donate a portion of their profits to charity, but in this case the donation would be more "personal" for the customer because each would have his or her own account. The business might also advertise that it is giving its customers Democracy Dollars instead of making its own political expenditures and risking a customer backlash as Target stores in Minnesota experienced in 2010. (The promotion might run something like this: "Here at XYZ Stores Inc, we believe YOU the customer should decide. We do not ourselves contribute to PACs or other political organizations but instead we will give YOU up to $X per year in Democracy Dollars, depending on how much you buy with us.")

People could then spend their Democracy Dollars on candidates of their choice simply by going online, using a confidential password, and allocating them to a political campaign or party of their choice. Sale of Democracy Dollars would be prohibited (making contributions easily revocable would discourage sale). Although there are endless hypothetical ways in which people could cheat and buy and sell Democracy Dollars, in the real world most people would not cheat because the maximum amount gained in one illegitimate transaction would be limited to $200. Cheating could be discouraged further if Congress were to support such a program by making it a crime to directly or indirectly offer compensation to someone in exchange for a political donation through Democracy Dollars or a similar program (compensating other people for political donations is already a crime if the person paying for the cost of a donation has exceeded his or her allowable donation to a particular candidate). Few political fundraisers would want to risk violating the law to get only $200 per violation, with the number of transactions increasing the chance of getting caught. Enforcement of such a law might be even more effective if it was the purchaser of Democracy Dollars, and the associated political campaign, that was subjected to prosecution, whereas the seller would not be prosecuted and instead would be given a small reward for reporting the transaction to authorities.

Deal with the District

YET ANOTHER APPROACH to campaign finance reform would be for citizen groups to seek binding contractual promises from candidates to reduce their dependency on special interests.

On at least some issues candidates for public office as well as officeholders could enter into legally binding contracts. Contracts could not seek to control what public officials do in their official capacity (a contractual commitment by a Congressman to vote a certain way would probably be unenforceable and if there were something given in return could be deemed a bribe). Contracts can, however, cover much of what people do to get elected (for example, how they run their campaigns, including whose contributions they accept). Contracts could also address another aspect of the corruption problem, which is what officeholders do after leaving office (for example, whether or not they become lobbyists and lobby their former legislative colleagues).

One way of achieving such a contract is for a group of voters in each congressional district to set up a corporation, limited liability company (LLC), or similar organization that would ask candidates for a particular office to contract with it in their personal capacities. The contract—called a deal with the district—could provide that the candidate would not accept campaign contributions from PACs, trade associations, or labor unions or individual contributions over a certain amount. The contract could also provide for liquidated damages (for example, twice the amount of the contribution) that would have to be paid by the candidate personally to the organization in the event of breach by him or his campaign. The advantage to the candidate from this arrangement is that he could tell voters that he has made an enforceable, and therefore more credible, promise in his personal capacity not to do things that corrupt the political system.

The organization could be named for the district (for example, Minnesota Sixth LLC) and should be open to membership to any voter in the district who pays a very small amount ($1 to $5) to help cover administrative costs. The members of the LLC would then elect its managers. The managers of the LLC would be responsible for enforcement of the contract. The candidate's campaign would pay a larger amount to the LLC, perhaps $500, to cover the administrative costs of the organization.

The candidate's agreement with the LLC would be set forth in two documents, a pledge distributed to voters that describes the terms of the contract with the LLC and the legally binding contract between the candidate and the LLC. The two documents would have substantially similar language, but the contract would be signed by the candidate and a managing member of the LLC and would specifically state the consideration provided by the LLC to the candidate in return for the candidate's promises. This consideration would include the LLC's efforts at its own expense to ascertain the candidate's intent to comply with the pledge, to explain the pledge to the candidate and his or her staff, and to publicize it as part of a voter education effort, as well as the LLC's ongoing efforts to ascertain compliance with the pledge by all candidates in the district who sign it.

The LLC or other organization enforcing this contract would probably have to be designated as for-profit to avoid restrictions under IRS rules governing a nonprofit organization's interaction with candidates for political office, but it could provide in its articles of organization that if it were to successfully recover contract damages for breach from a candidate or officeholder, any amount left over after taxes and legal expenses would be donated to a charity serving people of the district or perhaps to a reform PAC such as Mayday PAC.

At least one congressional candidate—John Denney, who ran for the Minnesota Sixth Congressional House seat in 2014—entered into such a contract that his campaign manager John Schwietz drafted. A copy of Denney's contract appears in Appendix B. He promised not to take any large campaign contributions from outside the state and if he won he promised not to lobby back to Congress after leaving office. Denney announced the contract only one week before the election, however, and he lost the election. Other candidates might try a similar arrangement, making somewhat different promises. Such contracts could cover just about any area of personal conduct or campaign conduct that affects the integrity of the political system, including acceptance of campaign contributions, lobbying and other personal conduct after completing a term in office, and holding investments that create conflicts with official duties.

Reducing the Cost of Campaigns

THE OTHER SIDE of the equation is the cost of political campaigns. How much bang for the buck do campaigns get for the money they raise? The more campaigns get for each dollar, the less dependent they will be on the special interest contributors who can provide them with more money, and the less time elected officials will have to devote to fundraising. Cutting costs of campaigns is an important but often overlooked part of the campaign finance problem.

The good news is that the Internet and social media (Twitter, Facebook, etc.) may already be making it easier for candidates to raise small-dollar contributions and to campaign. The private sector can also do a lot more to make less expensive communication possible for political candidates and their supporters. And government should avoid standing in the way.

For example, Google or some other search engine could make advertising on its home page available at cut rates or for free during the 60 days before an election, but only to candidates who sign a pledge not to take PAC money. Google has the technological ability to target ads to the location of the person conducting a search, so presumably local candidate ads would show up on the search engine home page if this approach were pursued. If such an arrangement were to be deemed a campaign contribution by Google under federal law, an organization similar to Mayday PAC could buy the advertising space from Google ahead of time at discounted rates, and then allocate it to candidates who met criteria of its choice. And if that arrangement were to still create legal problems for Google because of the discount, this may be one more example of how federal regulation of campaigns can do more harm than good.

Facebook could make available an application that would insert the user's preferred candidate ads—including links to videos—on a Facebook page 30–60 days before an election. The ads could be downloaded from the candidate's website. Other social media companies such as Twitter could follow suit, allowing users to run their own advertising—the electronic version of the bumper stickers and yard signs that give individuals an inexpensive way to express their support for candidates. Government could facilitate such initiatives with tax breaks for social media companies with programs that allow users to run their own political ads.

Finally, organizations such as the NFL, NBA, and MLB that hold valuable copyrights to video footage could join the effort by providing viewers with free access to video of old games or movies that include brief political ads from candidates who agree not to take PAC money in order to participate in the program. If these organizations require incentives to create such a program, private sector foundations could provide them with the monetary incentives they require.

Private sector businesses are often blamed for the campaign finance system, and unfairly so, because as pointed out in Chapter 6, many don't participate in the system at all or resent having to participate in order to "compete" in the realm of lobbying and government relations. In an age of rapid innovation in communications technology, the private sector can also be part of the solution to the campaign finance problem if business leaders choose to take this path and government does not stand in the way.

This book is principally about what political conservatives can and should do to fix the campaign finance problem, so discussion here of private sector innovations and solutions is limited. The United States, however, has the most innovative private sector in the world. The power of American entrepreneurs to help solve the money-in-politics problem should not be underestimated.

Epilogue

The Elusive Question:
What Is a Campaign Contribution?

MANY AMERICAN FAMILIES argue over politics at the dinner table. But for most American families, discussion, however contentious, is all that happens until the adults have a chance to vote on Election Day.

A few families have an opportunity to put money where their mouth is. Members of the same family may make campaign contributions to different and sometimes opposing candidates (as pointed out in Chapter 6, this is another way contributions by the rich sometimes cancel each other out). They may support PACs, 501(c)(4)s, and other organizations that back one candidate or another. Or they may spend their money in more creative ways to support or defeat a particular candidate.

One such family is the Mellon family of Pittsburgh, the descendants of Judge Thomas Mellon and Andrew W. Mellon, a very successful banker and businessman. Andrew Mellon was himself politically active, serving as treasury secretary under Presidents Calvin Coolidge and Herbert Hoover. The Mellon family at one point owned controlling interests in the Mellon Bank and Gulf Oil, as well as other companies, and has donated an enormous amount to philanthropic causes in Pittsburgh and around the nation, including the National Gallery of Art in Washington and Yale University.

Various members of the Mellon family have made campaign contributions of the more traditional sort—the type that are reported to the Federal Election Commission and that can be seen on its web page. But that is not the only way to support political causes and political campaigns.

Two of the Mellons confronted on separate occasions in the past two decades a question that arises quite frequently: what to do, other than talk about it, when a prominent politician is caught in a sex scandal. One approach is to ignore the scandal and focus on the political issues.

Another approach is to exploit the scandal for all it is worth, using the media and sometimes the legal system to embarrass the politician and end his career. Another approach is to have pity on the miscreant politician and do everything possible to cover up his sex scandal before someone else discovers it and tries to destroy him.

Sitting at opposite ends of the Mellon family dinner table, figuratively if not literally, were Richard Mellon Scaife, grandson of Andrew W. Mellon and very much aligned with him in Republican political allegiance, and Rachel "Bunny" Mellon, the widow of Andrew Mellon's son Paul Mellon. Paul Mellon was one of the most famous art collectors and donors in American history, and stayed out of politics, but many of Bunny's good friends over the years, including Jackie Kennedy and William and Hillary Clinton, were Democrats.

Richard Scaife backed Republican politicians for decades, most notably President Richard Nixon in both of his successful campaigns for the White House. Scaife was more libertarian than some Republicans on social issues (he supported Planned Parenthood), but like his grandfather he was very conservative on economic issues. He very much disliked President Bill Clinton.

President Clinton's sexual exploits and other scandals made him vulnerable to personal attack. He almost lost the Democratic nomination for president in 1992 over an affair with a woman named Jennifer Flowers. Then, after he took office in 1993, another woman, Paula Jones, publicly accused him of sexual harassment that allegedly took place while Clinton was governor of Arkansas. Jones sued Clinton, and lengthy litigation followed. One legal issue (whether a sitting president could be sued for conduct that occurred before he took office) went all the way to the Supreme Court (the court's answer was yes). According to *The Washington Post*[213] and other sources, a substantial portion of Jones's legal battle was at least indirectly supported by Scaife and his associates in the so-called Arkansas Project. Scaife also owned a newspaper, the *Pittsburgh Tribune-Review*, which was one of the first papers to report the Jones affair and the scandal that followed.

Is Scaife's supporting and publicizing a lawsuit against a sitting president in his first term a campaign contribution to the opposing political party that hopes to unseat the president in the next election? Depending on the nature of the lawsuit (lawsuits involving sex have staying power in

213 See, for example, Robert G. Kaiser, "How Scaife's Money Powered a Movement," *The Washington Post*, 2 May 1999.

the media), the lawsuit may be more effective in defeating the president than a direct campaign contribution to an opponent.

The Jones lawsuit weakened Clinton politically. Scaife and his allies must have known this lawsuit could hurt Clinton politically, and they probably wanted it to have that effect.

And Jones—a woman of very modest means—certainly needed this help if she were to pursue a lawsuit against the president. She alone was no match for the Clintons' resources. Things changed, however, if wealthy supporters stepped in.

Jones had another advantage in that because she was not a public official she could accept support for her lawsuit from anyone she chose. President Clinton, on the other hand, was under severe restrictions under federal gift rules. He had to pay his own lawyers or borrow the money to pay his lawyers. He could not turn to wealthy supporters to pay for his defense.

Lawyers cost a lot of money and the longer the lawsuit went on, the deeper the Clintons went into debt and the more the case hurt the president personally and perhaps his presidency. And this stress might increase the chance he would make a big mistake in defending himself in the case such as lying under oath (which he did). Clinton was backed into a corner by whoever, including Scaife, was supporting Paula Jones. And in that corner he did not fare so well. What saved him was that he was able to buy time and he was not that far into the corner by the time of the 1996 election.

Scaife's efforts on behalf of Jones were potentially an enormous help to the Republican Party, and probably would have been helpful in the 1998 Congressional elections if the Republicans had not overplayed their hand by impeaching President Clinton. Nowhere, however, are Scaife's expenditures on any of the Clinton scandals recorded as a campaign contribution, to the Republican National Committee (RNC), to Clinton's 1996 opponent Senator Robert Dole, or to anyone else. Indeed, there is no public record of how much money Scaife or any other donor contributed to this effort to discredit Clinton. Legally, it was not a campaign contribution.

Scaife also pursued another approach to supporting and opposing political candidates. The newspaper he owned, the *Pittsburgh Tribune-Review,* consistently backed Republicans, criticized Democrats, and reported extensively on the Jones scandal. And this was squarely within the protection of the First Amendment (even the minority on the Supreme Court that dissented in *Citizens United* would not have upheld laws that restricted newspaper editorials or the influence of newspaper owners on editorials). Scaife thus followed in the footsteps of Henry Ford, William Randolph Hearst, and other rich Americans who decades earlier owned newspapers and used them to project their views on politics.

Bunny Mellon, by contrast, liked Democrats. She was close to the Kennedys, particularly Jackie Kennedy. Bunny Mellon's passion was gardening, and she helped the Kennedys redesign the White House Rose Garden.[214] She was also close to the Clintons, although there is no evidence that she got involved on anybody's side in their personal affairs. Then, in the 2000s, as Bunny Mellon was well into her nineties, she got to know Senator John Edwards—the Democratic Party's nominee for vice president in 2004 and a candidate for president in 2008.

In 2008 Edwards was in trouble. The situation was potentially even worse than a sexual harassment suit. His wife had terminal cancer, and one of his campaign workers, Rielle Hunter, was pregnant—with his baby. Edwards needed help, and fast. Bunny came to the rescue.

Paying lawyers to defend Edwards in a paternity lawsuit or other litigation would have been pointless. Given his wife's medical condition, his career would be over as soon as the affair was disclosed. Edwards needed someone to provide sufficient financial support for Hunter that she would keep her mouth shut and not reveal that he was the father of her child. Bunny Mellon provided the funds. These payments to Hunter were made at the same time Edwards was seeking the 2008 Democratic nomination for president.

Were these payments a campaign contribution? Later, in 2010, federal prosecutors and a grand jury thought so. On June 3, 2011, Edwards was indicted by a grand jury on four felony counts of collecting illegal campaign contributions, one count of conspiracy, and one count of making false statements. In May 2012 Edwards was found not guilty on Count 3, illegal use of campaign funding from Bunny Mellon, and a mistrial was declared on the other counts. The Justice Department then decided to drop the case.

In the above examples, money originating from the same family fortune was thrown into both attacking and defending prominent Democratic Party politicians in sex scandals. None of this money was reported

---

214 Mrs. Kennedy years later left Mrs. Mellon some artworks in the first paragraph of her will:

I, JACQUELINE K. ONASSIS . . . FIRST: A. I give and bequeath to my friend RACHEL (BUNNY) L. MELLON, if she survives me, in appreciation of her designing the Rose Garden in the White House my Indian miniature "Lovers watching rain clouds," Kangra, about 1780, if owned by me at the time of my death, and my large Indian miniature with giltwood frame "Gardens of the Palace of the Rajh," a panoramic view of a pink walled garden blooming with orange flowers, with the Rajh being entertained in a pavilion by musicians and dancers, if owned by me at the time of my death.

Jacqueline K. Onassis, "Last Will and Testament of Jacqueline K. Onassis," Living Trust Network, 22 March 1994, livingtrustnetwork.com/estate-planning-center/last-will-and-testament/wills-of-the-rich-and-famous/last-will-and-testament-of-jacqueline-kennedy-onassis.html (accessed 15 September 2015).

as a campaign contribution to any candidate or party, and no court has held that any of it should have been reported, although in Edwards's case federal prosecutors believed it should have been.

There is one respect in which Bunny Mellon's payments to Edwards's mistress might, more than Scaife's support for the Jones lawsuit, be close to the type of arrangement covered by the statutory framework for regulating campaign contributions. These types of payments create a dependency relationship between the campaign and the person making the payments. But for the payments to his mistress, the scandal would have been exposed and Edwards's campaign for the presidency would almost certainly have failed. A dependency relationship between a presidential candidate and a 96-year-old woman whose passion is gardening might be relatively harmless, but one can imagine the uproar if an oil company, or the American Trial Lawyers Association, had made these payments. As much as Scaife contributed to the cause of unseating President Bill Clinton (it was a lot), a single candidate probably was not dependent on him alone for electoral success.

The impossibility of prosecuting Edwards in this case, however, illustrates another challenge for attempts to regulate campaign finance by restricting or even requiring disclosure of what people do with their money. A campaign contribution is usually easy to identify, but sometimes it is not, whether it is the payments by Bunny Mellon or those by Scaife to either squelch or fan the fire of a Democratic sex scandal. Scaife's media holdings, and similar holdings of other wealthy Americans on both ends of the political spectrum, illustrate another part of the equation, and one that is almost impossible to regulate consistent with the First Amendment right to freedom of the press.

What about someone making a nasty movie about a former first lady, set to run weeks before an election in which she is running for president? (This was the factual background in the *Citizens United* case, in which the operative language in the statute overturned by the court was "electioneering communication" rather than "campaign contribution.") The difficulty of drawing legal lines in these and other cases has led many people to conclude that there is little that can be done to stop a few rich people, unions, and corporations from spending money in the political arena. And the fact that the Supreme Court won't even allow legislators to try to address this problem has made this endeavor even more difficult. In sum, we really don't know how to define a campaign contribution, and we certainly don't know how to regulate one.

Reformers need to disengage from what is probably a pointless dispute with the Supreme Court over the constitutionality of restrictions on speech and expenditures. As the above examples illustrate, people with means will never run out of creative ways of supporting or opposing politicians. What reformers can do is diminish officeholders' actual or apparent *dependence* on specific sources of funds to get elected. It is this dependence that is the essence of corruption because it undermines both independent decision-making and responsiveness to the public. Creating additional sources of campaign funding through the "Taxation Only with Representation" statute or amendment described in Chapter 8 as well as through innovative projects such as Democracy Dollars described in Chapter 9, will help. So will private sector initiatives to lower the cost of campaigns, which could be encouraged, or at least not hindered, by government. It is in these directions that conservatives should go with campaign finance reform—directions that enhance rather than hinder individual participation and decision-making.

The objective is not to take away the free speech rights of people like Richard Mellon Scaife and Bunny Mellon or anyone else. People who can afford it can make a movie about a politician they like or don't like, publish an article about a politician in a newspaper they own, put something on a website about the politician, or say whatever they want however they like. People can contribute directly or indirectly to political campaigns. There presently are no meaningful limits on indirect contributions, and the Supreme Court is chipping away at limits on direct contributions. That is the world we live in and there is little that can be done to change it.

The objective here—and an agenda that should be embraced by all Americans—is first to make elected officials less dependent on money from a few special interests, and second to allow many more Americans to participate in funding political campaigns.

We live in separate families, some rich, some poor, and many in the middle. As families we sometimes discuss and disagree about politics, whether over the dinner table or somewhere else. As American citizens we also have many conversations with fellow citizens about political issues and candidates. We have to recognize, however, that too often the conversations that elected officials listen to are at the "high table" of campaign finance. At that table every American should have an opportunity to sit and participate in the conversation.

Appendix A

Proposed Constitutional Amendment

As discussed in Chapter 8, taxation should be conditioned on the fundamental right to meaningful representation. To accomplish this, state constitutions and the federal Constitution should include an amendment providing for Taxation Only with Representation. If a constitutional amendment is not feasible, however, federal and state legislatures can enact statutes that will accomplish the same purpose. Suggested language is below.

Taxation Only with Representation Amendment to the United States Constitution

Neither the government of the United States nor any state or subdivision thereof shall levy an income tax, sales tax, property tax, inheritance tax, or any other tax upon any natural person over 18 years of age who is a citizen of the United States or upon his or her estate unless the United States government or the state levying said taxes pays an amount totaling at least two hundred dollars within the same calendar year or within the immediately following calendar year to the campaign of one or more candidates for elected federal, state, or local office chosen by such citizen [for whom such citizen is also eligible to vote] [or who is running for office in the state in which the citizen resides]. A citizen's right to designate taxpayer-funded political contributions pursuant to this amendment is waived in any year in which the citizen fails to designate a recipient of such payment or dies before designating a recipient of such payment. Every five years after adoption of this amendment, Congress shall by statute or, in the event Congress shall not enact such a statute, the United States Treasury shall by regulation, adjust the taxpayer-funded political contribution amount to be more or less than two hundred dollars to reflect changes in the purchasing power of the United States dollar within the preceding five years.

Taxation Only with Representation Amendment to a State Constitution

NEITHER THIS STATE nor a subdivision thereof shall levy an income tax, sales tax, property tax, inheritance tax, or any other tax upon any natural person over 18 years of age who is a resident of this State or upon his or her estate unless the United States government or this State pays an amount totaling at least two hundred dollars within the same calendar year or within the immediately following calendar year to the campaign of one or more candidates for elected federal, state, or local office chosen by such resident [for whom such resident is also eligible to vote] [or who is running for office in this state]. A resident's right to designate taxpayer-funded political contributions pursuant to this amendment is waived in any year in which the resident fails to designate a recipient of such payment or dies before designating a recipient of such payment. Every five years after adoption of this amendment, the legislature shall by statute adjust the taxpayer-funded political contribution amount to be more or less than two hundred dollars to reflect changes in the purchasing power of the United States dollar within the preceding five years.

Taxation Only With Representation Act for Enactment by the United States Congress

THE UNITED STATES government shall not levy an income tax, sales tax, property tax, inheritance tax, or any other tax upon any natural person over 18 years of age who is a citizen of the United States or upon his or her estate unless the United States Treasury pays an amount totaling at least two hundred dollars within the same calendar year or within the immediately following calendar year to the campaign of one or more candidates for elected federal, state, or local office chosen by such citizen [for whom such citizen is also eligible to vote] [or who is running for office in the state in which the citizen resides]. A citizen's right to designate taxpayer-funded political contributions pursuant to this law is waived in any year in which the citizen fails to designate a recipient of such payment or dies before designating a recipient of such payment. Every five years after the enactment of this provision, the United States Treasury shall by regulation adjust this taxpayer-funded political contribution amount to be more or less than two hundred dollars to reflect changes in the purchasing power of the United States dollar within the preceding five years. The United States Treasury shall within 180 days of enactment of this provision promulgate rules and designate procedures for the purpose of implementing this provision.

Taxation Only with Representation Act for a State

NEITHER THIS STATE nor a subdivision thereof shall levy an income tax, sales tax, property tax, inheritance tax, or any other tax upon any natural person over 18 years of age who is a resident of this State or upon his or her estate unless the United States government, this State, or one or more other government entities levying said taxes pays an amount totaling at least two hundred dollars within the same calendar year or within the immediately following calendar year to the campaign of one or more candidates for elected federal, state, or local office chosen by such resident [for whom such resident is also eligible to vote] [or who is running for office in this state]. A resident's right to designate taxpayer-funded political contributions pursuant to this law is waived in any year in which the resident fails to designate a recipient of such payment or dies before designating a recipient of such payment. [insert inflation-adjustment provision] The [State Treasurer] shall, within 180 days of enactment of this provision, promulgate rules and designate procedures for the purpose of implementing this provision.

Notes:

1) The state constitutional amendment and state statute allow the federal government to pay the political contributions instead of the state government. States that enact such provisions thus have an incentive to urge the federal government to enact a similar provision by statute or constitutional amendment.

2) The state statute does not contain a specific inflation-adjustment provision, leaving this matter to the discretion of the legislature. The federal statute and the state constitutional amendment, however, do contain inflation-adjustment provisions.

Appendix B

Deal with the District:
A Legally Enforceable, Money-Back-Guaranteed Ethics Contract for Better Government

(**THIS VERSION WAS** signed by John Denney, 2014 Independence Party Candidate for Congress in the Sixth District of Minnesota.)

PURPOSE AND AGREEMENT

I _____ as candidate for Congress in the _____District of [State], and later, if elected, as a member of the United States House of Representatives ("Promisor"), agree to truly hold myself accountable to my constituents by making legally enforceable my campaign promises and subjecting myself to the below anticorruption provisions and penalties not currently enforceable against or applied to any candidate for or member of Congress.

In order to make these promises legally enforceable, I shall enter into a legally binding contract with [name of state followed by district number LLC] [for example Minnesota Sixth LLC] ("Minnesota Sixth"), a Minnesota LLC established for the sole purpose of enforcing this contract, providing that Minnesota Sixth has, at its own expense, investigated my intent to abide by these promises, and believes I will abide by these promises and that, if I break any of these promises, I agree to pay to Minnesota Sixth, out of my personal funds, liquidated damages as set forth below.

As provided in its Articles of Organization, for any such recovery Minnesota Sixth receives from any candidate or member for breach of contract, after paying all applicable expenses and taxes, Minnesota Sixth shall distribute all remaining amounts recovered to charities that serve, principally, the interests of the people of the Sixth District. The Articles of Organization of Minnesota Sixth shall provide that its managing members shall all be residents of the District who are committed to the principles set forth in this agreement.

ANTICORRUPTION PROVISIONS

Prohibitions and Promises

1. No Conflict of Interest Campaign Contributions. *Promisor shall not intentionally and directly solicit or Knowingly Accept any campaign contributions that create a conflict of interest ("COI Contributions") with Promisor's duty to represent, exclusively, the people of the District Promisor represents.*

2. Lifetime Ban on Lobbying Congress. *Promisor agrees to self-impose and adhere to a lifetime ban on Lobbying back to any member or staff of the United States House of Representatives or Senate for compensation after serving any congressional term.*

Definitions and Terms

1. Knowingly Accept *means to expressly accept or Impliedly Accept any contribution of any legal tender.*

2. Impliedly Accept *means to spend or cash any contribution, or to fail to Expressly Reject any contribution within 90 days of its receipt.*

3. Express Rejection *may be made in any manner reasonably calculated to give notice to donor and the public.*

4. COI Contributions *are campaign funds donated to Promisor by any political party, Political Action Committee (PAC),* *labor union, for-profit corporation, Special Interest Group, or individual not residing in the State of Minnesota who is not also a Family Member of Promisor.*

5. Special Interest Groups *are industry or advocacy associations or groups that focus on particular issues, or any other group that seeks through its contributions to influence legislation.*

6. Family Member *means any family member or immediate relative as defined by the Office of Personnel Management under 75 C.F.R. § 33491 (2010).*

7. Lobbying *shall have the same meaning as set forth in the Lobbying Disclosure Act of 1995 as amended.*

Penalties/Damages in the Event of Breach

Section 1 *Promisor must pay out of Promisor's personal funds, liquidated damages to Minnesota Sixth in the amount of twice the amount of the contribution in question, and furthermore, if elected, Promisor must pay liquidated damages in the amount of Promisor's entire congressional salary for Promisor's term as Member.*

Section 2 *Promisor must pay out of Promisor's personal funds liquidated damages to Minnesota Sixth in an amount equal to Promisor's entire earnings to date as a Member plus the agreed-upon amount of Promisor's first year salary as lobbyist.*

Signed: _____

Date: _____

Candidate

Note: This document is a pledge signed by the candidate. This is not a contract. The contract with the LLC is to have substantially similar language, is to be signed by the candidate and a managing member of the LLC, and shall state the consideration provided by the LLC to the candidate, including the LLC's efforts at its own expense to ascertain the candidate's intent to comply with the pledge, to explain the pledge to the candidate and his or her staff and to the public, and the LLC's ongoing efforts to ascertain compliance with the pledge by all candidates in the district who sign it. Any registered voter residing in the District should be eligible to be a member of the LLC upon payment of token consideration, and the members of the LLC shall elect its managers. The managers of the LLC shall be responsible for enforcement of the contract, payment of the LLC's expenses out of proceeds from recoveries for breach of contract, and distribution of excess funds to charitable organizations serving the people of the district.

ABOUT THE AUTHORS

RICHARD W. PAINTER is the S. Walter Richey Professor of Corporate Law at the University of Minnesota. He is also a director of Take Back Our Republic, an organization of conservatives working for campaign finance reform. From 2005 to 2007 Painter was associate counsel to the president and the chief White House ethics lawyer under President George W. Bush. His work on this book was supported in 2014 and 2015 by Harvard University, where he was a residential fellow at the Edmond J. Safra Center for Ethics.

JOHN PUDNER is the executive director of Take Back Our Republic. In 2014 Pudner launched the campaign of David Brat (R-VA) in the Republican primary for Virginia's Seventh Congressional District; Brat won the primary and was then elected to Congress. Pudner has written about and lectured extensively on a wide range of topics of interest to political conservatives, including campaign finance reform.